Since the mid-1960s there has been increasing awareness of the young child's potential for learning. The resulting flurry of ideas and activities has created a need for a comprehensive view of strategies for teaching young children. This book answers that need. It deals with curriculum ideas appropriate for children between the ages of three and seven; therefore, it can be used by those working with preschool, kindergarten, and early primary aged children. Activities are keyed to indicate levels of difficulty; most are accompanied by suggestions and variations that illustrate how teachers can make them more simple or complex to adapt to the individual needs of children. The use of inexpensive and teacher-made materials is suggested and explained. Reference material at the end of each chapter includes resources for both teacher and children. This comprehensive volume will help .id learning and will prepare them to develop their own programs for young children.

Special features include the use of many photographs and drawings to illustrate the text; numbered activities for easy references; cross-referencing of activities; and an identical section format for each chapter, which helps readers by allowing them to assign similar sections in each chapter.

JUDITH A. SCHICKEDANZ
Boston University

MARY E. YORK
Portland State University

IDA SANTOS STEWART
University of Houston

DORIS WHITE
Northern Illinois University

strategies for teaching young children

PRENTICE-HALL, INC., ENGLEWOOD CLIFFS, NEW JERSEY 07632

Library of Congress Cataloging in Publication Data

Main entry under title:

Strategies for teaching young children.

    Includes bibliographies and index.
    1. Education, Primary. 2. Kindergarten—
Methods and manuals. I Schickedanz, Judith A.,
LB1523.S77   372.1'1'02   76–21265
ISBN 0–13–851105–5

PRENTICE-HALL SERIES IN EARLY CHILDHOOD
Bernard Spodek, *Series Editor*

Printed in the United States of America

10   9   8   7   6   5   4   3   2   1

PRENTICE-HALL INTERNATIONAL, INC., LONDON
PRENTICE-HALL OF AUSTRALIA PTY. LIMITED, SYDNEY
PRENTICE-HALL OF CANADA, LTD., TORONTO
PRENTICE-HALL OF INDIA PRIVATE LIMITED, NEW DELHI
PRENTICE-HALL OF JAPAN, INC., TOKYO
PRENTICE-HALL OF SOUTHEAST ASIA PTE. LTD., SINGAPORE
WHITEHALL BOOKS LIMITED, WELLINGTON, NEW ZEALAND

contents

iii

134869

7 THE SOCIAL SCIENCES, 253

preface

THE last ten years have brought an increased awareness of the young child's potential for learning. There has been a concommitant proliferation of ideas about types of educational programming that might be developed to support such learning. This flurry of activity had created a need for a comprehensive view of programming that integrates considerations of child development and the structure of the content areas and recognizes the increased emphasis on the learning potential of the young child while maintaining the early childhood tradition of valuing the whole child. This book is an attempt to respond to that need.

The first chapter presents a sketch of the framework from which the program ideas were developed. Included in it are discussions of the authors' views about how children learn, the role of the teacher, and the purpose of schooling. Chapter two deals with planning and organizing for instruction and with evaluating children's learning. The remaining five chapters are organized around the following content areas: (1) Aesthetic Arts, (2) Language Arts, (3) Mathematics, (4) Science, and (5) Social Science. Within each of these chapters, the reader will find a discussion of the structure of the content area, skills and concepts in the content area that are appropriate for young children, and specific activities that serve as *examples* of ways a teacher can support children's learning in the particular content area. The classroom teacher or teacher educator who prefers an activity organization that integrates learning from several content areas can refer to the key provided in the appendix in order to find activities that utilize Water Play, Dramatic Play, Block Play, Woodworking, Small Motor Play, and Large Motor Play.

This book has been written primarily to meet the needs of undergraduate students studying early childhood education, although it would serve as a valuable resource for teachers already working in the field. The book helps the student who has had little background in child development or the content areas by including sections that discuss these considerations in each curriculum chapter. This makes the book appropriate for students in programs that integrate developmental and content area theory with methods or practicum courses, or those in which field work begins in the freshman or sophomore year before the student has completed theoretical work. Students in programs that require theory courses in development and the content areas before methods or practicum experiences will find the discussions useful in helping them see the implications of previous learning for their practical work with children. Teachers in the field will find the theoretical rationale for the practical ideas helpful in explaining and interpreting their program to parents, community, and colleagues.

Because the book deals with curriculum ideas appropriate for children between the ages of three and seven, it can be used by teachers of preschool, kindergarten, and early primary school children. The activities are keyed to indicate their level of difficulty, but most activities are accompanied by "Suggestions and Variations" that illustrate how teachers can make them more simple or complex to meet the needs of individual children.

. Activity suggestions rely heavily on materials that are inexpensive and teacher-made. Materials needed for each activity are listed and described, and often, several suggestions are made for materials that would work well for the same activity. Reference material at the end of each chapter includes resources for both teacher and children. The list of children's books indicated at the end of the Social Science chapter is annotated to help the teacher select those best suited for specific purposes.

ACKNOWLEDGEMENTS

The authors are indebted to many who have indirectly contributed to this book. First, there are the photographers. Jack Adams is affiliated with the University of New Hampshire Photographic Services. Jim Fety is a free lance photographer who is also a teacher at Rogue River, Oregon. Judi Jones is a teacher who enjoys photography as a hobby and a record-keeping device. We believe the pictures have captured the spirit of children and express ideas and feelings that are difficult to put into words.

There are also the children, and the teachers of children who contributed to the development of the book by providing opportunities for obtaining photographs and testing out ideas. These schools and teachers include the University of New Hampshire Child Development Laboratory, Durham, New Hampshire, Judi Jones, head teacher; E-Kosh-Kosh Day Care Center, Urban Indian Coalition, Portland, Oregon; the Harold E. Moon Head Start Center, Alexandria, Virginia; and the first grade classroom of Sharon Lewis, Beaverton School District, Beaverton, Oregon.

The writers are also indebted to Mrs. Julia Bursch, instructor of parent education classes for Portland Community College and former director of a parent cooperative center, for many of the diagrams and drawings and for her comments and contributions to the Expressive Arts Chapter.

Above all, we are deeply indebted to our teacher, Professor Bernard Spodek, who introduced us to the serious study of early childhood education and who remains interested in us and our ideas, and without whose support this book would not have been written.

J.A.S., M.E.Y., I.S.S., D.W.

1
conceptual
framework

SCHOOLS must provide a climate of openness and freedom, yet they must have structure and discipline; children must be valued as unique individuals, yet they must become involved in society; children must be supported as agents of their own learning, yet they need guidance and direction. In the following chapters ways to provide for these contrasting conditions are suggested. In the present chapter, basic ideas relating to assumptions about children and learning, the role of the teacher, and what children should learn in school will be discussed to provide the framework within which the remaining chapters may be viewed.

ASSUMPTIONS ABOUT CHILDREN AND LEARNING

Whenever plans are made for the education of young children, some fundamental assumptions are made about the nature of children and the way they learn. These assumptions affect the ways goals are formulated, activities are designed, materials are supplied, and time and space are organized. The assumptions on which the methods in this book are based are examined below.

Each Child Is Unique

Each child is a product of genetic heritage and experience. Individual children develop their own patterns of reacting to events. They have their own paces of living and learning and evolve their own concepts of who they are and what they can do. Inescapably, the experiences a child has in the classroom will have their effect. Different children, however, will approach new experiences in different ways. Teaching methods should allow children to be themselves.

Children Proceed Through Levels of Development

Each child proceeds through levels of development in physical, cognitive and affective domains. The child walks before skipping,[1] uses two-

---

[1]M. Smart and R. Smart, *Children: Development and Relationships,* 2nd ed. (New York: Macmillan, 1972), p. 218.

word sentences before talking fluently,[2] and develops trust before autonomy.[3] Although these illustrations are from the early years, the principle holds true for all subsequent learning.

There may be a variety of levels of development among children who are chronologically the same age. Similarly, children who are different ages may be at the same level of development in one or more areas. A teacher, whether working with a mixed-age group or a single-age group, needs a thorough understanding of all aspects of child development in order to be able to assess the levels of development represented by the individuals in the class being taught.

Each Child is an Active Learner

The determination to learn new skills is nowhere more obvious than in a child's learning to walk and talk, but those who study child behavior can point to evidence of a child's eagerness to learn in many other areas. Each child actively explores the surrounding environment. Children look, make sounds, smell, touch and taste; moreover, they repeat these behaviors over and over again. Piaget[4] calls the repetition of organized patterns of behavior **functional assimilation.** He has noted that it is the new or emerging pattern that tends to be repeated most often. Weir[5] has noted similar repetitive play with language. Montessori[6] has also reported observing children repeat actions with objects as many as ten, twenty or even fifty times.

The remarkable thing about all of the situations cited above is that in no case was someone making the child practice or work on a skill. The children seemed to do it on their own. This does not mean that adults are unimportant or even incidental to a child's learning. Adult input is absolutely crucial to childhood learning. Someone must provide a language model. Someone must provide social stimulation. Someone must adjust the physical environment to the child's ever-changing abilities. Someone must set limits. But what adults cannot do is hand over to the child knowledge that is complete and ready-made. Children must construct their own knowledge. David Elkind[7] has pointed out that for

[2]J. Deese, *Psycholinguistics* (Boston: Allyn and Bacon, Inc., 1970), pp. 53–65.
[3]E. Erikson, *Childhood and Society,* 2nd ed. (New York: W. W. Norton and Co., Inc., 1963), pp. 247–254.
[4]H. Ginsburg and S. Opper, *Piaget's Theory of Intellectual Development* (Englewood Cliffs, N.J.: Prentice-Hall, Inc., 1968), p. 30.
[5]R. Weir, *Language in the Crib* (The Hague: Mouton and Company, 1962).
[6]M. Montessori, *Spontaneous Activity in Education* (New York: Schocken Books, 1972), pp. 153–169.
[7]D. Elkind, "Misunderstandings About How Children Learn," *Today's Education,* 61, no. 3 (1972), pp. 18–20.

the child under six or seven this construction requires real, physical actions with real things. Gradually, the child's thinking processes become independent of such actions so that active learning in the physical sense decreases as the child grows older. Good education, however, should continue to support children's active interest and involvement in their learning.

Children Learn Most Easily
When the Educational Experience Matches
Their Cognitive Schemas

In the past, readiness to learn was thought to be determined by physical maturation alone. While physical maturation does indeed play a part, a child's developmental level is determined both by physical maturity and by experience. A child's experience and genetic timetable probably interact to build what Piaget[8] refers to as **cognitive schemas.** These are organized mental structures which determine a person's level of thinking. What these structures contain at any time determines the kind of educational experience for which a child is ready.

The reader should note that in the view sketched above, readiness to learn is determined by the developmental level of the child, *and* by the educational experience provided by the teacher. Readiness is not something that resides solely in the child. Sometimes when we say a child is not "ready," we may mean that the child is not ready to learn a specific concept or skill in the way we have presented it. The child may be able to learn these if we change our approach. At other times when we say a child is not "ready," we may mean that the selected concepts and skills are too advanced for the child. If this is the case, we must return to more basic ones. Finding an experience which fits with what the child already knows is what Hunt[9] has referred to as "the problem of the match." Hunt says that if learning is to occur, the educational experience must have an appropriate relationship to the information already accumulated in the child's mental structures. Experiences which provide too little new input will bore the child, whereas experiences which provide too much new input might frighten the child. When children react to an opportunity for learning with interest and delight or when their involvement is sustained, we can be reasonably certain that a good match has been made. A variety of activities and good individual guidance should be provided to increase the opportunities for such matches.

[8]Ginsburg and Opper, *Piaget's Theory of Intellectual Development*, p. 20.
[9]J. McV. Hunt, *The Challenge of Incompetence and Poverty* (Urbana: University of Illinois Press, 1969), p. 129.

THE ROLE OF THE TEACHER

The teacher's role should be consistent with the assumptions about children and the nature of learning described above. This means that in addition to the traditional roles of knowledge-imparter and disciplinarian, the teacher should be a decision-maker, a facilitator, and a planner-evaluator.

The Teacher as Knowledge-Imparter

Although children learn many concepts by active involvement or discovery, certain kinds of information cannot be learned in this manner. For example, children cannot discover which letter is named "A" and which is named "B"; someone must tell them which is which. In contrast, children can discover that containers of different shapes can hold the same amount of water simply by being provided with appropriate materials. A teacher must understand that there are different kinds of knowledge and that teaching strategies must be adjusted to conform to the knowledge that the child is learning in a particular situation.[10]

The Teacher as Disciplinarian

Learning is hampered in an atmosphere that is chaotic or personally destructive. It is the teacher's responsibility to help children behave in ways that promote self-respect and group cohesiveness. Everything a teacher does, from organizing the room and daily schedule to helping children solve disputes, will influence that teacher's effectiveness as a disciplinarian.

The Teacher as Decision-Maker

Sometimes it seems as though teachers have little decision-making responsibility. Lunch and gym schedules may influence the sequence of the daily classroom schedule, or the absence of materials or space may militate against including certain activities as class projects. Despite these common problems, teachers do make many decisions. Spodek[11], for example, has pointed out the number of decisions involved in a teaching behavior as simple as reading a story to a group of children.

[10]C. Kamii, "A Sketch of the Piaget-Derived Preschool Curriculum Developed by the Ypsilanti Early Education Program," in B. Spodek, ed., *Early Childhood Education* (Englewood Cliffs, N.J.: Prentice-Hall, Inc., 1973), pp. 215–29.
[11]B. Spodek, *Teaching in the Early Years* (Englewood Cliffs, N.J.: Prentice-Hall, Inc., 1972), pp. 5–11.

Decision-making ability is a crucial aspect of a teacher's total performance. All the ideas, suggestions, theories, and recommendations of experts necessarily apply to general cases. Even when procedures for dealing with individuals are described, these can only be for the "general individual." All such recommendations will be of little value without good decisions about when, how, and for what purposes they should be applied. When it comes to individual children, it is the teacher who mediates practice, for it is the teacher, not the expert, who is there.

The Teacher as Facilitator

The teacher who facilitates learning shows respect for a child's worth and competence. This kind of teacher provides a wide variety of experiences and materials to give children ample opportunity to interact with their environment and, further, encourages children to work together on projects they find interesting. Such teachers comment about ongoing activities, thus helping to raise to awareness and verbalization that which children are learning. They raise questions which will help children explore further. Finally, they make suggestions and provide materials that suggest ways to find answers to questions which children have raised.

The Teacher as Planner, Organizer, and Evaluator

Planning, organizing, and evaluating are closely related processes. Resources are organized to support planned experiences. Learning is evaluated to determine whether what was planned was accomplished. Evaluation becomes the basis for further planning, and new plans may require modifications in organization.

At the beginning of the school year the teacher plans activities which he or she believes will be of interest to children and enable them to accumulate new knowledge, learn new skills, and acquire new attitudes. This planning is based on the teacher's knowledge of children in general. As children engage in activities, the teacher collects data concerning each child's learning. She then uses these data to determine what new learning is appropriate.

WHAT CHILDREN SHOULD LEARN IN SCHOOL

Schools must make decisions about what children should learn. It is necessary for children to acquire characteristic skills and knowledge needed in their society. In most societies, this will mean that children need to become skilled in the use of their bodies, and to develop competence in such areas as oral and written communication, mathematics, the arts, and physical, biological, and social sciences.

The values of a society determine other knowledge and abilities which are desirable. If a society values obedient followers, its educational goals and methods will be quite different from those of a society which values independent and critical thinkers.[12]

Schools are expected to transmit knowledge and values and to help learners develop skills which will enable them to cope with the complexities of modern society. In many classrooms developmental considerations and democratic values are undermined as teachers fervently attempt to make sure that the next generation gains the information and skills it will need in order to function. It is hoped that in the chapters to follow, teachers can find ways to help children acquire necessary skills without violating either the children's developmental needs or the stated goals of this society.

ADDITIONAL RESOURCES

FROST, J., ed., *Revisiting Early Childhood Education*. New York: Holt, Rinehart and Winston, Inc., 1973.

HESS, R. D., and R. M. BEAR, eds., *Early Education: Current Research, Theory, and Action*. Chicago: Aldine Publishing Co., 1968.

HYMES, J. L., *Early Childhood Education: An Introduction to the Profession*. Washington, D.C.: National Association for the Education of Young Children, 1975.

KATZ, L., "Early Childhood Education as a Discipline," *Young Children*, 26, no. 2 (1970), pp. 82–89.

MUSSEN, P., J. CONGER, and J. KAGAN, *Child Development and Personality* (4th ed.). New York: Harper & Row Publishers, 1974

SPONSELLER, D., *Play As a Learning Medium*. Washington D.C.: National Association for the Education of Young Children, 1974.

SUTTON-SMITH, B., "The Role of Play in Cognitive Development," in W. Hartup and N. Smothergill, eds., *The Young Child: Reviews of Research*. Washington, D.C.: National Association for the Education of Young Children, 1967.

WANN, K., M. DORN, and E. LIDDLE, *Fostering Intellectual Development in Young Children*. New York: Teachers College Press, Columbia University, 1962.

12U. Bronfenbrenner, *Two Worlds of Childhood: U.S. and U.S.S.R.* (New York: Russell Sage Foundation, 1970).

2

planning, organizing, and evaluating

SUPPOSE we were to step into a classroom and watch a teacher interacting with children. We might observe the following:

The teacher asks questions of a child who is experimenting with objects in water. Another child approaches and asks how "ambulance" is spelled. The word is needed for a picture that is one of the drawings the child has assembled into a book. The teacher moves to the box of scrap paper nearby and finds a suitable piece on which to write the word. The child takes the paper and returns to the table to continue making the book. The teacher starts to walk across the room, then pauses to watch a child who is jumping across the room. "Do you want to try hopping all the way back?" asks the teacher. "Hopping is a one-footed jump." The child turns around and begins hopping back.

The math table is the teacher's next stop. The child who is placing pegs in a peg-board there has been selecting numerals from the large upright calendar nearby and making the corresponding number with pegs. The teacher had observed this while with another child at the water table and had heard the child say each numeral aloud before making it: "14, 15, 21, 27, 31." Noting that the child was placing the appropriate number of pegs in the board with ease, the teacher sits down beside the child and asks what number is on the peg-board. "Thirty-one," the child answers. The teacher then asks the child what number there would be if all four rows were filled with pegs. The child hesitates for a moment, and then answers, "forty." "That's right," says the teacher. The teacher then asks whether the child would like to make some very large numbers on the peg-board. The child says yes, and the teacher writes 45, 50, 55, 65, and 70 on a piece of paper. Handing it to the child, the teacher promises to return later to see how things are going and then moves on to a group of children involved in dramatic play.

There are many questions the visitor to the classroom might ask. Why were water and objects provided? Why pegs and peg-boards? Why was the child asked to hop back rather than skip or walk? Why were various children doing different things at the same time? How was it possible for these children to work without constant teacher direction and yet progress in their learning? How did the teacher know what each child was learning?

These questions are answered by teachers as they perform teaching behaviors which often go unnoticed by the observer. These behaviors can be categorized into three types of activities: (1) planning, (2) organizing, and (3) evaluating. The visible aspects of teaching that were noticed by the observer are influenced considerably by these three less visible activities.

PLANNING

Planning is thinking ahead. Planning includes thinking about *what* the teacher wants to happen, *why* it is to happen, *to whom* it is to happen, and *when* and *how* it will be made to happen. Why and to whom something should happen depends on the teacher's evaluation of what children have learned, of what is worthwhile for children to learn, and of what is appropriate for an individual child to learn. When and how the teacher will help learning to occur involves organization. It is in the planning process that planning, organizing, and evaluating merge.

Setting Goals

The question of what the teacher wants to happen is unique to the planning process and involves setting goals. Teachers determine goals for the children in their classrooms. They decide that children should learn to climb a cargo net and throw a ball, count objects and recognize shapes, handle a paint brush and work with clay, and share materials and listen while others talk. Teachers' goals are influenced by a number of factors. These include:

1. The teacher's assumptions about children, their learning, and the purpose of schools.
2. The age of the children in a teacher's class.
3. The community in which the school exists.

A teacher who views learning as a passive process will have goals differing from those of a teacher who views learning as an active process. When learning is considered to occur passively, goals often include helping children learn to sit still, be quiet, and be attentive to the teacher. In contrast, when learning is viewed as an active process, goals often include helping children learn to interact and talk with one another and to decide to whom or what their attention should be directed.

Similarly, goals will differ between two teachers when one views the sole purpose of schools to be to provide literacy skills, whereas the other considers the purpose of schools to include helping children develop a wide range of skills. Planning becomes more complex as the range of goals broadens.

The age of the children one teaches also affects goals. Although age cannot be used as a precise predictor of appropriate goals for specific children, the children's ages will influence the goals a teacher sets. A teacher of three-year-olds who hopes to teach them to tell time, to understand place value in math, jump rope, and to tie their shoes will probably not be very successful. These goals need to be modified to take the children's developmental level into account, and age is a good first indicator of what children's developmental levels may be. Although children's development cannot tell us what knowledge we should teach them, it can tell us something about when and how to teach those things we consider to be valuable.

A teacher's goals are influenced by the school community too. Communities vary in their expectations of what their children should learn and at what levels and in what ways they should learn it. Communities also vary in the skills required to live in them. Although one of the purposes of schooling is to enable children to cope with the larger community that lies beyond the specific one in which they live, the teacher of young children in particular needs to be aware of the child's immediate community and to adjust teaching goals accordingly.

After considering the above factors, teachers develop specific, tentative goals for the children in their classrooms. It is usually helpful to generate goals in terms of categories. Such categories may include mathematics, language and speech, small and large motor skills, peer relationships, adult relationships, self-help and work-study skills, social science, and science. Specific goals would be listed within each category. Not every child in the classroom will attain all goals. Teachers must always adjust and modify goals in relation to individual children.

It should be noted here that specificity of goals need not lead to highly prescribed learning situations for children. Teachers can and should think clearly and specifically about what it is they hope that children will learn, but this clarity of thought does not dictate that children must attain each goal in a specific and isolated fashion. Rather, children can spend much of their time engaged in experiences which contribute to several goals at the same time. A child who participates in a cooking project may learn some language, math, and science, and gain experience in working with peers as well. If the teacher does not think about the experience and its potential for learning, little learning may occur.

Planning as a Process

Good planning starts with goals. The content of the activities and experiences provided in a teaching program should contribute something to the children's development and learning. The plans that are made for implementing activities and experiences should also be related to goals.

Suppose we were to observe in a classroom. We might notice an activity using food coloring, water, and eye-droppers. Three containers of water dyed with food coloring are available (red, yellow, blue) as are several small empty plastic test tubes. The tabletop is covered with a layer of newspapers.

If we were to ask the teacher to explain why he provided this activity, the answer might be as follows:

> Some children in the class are still learning to recognize and name basic colors. This activity provides an opportunity for them to work directly with substances of different colors. The activity also involves the mixing of colors. Children who may already be able to recognize and name basic colors may not know some colors can be made from others. So they can learn that. In addition to contributing to children's understanding about color, the activity helps children develop fine motor skills. It's really quite difficult to manipulate an eye-dropper to obtain a small quantity of water and then squeeze out the amount you want. The activity is also a good one for helping children learn about vacuums and air. For example, the teacher can ask children what they think is in the eye-dropper that keeps water from entering before the bulb is squeezed, or why the water squirts from the dropper when the bulb is squeezed.

> I set up the activity so at least three children can work with it at one time. I want children to share ideas and information and have opportunities to explain things to each other. This activity is a particularly good one to encourage interaction among children. They become very interested in the changes that occur as the colored water is mixed, and they want to tell someone else what they did that caused this to occur. Often other children try to follow these directions to see if they get the same results. I make this activity available during activity time for as long as three or four weeks. This provides ample opportunity for children to have as many turns as they want. Some children spend a great deal of time there and take many turns. I want to encourage this kind of involvement and thoroughness in learning.

As we can see, this teacher had specific reasons for including the colored water activity in the teaching program. Some of these goals were met by the content of the activity. Other goals were met through the way the activity was implemented. This latter effect is known by the term **hidden curriculum** and is often overlooked by the teacher. Teachers should analyze activities in terms of all of their possible effects rather than focusing on the obvious effects of content. It is in the planning process that teachers develop learning experiences and activities that are congruent with teaching goals.

Making Plans

Broad general plans are usually made for the long term, and then details and modifications are made as needed from week to week, day to day, and moment to moment. For example, having decided that a play grocery store would provide good learning experiences for the children in the classroom, the teacher must decide when and how the activity will be introduced. It will be necessary to arrange for space and props and to determine what new knowledge children can gain, what seems to be of interest to them, and at what levels they can handle concepts that may be involved. The teacher must also decide what limits are appropriate: for example, the number of children who may be in an area at one time; times when the store is "open" or "closed"; and the kind of behavior that is to be expected of children using the store. These are broad plans that will have an effect on the activity for its duration.

More detailed plans for the store will need to be made, perhaps on a weekly basis. It might be decided that a trip to a local grocery store is necessary to help the children gain information. It might also be decided that children should purchase some items at the grocery store so that the roles of customer and cashier might be emphasized. Perhaps it is determined that fruit will be purchased because it must be weighed, and the teacher wants to encourage this behavior in the children's later store play. Decisions about what type of fruit and how much would then need to be made. The teacher would also need to make plans for use of the fruit when it is brought to the classroom.

The teacher must also determine which children will make the trip, what staff will go with them, and what mode of travel they will use. In addition, it will be necessary to decide what time of day the trip will be made, as well as when and how to explain to the children what is to occur.

No matter how carefully daily, weekly, or monthly plans are made, moment-to-moment decisions must be made as the reality of the specific situation emerges. It may begin pouring rain as the trip to the store is about to begin, and if the plan was to walk, the trip may have to be cancelled or delayed. Maybe the high school volunteer who was to take the children on the trip will become ill and call only half an hour ahead of time to say so. Perhaps one of the children who had been selected to go will be absent on the day of the trip or will unexpectedly become very upset about leaving the classroom. Or perhaps the day will start out bitter cold but then warm considerably, so that the teacher must decide whether snowpants go on the children or stay at school.

Experienced teachers can make these decisions on the spot. One of the ways to prepare for these moment-to-moment decisions is to make contingency plans. Wise teachers think to themselves, "If we cannot go to the store tomorrow, we can go the following day when we have another volunteer." "If we cannot use the fruit from the store for snack tomorrow, we'll have the graham crackers from the cupboard." "If John and Karen do not wish to make the trip, we will ask Carl and Greg if they would like to go." "If our thermometer reaches 32° we won't dress the children in snowpants for short walks."

It is absolutely crucial for a teacher or the entire staff to devote some time to making weekly plans. In addition, it is usually necessary for a teacher or staff to have at least a short time each day to discuss children and finalize plans. Sometimes teachers do this daily by talking "on the move" as they get materials ready for the day or put the room back in order at day's end. However it is arranged, time to talk and think about children and the program is a necessity.

Involving Children in the Planning Process

Children can contribute many ideas for classroom activities. If children are expected to become independent problem-solvers and planners, then they must be given opportunities to gain experience in these tasks.

Children could be included in planning for the store described above. By using discussions with the whole class and individual children, the teacher can include children in decision-making about where the store should be located in the room, what equipment can be used to build it, what items will make appropriate stock, and what limits will be necessary during store play. Children can also help decide what type of fruit might be purchased at the store, how it will be prepared back at school, and when it should be eaten.

Just as teachers must learn to make decisions from moment to moment, so must children. A question might arise regarding which child gets to pay the cashier for the fruit, or which child gets to carry the package back to school, or which child gets to press the button to make the street light change from red to green. Perhaps each child can purchase two apples each, and each child can carry the package for one block. Children can express their ideas, and alternatives can be discussed. Teachers can help children arrive at and implement satisfactory decisions.

Recording Plans

Teachers sometimes get into heated debates about whether or not plans should be written down. It is the opinion of this author that plans are more useful if they are recorded. If several staff members are involved in implementing the plans, recording becomes even more essential. Sometimes it is impossible for part-time staff to attend all planning sessions and impossible for full-time staff to brief them personally on what they missed. In these cases plans must be readily accessible and understandable in written form to insure that staff know what they are to do when they arrive to work with the children.

There are dozens of ways to record plans. Teachers must develop a method suitable for their particular situations. A weekly plan sheet for a preschool with one full-time teacher (Jan), one part-time assistant (Ted), and three high-school volunteers (Sara, John, and Steve) took the form shown in Figure 1.

Area \ Day	Monday	Tuesday	Wednesday	Thursday	Friday
Math	Chart Worms eaten by turtle. →				
Science	(Steve)		(Steve) Tubes, corks, water and food coloring.		
Language Arts			(Sara) Write dicta- tion.		
House Area	(Ted) Add Materials for table.	(Ted) Applesauce- Sharon & Tom	(Ted)	(Ted)	(Ted)
Blocks	Add transporta- toys.				
Art Table	Object painting		Add new objects for printing. →		
Music	Resonating bells.			(John)	
Story	(Jan) (Steve)	(Ted)	(Ted)	(Ted) (Susan)	(Ted) (Jan)
Group Time	(Jan)	(Jan)	(Jan)	(Jan)	(Jan)
Outdoor Play	Old tires for rolling down hill.		Visiting goat.		
Trips or Visitors					
Snack	Celery and peanut butter.	Applesauce	Juice and graham crack- ers.	Tapioca pudding.	Juice and raisins.

Figure 1. Teacher's weekly plan sheet.

This particular classroom was organized into learning centers (refer to the section of this chapter dealing with organization of space, begin- ning on page 17 and a wide variety of basic materials was always avail- able to the children. Therefore, the weekly plan sheet needed only to note additions in materials or special projects which were to be started or continued.

Part-time and volunteer staff assigned to specific areas of responsibility were also noted on the plan sheet. The full-time teacher was not assigned to any particular area, but was to move from area to area as needed. The staff member who has this duty is often referred to as the *floater.*

Because the high-school volunteers in this class were not available for planning sessions, additional information was provided to them through notes posted on a bulletin board next to the plan sheet. When they arrived to the classroom to work with the children, they first referred to the plan sheet and then looked for any notes posted for them. A note corresponding to the weekly plan sheet shown in Figure 1 might have read as follows:

Sara:

Hi. Thought you'd like a turn at the table where children usually sit when making books. A few children can do the writing themselves although you'll have to spell most of the words. In order to find out who can do what, just ask them if they want to write the words or if they want you to write. They'll let you know what they can do.

Try to get the children to tell you what letter the words they want start with. If they're stumped, don't hesitate to tell them.

I gave you a manuscript letter guide earlier in the year so you could practice. There's another one on my desk if you need it for reference. The children might become interested in it if you do use it and that will be good. There are dotted letter guides available on the language arts shelves if anyone wants to practice writing letters rather than or in addition to writing stories.

I've scheduled Ted for story so I can talk with you a minute before you must leave today.

Jan

Another plan sheet was also utilized in this classroom. It took the form of a "helpers' chart." It was posted in the classroom at the children's eye level. It was they who changed the names on the jobs at the end of each week. The name of each child had been written on three cards providing a small deck of name cards for each of the three jobs listed. The name card of the child who had finished the week as helper for the job was removed from the chart and placed on the bottom of the deck, and the name on the top of the deck was put on the chart to indicate the new helper. If a child's name already appeared on the chart for one job, his card, too, was put at the bottom of the deck and the next name was taken. Rubber bands were used to hold each of the three name-card decks securely.

In addition to the two planning charts discussed above, Jan, the full-time teacher in this classroom, kept a notebook in which she wrote ideas and tasks that were specifically for her reference. She typically wrote plans in this book for one week at a time, although she was careful to leave adequate space under the daily headings to add further plans as needed. The entries were reminders to herself of materials to bring, activities to suggest to specific children, or of specific children who needed special help or observation.

A teacher who works with kindergarten and primary-age children can utilize methods which involve children in recording plans for their work. Kindergarten children can keep their own plan sheets, which may be similar to the one shown in Figure 2. By referring to these records, each child and the teacher can determine work to be done.

Children in the primary grades can assume a greater amount of the responsibility for keeping plans for their work. They will usually be held responsible for the completion of a certain amount of math, reading, and writing every week. Plans for work can be kept in individual folders for each area of study. A child can place completed work in his folder and give it to the teacher, who can then place comments and suggestions for further work in the folder and hand it back to the child. In actual operation, assignments are given and work is evaluated by a combination of conferences and written messages.

Even though more responsibility for keeping written plans is assumed by children at the kindergarten and primary-grade levels, teachers will usually find it necessary to keep a separate book of some sort for reminders and ideas for their own reference. For example, there will be plans made that affect the group as a whole and which may not be noted in any individual child's plans.

ORGANIZATION

Organization is a tool for achieving goals and implementing plans. It determines in large part whether plans are successful and thus whether goals are attained. Teachers must learn to organize space, time, materials, and staff if they wish to be effective.

Organizing Space

Individualized classes may be organized into learning centers which provide for different types of activities to occur simultaneously in the classroom. Learning centers are clearly defined physical areas with space for working. They offer children a wide range of learning options. They allow children to practice skills, pursue topics of special interest, use different learning styles, and proceed at their own pace. They also foster involvement required to integrate and consolidate learning.

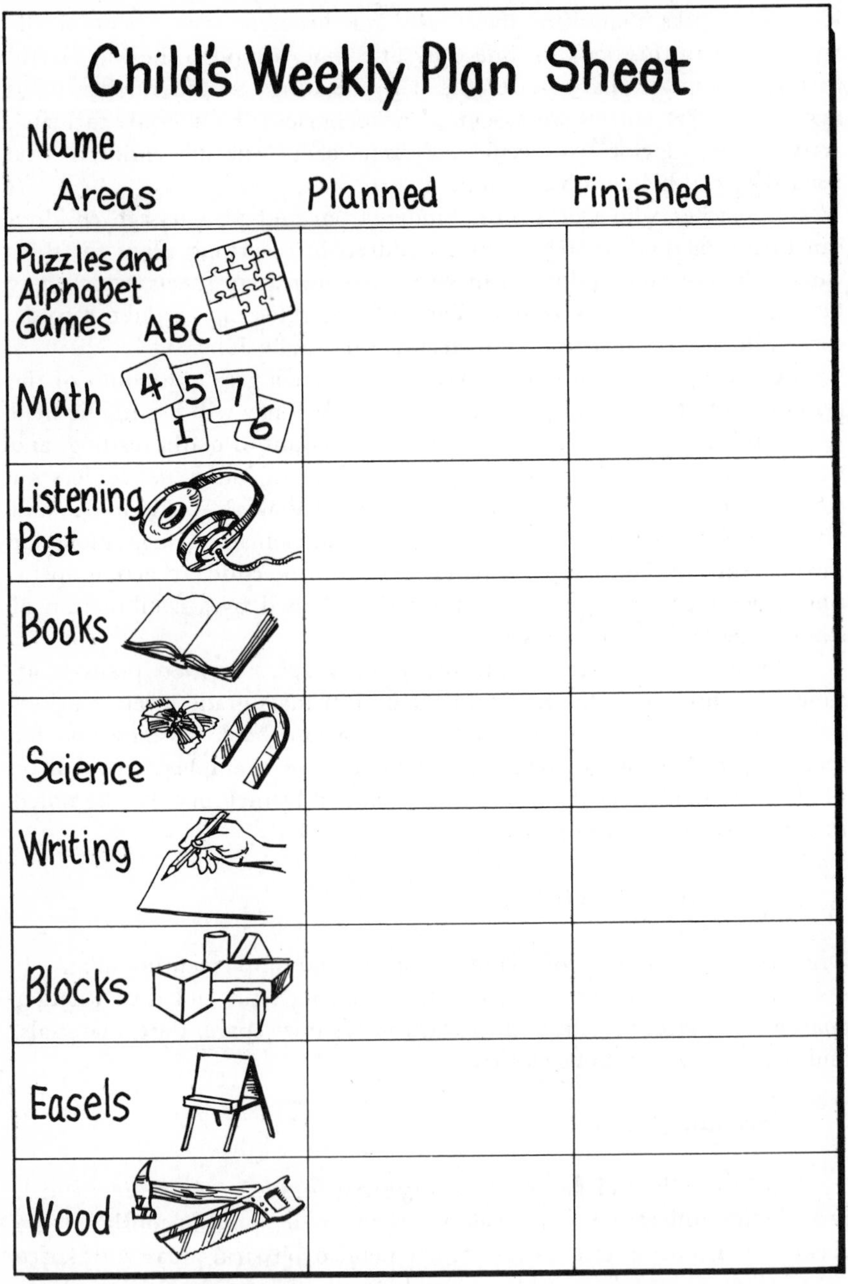

Child's Weekly Plan Sheet

Name ____________________

Areas	Planned	Finished
Puzzles and Alphabet Games ABC		
Math 4 5 7 1 6		
Listening Post		
Books		
Science		
Writing		
Blocks		
Easels		
Wood		

Figure 2. Child's weekly plan sheet.

Each center should be attractive, inviting, and well stocked with materials. For example, a mathematics center might contain counters, string, felt numerals, numeral cards, a 100's board, pegs and peg-boards, popsicle sticks and rubber bands, a pan balance, graph paper, geometric shapes, and geoboards. The center might also contain metronomes, clocks, hourglasses, and kitchen timers. All of these materials would be present in the center so that different interests and levels of ability would be provided for. They would be arranged for children to obtain what they needed with ease.

When the goals inherent in a center have been met, or when the materials in a center are no longer interesting to children, the center should be dismantled or reorganized so that more current interests and needs are reflected. As specific new interests arise and as children proceed with skill development, the teacher and children may plan together for new equipment and materials needed and for the placement of new centers.

SELECTING CENTERS. There are four major factors to consider when selecting centers for a classroom. These are:

1. The teacher's goals for children's learning.
2. Individual characteristics of the children in the class.
3. The length of the school day.
4. The demands of group living.

What teachers want children to learn will affect the centers chosen for a classroom. If a teacher values art and music, then space for these activities will need to be provided.

Center selection will also be influenced by the characteristics of the children in the class. For example, larger amounts of space within a center will need to be provided for younger children than for older ones. This may require that fewer centers be operating concurrently in a class of younger children. Differing amounts of space are also required for children with special needs, such as those confined to wheelchairs.

The selection of centers is also affected by the length of the school day. For example, in an all-day program provision must be made for storage of cots and cooking and eating facilities. Space needed for these activities may limit the number of centers which can be set up at one time.

Provisions for group living should also influence the selection of centers. Children need space to be by themselves, space to work with other children, and space to come together as a group.

ARRANGING CENTERS. After determining the different types of activities which will require classroom space, the teacher must arrange activity spaces within the classroom. Guidelines for planning the placement of areas include:

1. Locate electrical outlets and place areas for activities requiring electricity near them. For example, a listening center would need to be near an outlet.
2. Place the art area near a water source. If there is a sink in the room, the art center should be near it. If there is no sink in the room, the art center might be most conveniently placed by the door where access to hall sinks and bathrooms would be easiest.
3. Separate noisy activities from quiet activities. The library and mathematics centers should be separated from the block and dramatic-play centers.
4. Arrange the centers to divert traffic from areas where it would disturb work. It would be very distracting, for example, to have the main traffic patterns running through the block area.
5. Determine sources of light and decide what activities require it. For example, light is important for growing plants or doing close work.
6. Organize centers as distinct areas which are clearly defined.
7. Arrange areas to make them readily visible to the teacher. This permits the teacher to see when children need help or guidance.
8. Place interrelated areas adjacent to one another. For example, blocks may frequently be used to represent objects in dramatic play, or wheeled toys may represent the "work" that some member of the pretend family go to in the course of their dramatic play.

Sample plans which illustrate these guidelines are shown below in Figure 3.

Organizing Time

Traditionally, time has been blocked into small subject-matter or activity segments during which all children in a class engage in the same activity at the same time. This type of organization is not functional in individualized programs because all children are not learning the same thing in the same way at the same time. Even so, time is still structured or organized, although the organization differs from that found in traditional programs.

SCHEDULE COMPONENTS. A **schedule** provides the structure for the best use of student and teacher time. Components of a schedule are influenced by the same factors that influence the selection of activity areas (refer to page 19). For example, an extended nap might be needed in an all-day program for three-year-olds, whereas in a half-day program for five-year-olds a nap would not be needed. In all-day programs time

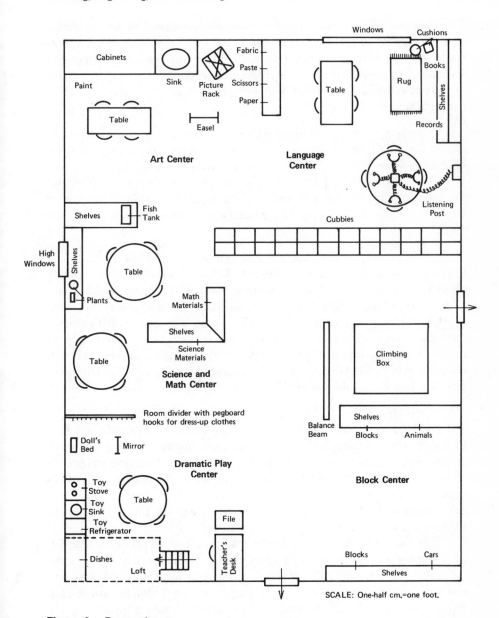

Figure 3. Room plan.

will have to be scheduled for meals, but in half-day programs it will not. Components which are typical of individualized programs for young children are discussed below.

Arrival. This is the period of time when children make the transition from home to school. In this time each child should have an opportunity to talk with the teacher or with other children and to move at individual speed into the day's activities. In schools where children arrive at different times, this period will be longer than when they arrive at the same time.

Planning meeting. This is a time for the teacher and children to clarify plans for the day. Sometimes they will review plans made earlier; sometimes they will need to make new plans. It should be kept short.

The teacher should be well informed about the work children did the previous day. During the meeting, the teacher provides guidance by asking questions and making suggestions which help children plan their day.

Activity and/or work time. The activity or work times constitute the major instructional time for the day. Rather than scheduling separate times for reading, mathematics, spelling, and so forth, the teacher sets aside a large block of time for these subjects. On any given day, some children might spend large amounts of time on a project which incorporates many areas of study, while other children may work specifically on mathematics, reading, or science. Over a period of time, all children will experience both kinds of days. This organization allows for attainment, practice, and consolidation of skills.

Evaluation time. This provides an opportunity for the teacher and children to discuss the day's work experiences and plan for what is to follow the next day. The discussion may involve sharing the day's events, bringing each other up to date on projects, and making judgments about work that has been done. As the children summarize their day's experiences, the teacher asks questions and provides information which helps them to evaluate their progress. They then use this evaluation to plan for the following day.

For example, the teacher might ask what a child did with the fish tank during activity time. The child might report having added some more water to the tank. The teacher would then inquire why it was necessary to add the water. The child might or might not be aware that water evaporates from the tank. The teacher should supplement the child's explanation if necessary. The teacher might then point out that the gravel in the tank was disturbed when the new water was poured in and ask whether anyone has an idea how new water could be added without disturbing the gravel. Children will usually come up with suggestions. Some will be reasonably on target, while others may not be. The teacher should accept all suggestions at this point by responding with a comment such as, "Yes, that might work." After a short time of brainstorming, the teacher should offer to provide materials at the water table so that the children can experiment to see how water can be poured from one container into another without disturbing the gravel the tank contains. There might be a clamoring of many children at this point to be allowed to do this. The teacher might respond by assuring the children that the materials will be kept out as long as anyone wants to experiment with them. The discussion then passes on to another topic.

Perhaps some cooking is to be done the next day and it is the procedure in this class for the cooks to check the ingredient supply one day ahead to make sure they have what is needed. The teacher might ask one of them if the cooks did check and if everything is there. The child might report that milk and two eggs are needed. The teacher might say that milk will be available from the school cafeteria, but that someone will need to bring the eggs. Two children volunteer to bring one each. It appears, then, that the cooking is all set for the next day, and the discussion moves on.

Evaluation sessions should be reasonably short; the length will vary with the age of the children and their ability to participate. Evaluation time is a crucial time in individualized programs. It provides a means for maintaining continuity in the children's lives. Children need to know what is going to happen next. In programs based primarily on textbooks and workbooks, the problem of continuity is solved. One simply goes on to the next page of the book or to the next book in the series. In individualized programs continuity is established by means of evaluation and decision-making procedures through which children gain a sense of what has been done and what some next steps are to be. Evaluation time provides one of the ways for this process to occur.

Nap time. This is a time during the day when children are expected to rest. Most preprimary children need to nap and this requires that they lie down. The teacher may realize early in the year that a few children do not require naps but will still need to rest. Occasionally, there will be a child who does not require either a nap or rest. Quiet activities should be provided for such children in a separate area where they will not disturb children who are sleeping.

Teachers often find it difficult to help children rest at naptime. Several techniques may be used to encourage children to rest. Sometimes a soft animal or book will help relax children before they fall asleep. Quiet music is also helpful in relaxing some children. Others will quiet quickly if their backs are rubbed.

Physical play. Young children are still learning basic motor skills such as climbing, skipping, throwing, and running. Specific provision should be made for such activity, particularly when limited classroom space reduces the range of activities which can be made available there.

Equipment facilitating the development of large motor skills should be provided. Teachers should encourage children to use this equipment independently. If some children do not play on equipment or participate in other rigorous activity, the teacher may engage them in activities such as jump rope, pitch and catch, frisbee, hula hoops, or games involving skipping, running and jumping. When restricted facilities or inclement weather prevent outside activities, provisions for comparable indoor experiences should be made.

Snack and lunch time. Because children burn up energy quickly, they need to eat frequently. Midmorning and midafternoon snacks should be provided. In full-day programs, lunch will also be served.

Snacks should be nutritious and varied. Nutritious foods such as milk or natural fruit juices, raw vegetables, fresh fruits, whole-grain foods, nuts, raisins, and peanut butter should be used. Since the growth rate of preprimary and primary children has slowed considerably from what it was when they were infants and toddlers and their appetites diminish accordingly, they should be served small portions. Those children who in fact can eat larger quantities can ask for more or take additional amounts when offered.

Snacks can be provided to the whole group at a specific time or made available early in the morning for a short period during which children may serve themselves. When snack is a group activity, it provides an opportunity for informal conversation between children and teachers. It should be remembered that children like to help set the table, prepare snacks, and serve them too.

Lunch in preprimary classes would be served much as has been described above. Care should be taken that meals are attractive, provide a variety of color and texture, and follow nutritional guidelines.

Music, movement, and story. These schedule components are somewhat self-explanatory. Experiences in music, movement, and story should be possible during activity/work time; however, because of constraints imposed by spatial requirements or noise, many teachers prefer specific time to be set aside for these also. For example, although musical instruments would be available to children during some portions of activity/work time and a teacher may guide some individuals or small clusters of children in working with these, a time is still set aside for musical activity involving all the children.

SCHEDULE SEQUENCE. Having determined the different types and lengths of activities which need a time slot during the school day, the teacher must determine their sequence. There are often external constraints on the sequence of a schedule. These include availability of shared resources such as gym facilities, eating facilities, special staff, and transportation accommodations. These fixed times should be noted first and other activities then filled in, and it is here that teachers have some flexibility. In determining how to arrange the schedule, the teacher should try to alternate active and less active periods, quiet and noisy periods, and periods requiring different kinds of participation.

Schedules for various kinds of programs are shown below:

Half-Day Preprimary Schedule

Arrival
Activity time (60–70 min.)
Clean-up (10 min.)
Group discussion and evaluation (10–15 min.)
Music and movement (15–20 min.)
Snack (10 min.)
Story (10–20 min.)
Second activity time or outdoor play (45 min.)

All-Day Preprimary Schedule

Arrival (can occur at different times for different children)
Activity time (60–80 min.)
Group discussion and evaluation (10 min.)
Snack (15 min.)
Story (15 min.)
Outside play (60 min.)
Lunch (30 min.)
Nap (90–120 min.)
Quiet time with quiet activities such as table games, puzzles, or art (30–120 min.; for those who do not sleep, this overlaps with nap time)
Music and movement (15–20 min.)
Snack (15 min.)
Physical play (outdoor or indoor 20–30 min.)
Story-records, film strips, movies, story-reading, puppet shows, flannel stories, quality TV programs such as *Mr. Rogers' Neighborhood* or *Sesame Street*

Primary Program Schedule

Arrival
Group planning meeting (15–20 min.)
Work-time (90 min.)
Group discussion and evaluation of work time (20 min.)

Lunch (30–40 min.)

Story read by teacher (15 min.)

Work time to continue work started in morning or begin new work (60–90 min.)

Gym or music (20 min.)

Group activity (student play or skit, puppet show, etc.) (20–30 min.)

Clean-up

In the above schedules active and less active periods have been staggered throughout the day. Activity time allows for moderate activity, whereas group discussion and evaluation which follow provide for relatively little activity. Story time would probably be the least active period of the day and it is followed by a more active period.

Quiet and noisy periods correspond closely to the less active and active periods, although there are some exceptions. Snack and lunch may be inactive, but not quiet. On the other hand, movement may be quite active, but quiet.

The kind of participation required of children in the activities listed also varies. During activity time, children participate individually or in small groups and make decisions about what they will do. This is followed by group discussions which require that children wait their turn to talk and remain quiet while others speak. Snack and meal times are group activities too, but they do not depend on the same type of participation or performance that as group discussion does. Lunch is followed by story time, which requires a different group effort.

Organizing Materials

SELECTING MATERIALS. The task of selecting materials is one of the teacher's major responsibilities. Materials should be selected on the basis of the following considerations: (1) safety, (2) durability, (3) cost, (4) instructional qualities, and (5) flexibility.

Safety. Materials used by children must be safe. Teachers should be alert to materials and equipment made with toxic materials such as lead paint. Materials should also be inspected to make certain that pieces do not come apart to expose nails and pins. The age of the children who will be using the equipment should also be remembered when teachers select materials for the classroom. Although pointed scissors may be used safely by an eight-year-old, they may be dangerous in the hands of a three-year-old.

Durability. Equipment used by a group of children will receive hard wear. The durability of learning equipment will be greater if suitable materials are used in its construction. For example, wooden blocks and puzzles last much longer than cardboard blocks and puzzles. Even durable materials deteriorate, however. It is essential, therefore, to be sure that materials are used and cared for properly. Paint brushes left in paint cups overnight soon become bent at the ends. Loose screws soon fall out and result in lost pieces.

Teachers can further the life of some materials and equipment. Paper materials can be laminated. Writing or drawing used to make teaching aids can be done with ink or a felt-tip marker, which leave marks that remain clear and dark, rather than with pencil or crayon, which do not. Paint and varnish can be used to prolong the life of materials made of wood or metal.

The containers in which materials are stored can also affect how long the items will last. Materials purchased in bulk or which arrive in flimsy containers will last longer if transferred to more suitable containers. If containers are too small for the amount of material stored in them, it is likely that some pieces will be spilled, damaged, and lost. The size of the container can also affect the care with which materials are put away, and thus, the amount of wear and tear they receive. Large Leggo pieces and one-inch cubes are often put away more carefully if they fit exactly into the storage containers. Similarly, materials with two distinct parts, such as lotto cards and pictures to match, will be put away more carefully if their storage containers are compartmentalized. Sometimes a smaller box inside a larger one works well. If the materials can be stored in this way, dumping and sorting by the next user is avoided and the materials receive less wear.

Teachers must also guard against the loss of a piece or two from a toy or game. For example, the loss of a puzzle piece ruins a puzzle. Putting a matching symbol, such as a number, on a puzzle frame and its pieces helps to keep them together. Carefully checking equipment each day at clean-up time can help rescue items before they are swept up or thrown out by mistake.

Cost. The question of durability can present a dilemma for the teacher because it is often directly related to that of cost. Wooden unit blocks are expensive in terms of initial outlay, whereas cardboard building blocks are not. Many teachers purchase the cardboard blocks only to find that they do not withstand children's play. In the long run, the wood blocks might be a better buy.

When teachers face children every day and they need materials and equipment immediately, they often trade durability for cost. This is unfortunate because teachers can often find or make things which work as well as the cheaper items they buy. Department stores, for example, are

Appropriate containers for materials encourage good care.

good sources for sturdy oblong boxes used as packing material. These
make very adequate cardboard blocks. The only cost is that of the tape
required to secure the box ends. In the short run teachers have blocks,
and in the long run they will be able to put more money into equipment
and materials which are of high quality. Over a period of years the
teacher will have a much better equipped classroom than if money had
been spent on lots of inexpensive materials to begin with.

Instructional qualities of materials. Teachers should also consider
the instructional qualities of materials. The consideration applies to
equipment and materials designed for specific instructional goals. It is
not uncommon for such materials to be designed so that children become
confused. Materials designed to help children detect initial consonants
should not include pictures of items whose names begin with consonant
blends and digraphs. "Shoe" is not an appropriate word to help children
learn the sound represented by a single s. "Sun" and "superman" are.
Similarly, arm balances designed to help children discover number relationships must be sensitive enough for children to receive accurate information.

Teachers also need to judge instructional qualities of materials in terms of the range of opportunities they provide. Materials should provide learning opportunities for children operating at different levels. This is not so problematic with flexible materials such as blocks or clay, because children are able to adapt these to their own ideas. It is an important consideration, however, with items such as puzzles, books, and materials designed to teach specific skills. It is wise to purchase only one of anything that can be used for just one purpose or which is only appropriate for children at a particular level. If a certain initial-consonant teaching aid can only be used for this purpose, only one set may be purchased. Pegs and peg-boards, on the other hand, can be used to help children at various levels understand many math concepts, and so it may be wise to purchase several sets.

Flexibility. Materials with specific attributes and purposes need to be included in a classroom. Puzzles, beads, books, records, a pan balance, magnets, and many other materials are quite specific in their design and use. In addition to these specific materials, classrooms should have abundant supplies of materials that lend themselves to many uses. Water, sand, blocks, cubes, clay, and paint are examples of materials which have flexible uses.

SOURCES FOR MATERIALS. Teachers must know where to obtain materials at reasonable or no cost. Educational equipment companies supply catalogues of their products and often display them at conferences. Teachers can use these catalogues and displays to become familiar with and select materials.

Teachers also need to know where to obtain free materials they want. If a teacher knows where to look for what he wants, this process can be simplified. Sources for free, natural and waste materials are listed below.

1. Lumber yards
   Scrap lumber, sawdust, sturdy cardboard boxes, wood shavings
2. Department stores
   Ribbon and paper scraps, drapery and carpet swatches, packing materials, display racks, cardboard boxes
3. Hospitals or clinics
   Heavy paper from X-ray films
4. Pharmacies
   Bottles of all sizes and shapes, small boxes
5. Telephone company
   Colored wire, cable spools, telephone poles
6. Hardware stores
   Wallpaper books, paint chips, linoleum samples

The natural environment can provide materials and equipment at little or no cost.

7. Printing companies
   Scrap paper
8. Gas stations
   Tires and inner tubes, ball bearings, car parts
9. Furniture stores
   Packing crates, scrap lumber, fabric scraps
10. Factories
    Foam rubber, plastic, leather, metal scraps, spools, wire, wood, paper
11. Out of doors
    Acorns, buckeyes, flowers and weeds, birds' nests, cocoons, leaves, pebbles, bark, pine cones, shells, trees (see photo above for example of how trees may be used as playground equipment)
12. Home
    Fruit and meat trays, egg cartons, coffee cans, tubes from towels and toilet paper, scrap fabric, empty food containers, old clothes, cardboard, magazines, newspapers
13. Chambers of commerce
    Maps, posters, information about their locale
14. Travel agencies, airline and railway companies
    Maps, schedules, colored posters

MATERIALS AND CLASSROOM STRUCTURE. It is possible to create as well as avoid problems by organizing materials in different ways. The arrangement of materials suggests something to children. It is extremely important for the smooth running of individualized programs that classrooms not be in disarray. Cluttered shelves suggest that materials do not belong in a particular place. In such rooms children are not apt to put things away. This makes it difficult for the next person to find the materials that are needed. Clutter also suggests to children that quality work is not expected. If quality work is expected, and it should be, then a quality environment is essential.

It is fairly easy to keep materials organized in some reasonable fashion. Designating specific and permanent storage places can help. For young children, pictures can be used to label storage areas. If woodworking tools are stored on peg-board hooks, their forms can be cut from colored contact paper and placed on the peg-board. These forms indicate specific places for the saw, hammer, drill, and screw driver. This reminds children where the tools belong. A similar technique can be used to label block shelves. It can also be used to label shelves for the placement of containers of crayons, paste, and magic markers.

Organization of materials can also affect the amount of traffic within a classroom. If items such as pencils, crayons, paper, and paste are placed

Equipment can help the teacher extend his time.

in all centers which require their use, rather than in just one center, traffic can be reduced considerably. In addition, this multiple placement reduces the extent to which items are lost or misplaced, because items are used near the place they are stored.

The organization of materials in a classroom can affect how children group themselves, and therefore, how they interact. For example, the quietness in the quiet area will depend in part on the number of children who congregate there. A teacher who wants to insure that small groupings will form in the quiet area, but does not want to enforce this personally all the time, can present materials in ways which suggest that only two or three children should work with them at the same time. For example, individual sets of crayons for illustrating stories might be placed in juice cans or plastic cups rather than all being together in large coffee cans or food jars. This arrangement suggests that a certain number of children are to use crayons at one time. If two sets are available, it suggests that only two children may work. If there are three sets, it suggests that three children may work. The number of chairs at a table, cushions in a library area, or smocks in the art area can have the same effect. In classes where small rugs are used as individual work spaces, the

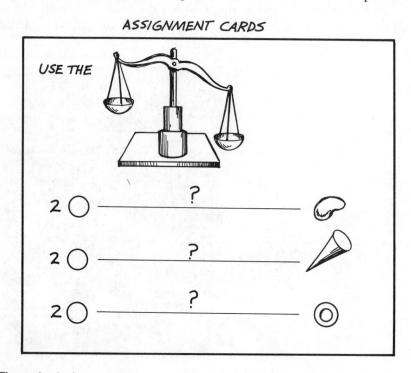

Figure 4. Assignment cards.

Figures 5 and 6. Assignment cards.

number of these in an area defines the number of people who may work there.

USING MATERIALS AND EQUIPMENT TO SAVE TIME. A teacher can extend instructional time by utilizing equipment and materials which can assume some instructional duties. A listening post can provide opportunities for children to hear stories without requiring the teacher's time. Self-correcting skill materials may also be used. A game for matching initial consonants could be made. The consonants should be written on cards. Pictures of items which begin with phonemes represented by the consonants should be pasted on another set of cards. Each consonant and picture-card pair can be color coded to enable children to check their own work.

Assignment cards are also useful devices for making a teacher's time go further. They are cards with questions or instructions pertaining to an activity. They are easier to use with primary school children who can read, but picture assignment cards can be used effectively with younger children. Several sample assignment cards are illustrated in Figures 4, 5, and 6.

By using materials similar to those described above, the teacher is using indirect instructional methods. Equipment and materials can help a child gain a skill or acquire information without constant and direct supervision from the teacher. These items free the teacher during the school day to be able to spend time with children on tasks which they cannot do alone. Even though such equipment and materials can be valuable as extenders of the teacher's instructional time, the teacher is still the key to instruction. Indirect instruction is only as good as the teacher's judgment about what kinds of experiences will be helpful to children and about what materials and equipment can provide good instruction.

MAKING MATERIALS GO FURTHER. The way in which materials are introduced into the classroom can affect their use by children. Children can explore an activity more completely if materials are presented carefully. By developing and extending activities over time, teachers can save preparation time because they can begin thinking in terms of small modifications of what they have, rather than in terms of major overhauls.

Clay, for example, may first be made available for several weeks without tools. The novelty of a new material will be sufficient to keep the children working the clay with their hands. Interest in this mode of exploration may last for several weeks. When it seems to be waning, one or two types of utensils such as cookie cutters, rolling pins, plastic knives, clay stamps, or wooden clay tools can be added. This addition changes the clay activity just enough to renew interest. After several more weeks, interest can again be revived by adding different utensils or tools. One reason why this procedure works so often to renew interest is that with the new tools children find new ways in which to work with the materials. New problems are created and must be solved.

The same principle can be applied to many other activities. New props for block play and dramatic play can be added from time to time. New utensils can be added to the sand and water play areas also.

Another way in which materials can be made to go further is to think of multiple uses for them. Dominoes can be used for several math skills, such as matching one to one, addition, subtraction, and multiplication. Cards from a rook deck can be used for a variety of mathematical skill games or as numeral cards with boxes containing different sets of materials. All of the felt letters that come in a set are not needed at the felt board. At least one letter from each set could be glued to a cardboard square to make a set of tactile cards.

Organizing Activities

The organization of an activity has a great impact on how effective it is. Sometimes the content or the idea of an activity is excellent and the potential for learning is high, but because the teacher fails to organize the activity carefully, children are unable to profit from it. For example, recently this author observed in two different classrooms where an identical activity had been prepared for the children. The activity in both cases was a "fishing game." Fishing poles had been made from dowel rods, string, and magnets. "Fish" had been made from heavy paper, and paper clips had been inserted into each one in the mouth area. Children were to catch the fish by connecting the magnet and the paper clip. In both classes, the activity was provided as one of many choices during an activity period.

In one class, the student helper placed the fish in a small area on the floor and gave the poles to children who wished to fish. As the children fished, they sometimes stood very near the fish or even stepped on top of them. They also tangled their lines from time-to-time, and bumped each other's arms. The teacher tried to help the children solve these problems by suggesting they "stand back," "watch out," and "be careful." The children responded to these suggestions very little and in general continued to have difficulty. The teacher grew impatient as conflicts continued to arise, and finally began telling children they could not fish if they did not do it "right." A fishing pole was taken away from one child who continued to step into the pile of fish on the floor.

In the second classroom, the teacher made a large "lake" on the floor with masking tape. She placed the fish inside the boundaries. Sometimes, as children fished, they would step over the tape and the teacher would warn them in a playful tone that they would get wet if they didn't get out of the lake. Children quickly stepped back beyond the tape line when the teacher pointed this out, although the teacher did have to repeat the warning several times during the activity when children forgot to stay out of the lake. The circle made by the tape was big enough that children had plenty of room to fish without bumping into each other, and this spacing seemed to prevent tangled lines too.

The simple addition of a lake made with tape seemed to make a difference in helping children be either successful or unsuccessful with this activity. It may have worked well because it appealed to children's sense of make-believe, or it may simply have provided more specific information about what to do than was the case with verbalizations such as "stand back," "watch out," and "be careful."

The difference in organization of the two fishing games seemed to have an impact on the children's learning. In the first classroom, the teacher spent so much time correcting children's behavior that she and the children had little time to talk about anything else. In the second classroom, however, the teacher asked individual children questions about the number of fish they were catching, about their color, and about the types of fish they might be. She also asked if they had ever been fishing and what must really be placed on the end of a fishing line if you want to catch a fish.

A teacher who plans an activity might ask what type of behavior is to be expected in relation to the activity. The teacher should then analyze how to organize the activity to make it easy for children to meet the expectations. Many times it is only after the activity has been tried that its difficulties are apparent. When difficulties do arise, we must be careful not simply to blame the children or chalk it up to a bad day. Sometimes children are to blame and sometimes it is the day, but often it is failure on the teacher's part to organize the activity in a way that helps children relate to it in the way the teacher expects. Good teachers analyze activities and make adjustments which improve them.

Organizing Staff

Teachers who wish to provide individualized instruction are aware that a small amount of individual instruction is more effective than much longer periods of large-group instruction.[1] Yet, faced with as many as thirty children in a kindergarten or primary classroom, a teacher may well despair of finding time to spend with each child. In most pre-kindergarten classrooms the teacher has a paid assistant, and in many kindergarten and primary classrooms paid aides are a part of the staff. When this is not so, volunteers may provide the solution. Parents, high-school students, or retired persons may be called on to volunteer their services. Whether a teacher is working with paid staff or with volunteers, skill in using such help to best advantage is required.

[1]M. Blank and F. Solomon, "A Tutorial Program to Develop Abstract Thinking in Socially Disadvantaged Preschool Children," *Child Development*, 39, no. 2 (1968), pp. 379–389.

UTILIZING STAFF EFFECTIVELY. Good communication among staff is a must. Only when assistants are aware of the teacher's purposes, plans, and methods can teacher and assistant work together as a smoothly functioning team. To achieve this, the teacher should be prepared to spend time with assistants when children are not present. Staff meetings for program planning, when the teacher can communicate plans and desires and elicit ideas, suggestions and feedback about children from assistants, should be scheduled periodically. In addition, a relaxed chat over a cup of coffee after the children have left may do much to help the teacher gain insight into an assistant's strengths and allow the assistant a chance to ask questions.

Even though the ideal is to include all staff—part-time, full-time, and volunteer—in program planning, there are times when it is not possible. Then there should be some way to inform everyone of plans made or changed. A plan sheet such as the one on page 15 is one way; providing a "mail" box for each assistant where notes may be left is another (see page 16 for an example of a note left for a high-school volunteer).

To utilize volunteers effectively, it is particularly important to communicate a feeling of welcome, need, and appreciation. It is wise to suggest that a new assistant, whether volunteer or paid, take time to observe the class without participating and to follow the observation with a conference during which the new assistant can ask questions. Schedules for specific and regular times for the assistant to be in the classroom should then be arranged. Asking volunteers to notify the teacher when they cannot be in the classroom as scheduled serves the double purpose of emphasizing to them the importance of their help and allowing the teacher to make alternate plans. As has been suggested in the section on planning, it is important that assistants have a clear idea of what the teacher expects them to do.

Children as a source of help. Children themselves may also be utilized as teachers. If there is one child who is beginning to learn addition facts and another who needs additional practice, they could both benefit from working with flash cards. The beginner holds the cards with the facts and answers, which is what beginners need, while the other child is quizzed on recall, which provides a chance for practice and review. When children have developed a particular skill, teaching another child increases their feeling of self-worth and develops their ability to conceptualize what they have done.

In addition to helping with some of the instruction, children can be helpful in other ways. They can be responsible for many of the details of classroom life. If rooms are arranged by the teacher to make it possible, children can get materials out, put them away, and clean up. For

Children can teach each other.

example, there is no reason for a preschool teacher to spend time tying or snapping children's paint smocks when simple, pull-on designs can be made. Similarly, a teacher does not need to spend time digging out blobs of paste onto pieces of paper each time a child needs some, when adequate amounts to last several weeks can be made available in small jars which can be stored on a shelf for children's use.

People to make things. Though not all volunteers have the patience or desire to work directly with children, many would be happy to provide other kinds of help. Many of the preparation tasks that teachers perform are not particularly difficult but require a substantial amount of time. It would be helpful if someone other than the teacher could do this work. There are many resources for such help. One frequently overlooked resource is older people. If older people live in group centers, they usually welcome requests for help to make things. Older people often have time on their hands and would like to contribute.

Parents too can help make things. Parent workshops are a good strategy for using their skills. Parents may visit with each other and the teacher while making materials. Workshops have the additional benefit of acquainting parents with materials their children will be using.

Teachers should not overlook the fact that it is difficult for some

parents to attend meetings and workshops at school. This does not necessarily indicate a lack of interest on the parents' part. It is often possible
for these parents to make things for the school while they are at home,
and teachers should make this option available. This strategy for parent
help can in fact be quite beneficial to the child. Sometimes the child can
assist the parent in making items for school. When this is not possible,
the child often is very aware that the parent is making something for
school and will often feel proud and special.

EVALUATING

The primary purpose of evaluation is to provide a basis for individual
guidance. Each child is evaluated in order to determine strengths and
weaknesses so that school experiences can enhance learning.

What to Evaluate

In order to evaluate a child's learning in any area, the teacher must
have a clear idea of the goals for the child's learning. Progress or growth
assume a direction. They assume movement from one level to another.
When a child's learning is evaluated, three steps are involved: (1) information is gathered to determine the child's skills and understandings,
(2) a comparison is made between the present assessment and previous
assessments, and (3) a comparison is made between the present assessment
and goals for the child's learning.

Although these steps are based on an underlying structure which
requires an organized idea of a progression in understandings and skills,
this does not mean that children's learning must be rigidly sequenced.
At any point in a child's learning, for example, there are many next
steps in mathematics. If a child can recognize and name sets with number
properties up to five, the child is probably ready to: (1) learn to recognize
and name sets greater than five, (2) learn about the relationships among
numbers from one through five, or (3) learn to recognize written numerals
for numbers through five and match them with the proper sets. In addition to these options in the area of number and numeration, the child
would also be able to benefit from beginning experiences in measurement and geometry. The child would not, of course, be ready for concepts
of base ten or place value, or for work with computation on paper. These
skills would be too far beyond the child's present capabilities. There is,
however, a wide range of skills with which a child can cope at any given
point. Children need not be restricted to specific steps along a narrow
path.

Obtaining Data

In order to evaluate a child's learning, the teacher needs to secure information about what the child knows or can do. There are basically two ways to collect such data: (1) directly through observation, and (2) indirectly through written work or other products. The nature of the skill or understanding that is to be evaluated will determine in part which method is used. For example, a teacher must observe directly to determine whether or not a child can name sets correctly if the child is not yet to the point of reading and writing their names. On the other hand, it would be extremely difficult to think of a way to collect data about computation skills without the use of pencil and paper. The teacher could look at this type of work after it has been completed by the child. It will not be necessary to watch as the child does the computation, although watching may on occasion help understand reasons for the child's errors or give clues to the child's thinking.

Sometimes it is helpful to combine direct and indirect methods of data collection. For example, in collecting data about a child's ability in art, the teacher might find it helpful to observe while the child works on an art project as well as to examine the finished product.

Organizing and Storing the Data

ACTUAL WORK. It is relatively easy to organize and store much of children's work. A file folder can be made for each child and samples of drawings, paintings, and writing can be inserted. If the work is dated, the teacher can then see the child's progress in a particular area over a period of time.

Some kinds of products cannot be saved, whereas others present a storage problem. Constructions made of unit blocks and Leggos must be dismantled so the materials can be reused by other children. Sculpture does not fit into a folder. A camera can be a very useful tool for recording these kinds of work.

OBSERVATIONS. It is more difficult to organize and store data obtained through observation. The difficulty comes from the necessity of noting in some way what is observed. Some things are difficult to put into words. All events take time to record. There are ways to make this type of record-keeping less tedious, however.

Before one can decide on ways to record data collected through observation, one must have some understanding of the kinds of information it is possible to collect. A sample of what a teacher might learn through observation is shown below.

Perhaps a discussion is conducted and the teacher notices the expression on several children's faces. John is gazing off into the distance, although he occasionally turns his face to a child who is talking. As Jim talks, he is smiling and maintains direct eye contact with the teacher. Maria yawns and rubs her eyes.

As children work independently, the teacher notices that Susan has started her third activity without having finished either of the first two. John is in the blocks with Tim, and José is separating Cuisenaire rods into piles. The teacher heard Shawn tell Tom he could not play with him any more if Tom did not give up the wooden truck and also saw Tom hand it over.

Stopping to work with one child and then another, the teacher noticed that Ian lost the concept of one-to-one correspondence when there were more than four objects to count, that Shawn called the numeral three, "two," and that Tim could think of four words besides his name that start with a "t." When asked how he learned to use a hammer so well, Ian responded by saying that his brother "teached" him.

The above is just a small sample of the information a teacher might collect during a day. Such information is not gathered during formal observation periods, although a teacher might at times step back from a situation and just observe. Most observations will take place while the teacher is doing other things. Teachers should learn to trust the information they obtain in this way. While they should not jump to conclusions when they observe one isolated behavior, they can watch for repeated indications that a child is functioning in a certain way.

The teacher needs some way to record and organize all the data collected through observation. Many types of information can be adequately recorded on a checklist. Information related to concepts and skills in subject-matter are easily recorded in this manner. The teacher constructs the checklist on the basis of goals he has for particular areas of study. A partial checklist for math skills is shown in Figure 7.

The teacher would have a checklist for each child which can be kept in the child's folder. When data are collected through observation, it would be indicated on the checklist that on a particular date the child showed evidence of having a particular skill or concept. When dates are noted several times in the boxes opposite a skill, the teacher can be rather certain the child does in fact have the skill.

It is important for such checklists to be detailed and specific. For example, it is not as helpful to have one item, "Can count," as it might be to have two items, "Counts to five," and "Counts to ten." It takes a long time for a child to learn to count to ten. Teachers need to know how far a child has progressed in order to give appropriate guidance. On the other hand, if checklists are too specific, their length will be burdensome.

Checklists are also helpful in recording data about children's re-

Name:					
Classifies					
Matches one-to-one					
Names sets to three					
Counts to five					
Names sets to five					
Counts to ten					
Combines sets to four					
Names numerals to five					

Figure 7. Math skills checklist.

actions to classroom routines, their physical abilities and health, their social-emotional behavior, and where they spend their time in the class-room.

Checklists are usually inadequate to record all the details a teacher might think important. Perhaps a child rarely cries except when required to attend gym class. Maybe another child accepts rules except when play-ing or working with a specific classmate. Yet another child may rarely lead in indoor play, but often leads in play outdoors. These qualifica-tions or details of behavior are important. They provide the necessary clues which a teacher would need in order to influence the children's behaviors in any way. In addition, they are idiosyncratic. They apply to individual children, not generally to everyone in the class. This is why it is difficult to construct an adequate checklist to handle this type of infor-mation. Children keep doing things for which there is no appropriate item to check. Clearly, another type of record is required.

Anecdotal records provide a structure for handling the type of data described above. Anecdotal records are detailed accounts of events. They should include important details of the setting as well as the event itself. Teachers should avoid recording their own conclusions about a child's behavior. Only the behavior itself should be noted. For example, rather than noting that "Johnny was happy outside today" the teacher should note, "Johnny jumped from the second bar of the climbing apparatus and laughed and smiled as he said, "Hey, did you see that?" Similarly, it will not be helpful to note that "Susan was awful today." Three weeks later the teacher will not remember what Susan did that was awful. If teachers hope to support children's learning, they need good, detailed information which tells them specifically where an event occurred, under what conditions it occurred, and with whom it occurred.

The actual form of an anecdotal record does not matter. Complete sentences and neat handwriting are not necessary for such records when they are for the teacher's own use. When several teachers work together with the same group of children, legibility may be important, but when they do not have to be concerned that someone else be able to read their records, they may use shorthand, abbreviations or any other system for making the writing less tedious. Entries may be kept on small pieces of paper which can be inserted into the child's file. Each entry must be dated to have value.

Sometimes teachers have difficulty remembering what they have observed during the day. For this reason, some teachers carry pads of paper in their pockets so they can jot notes as they teach. Teachers do not have time to record events in their entirety as they jot, but sometimes these notes can serve as reminders for later. For example, a note which simply says, "Jill, blocks," might help a teacher remember a particular incident.

TESTS. Numerous tests are available for assessing children's abilities. Most of these have been standardized; that is, a great deal of data have been collected with the test in order that statements can be made about how most children of a particular age perform on the test. If a test is standardized, the teacher can judge how a child compares with other children in general, or how an entire class compares with similar classes in other places.

There is a great deal of controversy about the use of standardized tests. Perhaps the most frequent criticism is that they are culturally biased. This means that information on the tests is much more familiar to children from some groups than from others and that the tests have been standardized on groups who are familiar with the information. Recently, attempts have been made to develop "culture-free" tests.

It is unclear at the present time whether "culture-free" tests are in fact culture-free. Even if group bias can be eliminated from standardized tests, other errors would remain. For example, a kindergarten teacher once told about an unusual response many children in her class made to a test item. A series of questions on the test required that the child relate two objects. One picture was enclosed in a box to the left of the page, and to the right was a row of three pictures. The child was to select one picture from the row that represented an object that belonged with the key picture in the box. One of the key pictures was a shoe. The pictures from which the children were to choose a related picture included a sock, a chair, and a dog. The "correct" answer was the sock. Presumably, shoes and socks go together because they are both worn on the foot.

Most of the children in this class missed the item because they selected chair to go with shoe. The tester was somewhat alarmed at the apparent inability of these children to grasp such a simple relationship and expressed that concern to the children's teacher. Upon receiving the information, the teacher laughed and said their answers made perfectly good sense to her. She had been in the last months of a pregnancy during the first part of the school year and was unable to bend over to tie shoes. If someone requested help, she always asked the child to put the foot with the untied shoe on a chair so she would not have to bend down to the floor. Thus, because of their experiences, children in this class learned that chair and shoe were related. The culture of this classroom influenced the views of the world developed by these children. This in turn influenced their responses to a test which was not constructed to accommodate such idiosyncracies.

The above story illustrates an important point about tests, standardized or not: *it is important for teachers to look at the errors children make on tests to determine if they make sense.* It is possible for a child to get an item right for the wrong reasons and to get it wrong for the right reasons. At one time Piaget worked with the IQ test developed by Alfred Binet. He became curious about why certain errors were made and he began looking for the underlying cognitive structures which might explain them.

Many tests are composed of several sub-tests and the child's score on the test is obtained by averaging or totalling the sub-test scores. Simply knowing this overall score is not very helpful to the teacher. Children who obtain similar overall scores can have quite different scores on individual sub-tests. Thus, when children are grouped for instruction on the basis of an overall test score, the diagnostic value of the test is lost.

JUDGING THE DATA. Evaluation requires making a judgment about the data one has collected. Judgments involve deciding whether or not a child is making adequate progress towards certain goals. For example, a judgment regarding the data discussed in the observation on page 41 might be that Shawn is not doing very well with names or numerals. He learns quickly and his interest in school is high. The teacher thinks he should be farther along. Another judgment might be that Ian's overgeneralization of verb endings is a typical pattern for a four-year-old and that he is progressing well in language development. A third judgment might be that Tim's ability to detect initial consonants is quite good and that he could profit from experiences to develop more ability in this area.

The above judgments are then used as a basis for planning. The teacher might plan to try to encourage Shawn to play numeral bingo with a friend who knows numeral names very well. He might also plan to mention to Ian's parents that his language is typical for a child his age, and might suggest that they do nothing more than repeat Ian's statements using the standard verb form. For example, if Ian says, "My brother teached me to saw," the parent might respond by saying, "Oh, your brother taught you to saw."

The teacher might also plan to construct some initial consonant picture cards for Tim to extend his skills and plan to give these to him at the end of tomorrow morning's planning meeting.

The above decisions indicate the teacher has made some judgments about the data that were collected. All the information in the world about a child is not very useful if the teacher cannot make some judgments about what it means in terms of the child's progress in learning and what it means in terms of appropriate learning experiences which should be planned for the child.

ADDITIONAL RESOURCES

ALMY, M., "Assessing Development and Learning," in *The Early Childhood Educator at Work*. New York: McGraw-Hill Book Co., 1975, pp. 220–243.

CARINI, P., "The Prospect School: Taking Account of Process," *Childhood Education*, 49, no. 7 (1973), pp. 351–356.

COHEN, D., and V. STERN, *Observing and Recording the Behavior of Young Children*. New York: Teachers College Press, Columbia University, 1973.

DURKIN, D., "Classroom Diagnosis," in *Teaching Them to Read*. Boston: Allyn and Bacon, Inc., 1971, pp. 402–431.

EVANS, E., "Some Frequently Used Tests in Early Childhood Education Research," in *Contemporary Influences in Early Childhood Education*. New York: Holt, Rinehart and Winston, Inc., 1971, pp. 337–347.

Farallones Designs, *Making Places, Changing Spaces, In Schools, At Home and Within Ourselves*. New York: Random House, 1971.

Found Spaces and Equipment for Children's Centers. New York: Educational Facilities Laboratories, 1972.

GOTTS, E., "A Test of Accountability and an Account of Testing," *Childhood Education*, 49, no. 7 (1973), pp. 338–342.

HAWKINS, F. P., *The Logic of Action*. Boulder, Colo.: Mountain View Center for Environmental Education, 1969.

HONIG, A., *Parent Involvement in Early Childhood Education*. Washington, D.C.: National Association for the Education of Young Children, 1975.

KRITCHEVSKY, S., and E. PRESCOTT, *Planning Environments for Young Children: Physical Space.* Washington, D.C.: National Association for the Education of Young Children, 1969.

MILLER, B., and A. WILMSHURST, *Parents and Volunteers in the Classroom: A Handbook for Teachers.* Palo Alto, Calif.: R and E Research Associates, Inc., 1975.

RUDOLPH, N., *Workyards: Playground Planned for Adventure.* New York: Teachers College Press, Columbia University, 1974.

SANOFF, H., J. SANOFF, and A. HENSLEY, *Learning Environments for Children.* Raleigh, N.C.: Learning Environments, 1973.

SARGEANT, B., *The Integrated Day in an American School.* Cambridge, Mass.: National Association of Independent Schools, 1972.

SEEFELDT, C., "Boxes are to Build . . . a Curriculum," *Young Children,* 28, no. 1 (1972), pp. 5–12.

STONE, J. G., *Play and Playgrounds.* Washington, D.C.: National Association for the Education of Young Children, 1970.

TAYLOR, J., *Organizing the Open Classroom: A Teacher's Guide to the Integrated Day.* New York: Schnocken Books, 1972.

WURMAN, R. S., *Yellow Pages of Learning Resources.* Philadelphia: Group for Environmental Education, Inc., 1972.

3

the
expressive
arts

YOUNG children should be provided with both receptive and expressive experiences in the fine arts. Music, painting, sculpture, drama, and dance are as important as the other areas discussed in this book. Indeed, there is an interrelationship between the expressive arts and other subjects. Pictorial representations are the first means of putting thoughts into graphic symbols; the singing of songs may add words to a chlid's vocabulary; exploring sounds is as much related to science as to music; and drama and dance are effective in helping children express themselves.

This chapter is designed to help teachers understand (1) the values of experiences with expressive arts, (2) levels of development in appreciations and competencies related to the expressive arts, (3) goals appropriate for young children, and (4) methods and activities which can be used to help children learn about visual arts, music, dance, and drama.

VALUES OF EXPRESSIVE ARTS EXPERIENCES

A Means of Expressing and Communicating

Often, young children have thoughts and feelings they are unable to express in words. Happiness, joy, sadness, hurt can be expressed in body movements, in song, and in working with paint or clay. While such self-expression may satisfy the child's own need without the conscious intent to communicate her thoughts or feelings to others, the child's actions do in fact communicate these to the sensitive teacher. At other times, the child may use art media to tell a story or communicate impressions of an experience to others.

Aesthetic Appreciations

The foundation for appreciation of beauty may be laid when the child is young. The teacher who brings order and beauty into the classroom through the arrangement of furnishings or the addition of a bouquet of flowers, a masterpiece of art, or recordings of great music expresses aesthetic appreciation. Such a teacher's comments about the children's work may also help in the development of aesthetic appreciation.

An Acceptable Way to Reduce Tension

Children are often under far more pressure than we realize. The demands of the family, the strangeness and confusion of a new situation, the imposed need to learn to control emotions all tend to make children tense. The fine arts are a potent means of expressing hurt and anger in acceptable ways.

Increased Perception
and Concept Development

In order to express a sight, a sound, or a complete experience in an art form, one must sharpen one's observation and recall it. The interaction among the five senses and the brain as the child experiences and recalls experiences leads to more accurate representations in art forms.

Enjoyment of Art Activity for Its Own Sake

As a teacher encourages young children's self-expression in art forms, the children develop confidence in their own ability, which may result in the enjoyment of art activities for their own sake. The long-term benefit of teaching art at an early age may be a lifelong worthwhile leisure-time activity.

Appreciation of Cultural Heritage

The values, life-styles, and flavor of a people is reflected in their art. The immortality of countries and communities resides in their art. This art becomes the cultural heritage of the descendants of those people. Through knowledge and appreciation of their own cultural heritage, children develop a sense of pride as a representative of that culture.

CHILDREN AND THE EXPRESSIVE ARTS

The competencies children are able to develop in the expressive arts are influenced by their level of development. Skill in visual arts is related to the child's perceptual and cognitive development. Skill in movement and dance depends on the child's physical growth and development. Skill in music depends on perception, concepts of number, the ability to use symbols, and the ability to place things in a sequence. Finally, skill in drama requires the ability to use language, to sequence events, and to coordinate actions of several people.

As children are introduced to new experiences in any area of the fine arts, they should be permitted a period of *exploration* followed by a period of *integration*, which is then followed by a period of *creation*. In other words, children should not be immediately asked to make or do something. Actually, the cycles of exploring, integrating, and creating continue as long as people continue to study an area of the fine arts. Each cycle occurs at a more complex level, however. Problems encountered while making something often lead to more exploring to learn more about what the medium will do.

Although the above stages are helpful as general guides for ways to approach fine arts with children, there is also specific information related to the development of children which has implications for judging what kinds of experiences will be most successful with children at a particular developmental stage. This information is discussed below for each area of the fine arts.

Children and the Visual Arts

In the visual arts, materials are used to make representations of things. In order to make a representation of something, or to appreciate a representation made by someone else, it is necessary to have a good image of that which is represented. Children develop these images very gradually.

Young children's first involvement with visual arts materials is not for the purpose of making representations of anything at all. They become completely caught up with manipulating the materials. They make random scribbles with crayons or pencils. They may paint with tempera over an entire piece of paper until it is so thickly coated it will crack when dry. They pound, squeeze, or tear off small bits of clay. However, they make "nothing." This does not mean that what they have created is not highly valued by them, for it is. But if you were to ask what the child had made, you would receive a blank stare. Such a question is inappropriate to ask children at this level, for they are not making a representation of anything. It is what it is; nothing more; nothing less. This stage is appropriately called the **manipulative** stage.

Somewhat later, usually by the age of four, children begin to organize their visual art creations. They may make lines, dots, or large separated areas of color with tempera paint. Collages may show areas where similar materials have been placed in close proximity on the paper. Even yet, however, the child is not using media to make representations of something. Children at this stage are still experimenting. But they are learning to control and organize their work. This stage is sometimes called the **design** or **patterning** stage.

There comes a time, often during the fourth year, when children do begin to make a picture or model of something. At first, the representation does not resemble the thing represented well enough for another person to determine what it is. Children will voluntarily tell you, however, and it is this naming behavior that first indicates that children are truly using the medium for representation. This stage is sometimes called the **naming** or **symbolic** stage.

During the fifth or sixth year, and often somewhat earlier, children's art work begins to resemble the objects represented. Because children's mental representations of things are often incomplete, however, their graphic representations lack detail and often do not match many aspects of reality. For example, a picture of a cat may contain only a circle for a head, a line for the body, and two lines for legs. In addition, the drawing may have been made with red or blue crayons rather than black or brown despite the availability of both. As children's mental representations become more accurate and complete, their pictures become more accurate and complex.

In addition to making progress in terms of including details of objects represented, children make progress in their ability to plan and coordinate the parts of individual objects. For example, in early pictures a cat's legs may be drawn as if they extended from the cat's head rather than the body, just as a child's picture of a person will often show appendages attached to the head. In addition, parts may be jumbled. For example, eyes, ears, nose, and mouth may all be drawn on a head, but not arranged accurately. It is as if the child thinks of one item at a time, draws it, and then goes on to another part. Perhaps because the child does not plan the whole before starting, he or she often does not leave room in the appropriate places, so just draws features where there is space.

It may be that the preschool child does not appreciate the spatial arrangement of parts of things, but rather experiences each separately. Research with infants, however, would indicate this is not the case, because it has been found that they prefer faces in which features are arranged correctly over those in which they they are not.[1] But creating a representation requires more than the perceptual skill of visual discrimination. It requires processing, organizing, and creating the arrangement oneself. It must be these skills which the young child is in the process of obtaining.[2]

Not only must children learn to coordinate parts within an object,

[1] R. L. Fantz, "Visual Perception from Birth as Shown by Pattern Selectivity," *Annals of the New York Academy of Sciences,* 118 (1963), pp. 793–814.

[2] J. Piaget and B. Inhelder, *The Psychology of the Child* (New York: Basic Books, Inc., 1969), pp. 63–68.

but all the objects within a picture as well. For example, if one of a child's early pictures contains a flower, a house, and a child, the child or flower may be bigger than the house. Gradually, the actual relationships are represented more accurately, but it will be a very long time before the relationships will be to scale.

In addition to these size relationships, there are other relationships which present problems. For example, if you look at a house from the outside, you cannot see the inside. If you look at the outside of a closed truck, you cannot see what is inside. Yet, children under six or seven make pictures that contain these contradictions. They show you everything at once; the inside and the outside, the front and the back, or the top and the side view too. As Piaget's[3] mountain experiment has shown, they do not understand that what can be seen at any one time depends on the view from which one is looking. At first, children include all views they may be familiar with in the same picture, and the contradiction is not appreciated by them. Later, when their understanding of space is more developed, they will select a point of view and stick with it.

Children's art work is also influenced by their ability to distinguish between the coordinates within objects and coordinates in external space. Coordinates refer to horizontal and vertical axes. Young children have no appreciation for coordinates in space external to objects. For example, in Piaget's[4] tilted bottle experiment, young children drew water lines in tilted bottles in terms of the coordinates of the bottles themselves, not external space.

These miscalculations are revealed in young children's pictures. Chimneys on houses jut out peculiarly because children orient them to the roof line they have drawn rather than in terms of the space around the house. Trees on mountain sides are given the same type of orientation. Only after children gain an appreciation for space as a total system and realize that objects are themselves in a coordinated space do these features disappear from their drawings.

Perhaps the most difficult understanding required for work in the visual arts is that involving the relationships of objects on a plane from foreground to background. The first pictures of young children contain no technique for organizing objects on a plane. Objects simply float in space. Later, around age six, a baseline usually appears. Sometimes this is simply the base of the paper, or it may be grass or water on which other objects rest. Still later, children will use multiple baselines in order to indicate that all objects are not at the same point on the plane. By the

---

[3] J. McV. Hunt, *Intelligence and Experience* (New York: Ronald Press, 1961), p. 220.

[4] J. McV. Hunt, *Intelligence and Experience*, p. 222.

age of eleven or twelve, children are using the technique called perspective, which requires sophisticated understandings of objects in space.

Teachers should keep this developmental information in mind when they teach visual arts. The making of representations is a highly cognitive activity, and what children are able to create will depend in large part on their knowledge about things and their ability to plan, organize, and create. In other words, the ability to make graphic representations depends on the ability to think. In turn, art experiences provide opportunities for planning, organizing, and creating. Contrary to what is often assumed, art experiences probably make a substantial contribution to cognitive development. It is this aspect that is slighted when children are given outline pictures to fill in or are given specific directions to follow. When these latter methods are used, the thinking has already been done by someone else.

Children and Movement and Dance

Movement and dance involve skillful use of the body. The physical growth and development of the child is, therefore, crucial to skill development in these areas.

Physical growth and development occur in a very orderly fashion. The child must learn to control the movements of arms and hands. At first, movements are not specific or directed. The whole arm moves in a rather jerky fashion, and the hands move only as awkward extensions of upper arm movements. By the last half of the first year, hand and finger movements are no longer extensions of arm movements, but are independent. The child's wrist, however, is still a mere crease between a chubby arm and an even chubbier hand. The tendons that are noticeable on the back of an adolescent or adult hand are not apparent on the hand of a young child.

The lack of independence in the structure of the hand and arm in the young child can be seen in the imprecision of the movements made by the child's hands. As the wrist, hand, and fingers lengthen in the child from age four to six, skill in their use increases.

The child must also learn to move about in space. The sequence of skills which culminates in locomotor skill starts with children's ability to lift their heads off a surface on which they are placed prone and proceeds through such abilities as sitting up, pulling up, standing alone, walking, and running. All of these require balance, and this is achieved quite differently by a young child than by an adult. As the child's trunk, arms, and legs lengthen in the years between two and five, the center of gravity shifts lower and balance becomes easier. The ability to move with speed, stop abruptly, and change directions while moving also improves as body proportions change.

Tissue growth also changes as children get older. During the first years, most weight gain is realized in fat tissue. After the first year, this fat production decreases rapidly, and bone and muscle tissue begin to grow at a faster rate than earlier. During the fifth year, about 75 per cent of the child's weight gain is realized in muscle growth.[5] These changes have an effect on children's strength and ability to control their bodies. As children get older, strength and control gradually increase, and this pattern continues on through adolescence.

Physiological processes such as heart rate, blood pressure, and respiration also change with age.[6] These processes affect stamina. Generally, young children do not have as much stamina as older children, and this can be seen in the faster rate at which they become fatigued. As these basic physiological processes change through childhood and adolescence, stamina increases.

When teaching movement and dance, the teacher should carefully consider the physical growth and development of the child. Characteristics we often associate with movement and dance, such as grace and smoothness, come slowly in children for the reasons discussed above. Younger children will need more space than older ones because they cannot control their movements as easily and, therefore, often accidentally topple or run into someone. If fatigue is to be avoided, younger children will also need more alternations than do older children between movements that require much exertion and those that require little.

Though skills in movement and dance depend on physical growth and development, experience in movement and dance also contributes to physical growth and development. It was stated earlier (page 4) that development results from the *interaction* of both maturation and experiences. Therefore, the wise teacher does not wait until seeing a child skip to introduce uneven rhythms in movement, but such a teacher knows better than to try to introduce skipping to a young three-year-old who is just getting a good feel for even rhythms such as running and marching.

Children and Music

The learning of skills in music is influenced by the child's development in many areas. Perceptual development is required if children are to discriminate among various tones, intensities, rhythms, and speeds. These are the elements of musical composition.

[5]H. Thompson, "Physical Growth," in *Manual of Child Psychology,* 2nd ed., ed. L. Carmichael (New York: Wiley, 1954), pp. 292–334.
[6]Thompson, "Physical Growth," pp. 292–334.

There seems to be a physical basis for the development of the ability to produce vocal sounds that match tones made by an instrument or another person (tuneful singing). There is evidence[7] to suggest that young children match the three or four tones above and including middle C most easily and only gradually gain the ability to extend their range upward. If children are not given opportunities to match tones within the appropriate range, they have difficulty learning to sing tunefully.

There is also an obvious physical base required for learning to play many musical instruments. Dexterity and strength in the hands and fingers is required to play many instruments. It is not surprising that instruments such as drums, bells, triangles, and cymbals are among the more common ones found in classrooms for young children. Around the age of eight many children can begin to learn to play instruments that involve considerable finger movements. Instruction on a recorder or piano would be appropriate at this time.

Finally, there are cognitive skills required to deal with music. Music requires basic cognitive skills such as sequencing and organizing. Music composition also involves concepts about measurement of time. Music occurs in a time span, and notes are given a time value. Finally, musical notation is a complex and abstract symbol system.

Young children begin to understand these aspects of music as they sing songs, move their bodies to music, and create their own music on simple instruments. Preprimary children can learn to discriminate among songs. This indicates that they can detect differences in the sequence and coordination of the elements of music. They can also make body movements which indicate they know the difference between music that is high and low, fast and slow, loud and soft, or even and uneven. It is these learning experiences that are appropriate for preprimary children. Formal instruction in musical notation is inappropriate for most children before the primary grades.

Children and Drama

Skills in drama depend on children's abilities to organize and sequence, to take on roles, and to use language. Since language development is discussed in detail in the Language Arts Chapter (page 109), only role playing, sequencing, and organizing will be discussed here.

Children first begin to "pretend" around the age of two. These first pretendings are often reruns of their own actions: they pretend to eat when they are not; they pretend to cry when they are not, or they pretend

[7] R. Smith, *Music in the Child's Education* (New York: Ronald Press, 1970), pp. 16–24.

to be asleep when they are not. This is soon followed and combined with projection of these actions onto other objects: the doll eats; the doll cries; the stuffed dog sleeps. Children also begin to use objects to stand for other objects which they do not resemble: a plain block is called a "car" or a "cup."[8]

Finally, children begin to pretend that they are someone else. They are a mother or a father, the baby or the sister, a fireman or a garbage collector. Such role taking usually appears by three-and-one-half or four.

The organization of this role-play behavior into a coherent flow of events is a difficult task for young children. Typically, three- and four-year-olds playing together go about their role playing without much regard for the actions of the other children. They play in the same physical space, but not really together. Later, usually during the fourth year, children begin to coordinate roles. They are able to do this by talking plans over with each other. "You go to the store, and while you're gone, I'll pack for the picnic." "You feed the baby while I fix dinner for us." "I'll mop the floor while you're out washing the windows so you won't walk all over it." This type of organization requires the ability to sequence and coordinate actions as well as to use and understand language.

In this type of role play, children perform the actions and say the words they have seen and heard, recombining these in their own unique ways. The roles are, then, their own creations, not reproductions of roles created by a story writer or a film maker. Indeed, children are not yet able to play out such unfamiliar roles. It is only in the primary grades that children should be asked to dramatize roles and events that are unfamiliar to them.

GOALS AND SKILLS FOR INSTRUCTION IN THE EXPRESSIVE ARTS

There are two major goals for teaching expressive arts: (1) the development of skills for self-expression and creativity in art forms and (2) the development of aesthetic appreciation. To attain these general goals, the teacher needs to identify specific objectives or competencies which young children may be expected to gain. In the following paragraphs, some appropriate specific objectives are suggested.

Visual Arts

To use art media with ease and enjoyment and to produce work that is personally satisfying are appropriate objectives for young children

[8]J. McV. Hunt, *Intelligence and Experience,* pp. 180–182.

at any level of development. Such objectives are gained through experiences and guidance, both of which are discussed later. The production of work which communicates thoughts and feelings to others is a competence which may begin to appear around the age of four or five, and the work can be expected to become increasingly more complex, recognizable, and reflective of the child's world.

Finally, in the production of art work, children will need to learn the technical aspects of working with various kinds of materials and tools. In addition, they must learn how to care for them properly. Even the youngest children can begin to understand how to control and care for materials and tools. This may include, for example, suggestions for preventing drips in a painting and for washing the paint out of a brush.

In developing aesthetic appreciation, the teacher should encourage responsiveness to what the child sees in the environment. The teaching aim is to help the child become sensitive to and enjoy natural and manmade beauty. Basic to such enjoyment is the ability to identify distinguishing features. To develop the ability to identify forms, shapes, colors, and sizes is a realistic goal for three- to five-year-olds, whereas older children may be expected to develop ability to identify and appreciate the additional features of design and balance. Asking children to help set up an aesthetic display (see page 80) will help children attain this ability.

Children should also be helped to develop personal standards for judging the merits of their own and others' artistic efforts. This starts with simply being able to say, "I like this better than this," and develops into the ability to say, "I like this because _____," giving a reason in terms of specific features of the art object or of the affective response it evokes or both.

Music

From well-planned experiences in music we expect children to develop some musical competence. The level of competence that can be expected will depend on the children's age, experience, and special talents.

Basic to developing musical competence is the ability to distinguish variances in pitch, volume, tempo, and rhythm. Children from three to five can learn to distinguish high from low tones, soft from loud tones, those played in rapid succession from those played more slowly, and those played at equal intervals from those played at unequal intervals. When movement and music are combined, it will often be bodily movement that will tell you that the preschool child can make these discriminations. If appropriate descriptive labels are given, the child will later be able to describe such differences verbally (high–low; fast–slow; loud–soft; uneven–even).

Children should also develop ability to distinguish between dissonance and harmony, noise and music. One measure of this ability is the way children play a xylophone or a piano. Does the child tend to select one note at a time? Which combinations of notes will be repeated, and which rejected?

By the time children have reached seven or eight years of age, they may be expected to gain competence in reading musical notation and in producing music independently, if experiences and activities to teach these skills are provided.

Although young children may be able to respond to music with various expressions of pleasure—dancing, listening quietly with an expression of contentment, keeping time with a foot, hand, or head—there are some specific goals which the teacher should keep in mind in planning a program. For younger children as well as older children the ability to distinguish among and recognize melodies is one such goal. Another goal is the ability to associate affective responses with characteristics of music.

A third goal is the ability to identify instruments by name and sound. This ability adds much to the enjoyment and appreciation of instrumental music. Even preschool children can learn to identify instruments as long as those presented differ substantially in timbre. For example, young children can easily distinguish a snare drum from a trumpet and a trumpet from a piano, although they would probably have difficulty telling the difference between a bass drum and tympani.

As children are given more experiences, they can learn to distinguish between instruments very similar in timbre. For example, six- or seven-year-olds who have had two or three years of experience in listening to and identifying instruments in music can easily tell the difference between a clarinet, a flute, and a piccolo.

Dance

The hoped-for competencies in dance include the ability to use the body with grace and coordination; to respond with appropriate movement to words, music, and rhythms; and to participate with ease and enjoyment in singing games, folk-dancing; and to express moods and concepts with movement. As with all the arts, teachers must determine appropriate levels of competence which they feel are reasonable for the children they teach.

From experiences with dance children should gain the ability to enjoy dancing either as a watcher or a participant. An aesthetic appreciation which is basic to the child's ability to participate in movement activities and which should be developed is awareness of movement in nature: wind blowing trees, birds flying, animals moving, plants growing. As a watcher the child should develop the ability to interpret moods expressed by movement and to see the relationship between rhythms in music and certain steps: i.e., skipping, hopping, running, walking.

Drama

Opportunities for dramatic play should result in helping the child to verbalize thoughts and feelings and to relive experiences. This may be enough for children under four. For older children, the ability to plan a sequence of actions, to assume a role in agreement with others, and to use a variety of props and costumes appropriately are additional abilities which usually develop. Children from about four-and-one-half years of age and up should also be able to assume the role of a character in a familiar story, recall the sequence of actions in the story, and work with others in the dramatization of the story. Guidance and activities which will lead to the development of these competencies are discussed later in this chapter.

Some competencies which should result from guided experiences as watchers as well as participants in dramatic activities include gaining a sense of story continuity and drama, distinguishing between fantasy and reality, and having a growing sense of discrimination in choosing dramatic presentations to watch.

METHODS AND ACTIVITIES FOR INSTRUCTION IN THE EXPRESSIVE ARTS

Since each area of the expressive arts is unique, methods and activities will be discussed specifically for each area. The first part of each discussion will deal with methods and materials in general terms. This is followed by specific activities which illustrate how the methods and materials can be used.

Guiding Work in the Visual Arts

Teachers should have a concept of art which goes beyond craft projects or coloring outline pictures. There are many craft books to help the teacher who is looking for these kinds of ideas, and we will not deal with these here. Crafts do have an important place in the classroom: they help the child develop eye-hand coordination, skill in using small muscles, and a sense of accomplishment and pride, and provide experience in working with different kinds of materials. Only in a limited sense, however, can they be considered the expressive art which is consistent with the goals and values indicated earlier. Only insofar as children are free to use the materials given them can crafts be considered to provide opportunities for self-expression.

THE VISUAL ARTS CENTER. A well-planned and stocked art center leads to self-reliant and responsible use of art materials. A portion of the room where children may work undisturbed by others and without interfering with others' work should be selected. A wide variety of materials, including commercial as well as homemade, should be available. The materials should be stored in appropriately labeled boxes. (Lists of suggested materials may be found on pages 63–65).

The teacher should not put out a vast selection of materials at the beginning of the year. Too large a selection is bewildering. A moderate selection of commonly used materials may be put out first and other materials introduced as children are ready for them. As each set of materials is introduced, instructions on their use should be given. In a planning period, the teacher should explain where the materials will be and under what conditions they may be used and may also demonstrate good ways to use materials and ways to care for them.

A complete art center would include easels for water-mixed paints and separate flat surfaces such as tables, desks, or wide low shelves for cutting and pasting work, for clay modeling, or for drawing with crayons, pencils, or chalk. A large area of floor covered with a sheet of heavy plastic or linoleum is great for working on large pieces such as murals or scenery for a play. If there is not enough space inside the room, larger pieces may be taken into the hall or outside.

In the case of unfinished projects, materials may be left out ready for work another day. Before stopping such work for the day, children should leave the area in order. Caps should be put on bottles, brushes should be cleaned, and materials which will not be needed should be put away. Being able to find materials in good condition on the following day helps to continue the work. When projects are finished, all materials should be returned to assigned storage areas and surfaces cleaned.

In order for children to clean up easily by themselves, materials for such clean-up must be accessible. There should be a nearby source of water. Sponges, rags, soap, paper towels, and buckets should be available. Though children should be expected to do their own clean-up, cleaning should not be such a tedious chore that it deters children from working in the art center. A cheerful assist from the teacher is often needed.

SENSITIVITY TO CHILDREN'S FEELINGS. In guiding the art of young children, the teacher must develop sensitivity to their readiness to accept suggestions. One primary rule to follow is to determine how children feel about their own work. Is a child satisfied or dissatisfied? This is often tricky: the child may verbally deprecate the work, but in actuality may be saying, "I hope you like it." Sometimes young children are unable to verbalize their own feelings adequately. Gentle, sensitive questions and comments may help to draw them out. The teacher as teacher helps children improve their work by offering suggestions.

HELPING THE CHILD SEE THE WORLD. As children move into the representational level, they need help to become more aware of the color, shape, form, and other characteristics of the environment. The sky isn't always blue or all blue; clouds have many different shapes and colors. The teacher through comments to children about features of the environment helps them look selectively at different features. Eliciting comments from the children helps the teacher also to see the world through the children's eyes and appreciate those things to which individual children respond. Because the aim is to help children focus on selected features of the environment to include in their drawings, the teacher must avoid telling the children what to draw. Children's responses to features of the environment should be elicited through questions about what they see and like.

There is also a kinesthetic form of "seeing": the feel of things which translates into drawing. "How does it feel to bend over and touch your toes?" "Is your head above or below your knees?" "How does bark feel?" "Is it smooth or rough?" As children perform these actions, they become more aware of the nature of things.

HELPING CHILDREN CONTROL MATERIALS. Only by having ample opportunities with art materials do they come under the child's control. The teacher may make suggestions to children about how to hold their brushes loosely so the color flows from the tip rather than scrubbing it into the paper; about how to hold the brush against the edge of the jar before transferring paint to the paper; about how to wash the brush in clean water or use separate brushes to keep colors clean. Such tips help children learn to control materials. Teachers should realize, however, that such tips may be followed by older children more than by younger ones. It's not easy to hold the brush loosely if you have little skill in the use of your hands. Younger children tend to grasp the brush tightly with a fist grip and make wide strokes using the muscles of the upper arm.

HELPING CHILDREN COMPLETE PROJECTS. Often, a child starts a project, works on it awhile, and brings it to the teacher before it appears complete. For example, an incomplete human figure is drawn near the edge of the paper. Children may be acting from a variety of motives in bringing their picture to the teacher at this point. A child may be tiring of art work and wishing to go on to something else. The child may also be wanting suggestions which would help add more to the work. Children's motivations can be determined by conversing with them. Finding that a child needs help to continue and desires to do so, the teacher asks questions designed to lead the child to elaborate. "Is it winter or summer?" "How could you show it is winter (summer)?" "What is the girl wearing?" "Does she have a friend with her?" These are a few questions which might lead the child to think of other things to add to the picture. If it is a non-representational effort, a question such as, "What colors would look nice with what you have?" might help the child move on.

Some children, however, seem not to know when to stop, but keep adding to the work until the colors become muddy or the picture is cluttered. These are typical behaviors of preschool children and they should be accepted most of the time. Older children, however, may be helped to recognize when a picture has reached that point at which it looks complete. The teacher's well-timed appreciative comment may help the child develop a sense of completion. For instance, when a child stands looking at her picture as if uncertain, the teacher might say, "I like your bold blue curved line and this bright yellow splash. It makes a pretty design."

CONSIDERATION IN PRESENTING MODELS.   What models should be presented to children? Should a model be used at all? This is a matter of some controversy. In some cases, the act of studying the drawings of another helps children gain a skill which is transferrable to drawing pictures they decide on. Much depends on the teacher's response to the child's efforts. If come children have met with appreciation of their efforts and so have developed self-confidence, they may learn from looking at the work of others or watching adult artists at work. But for others, the presentation of an adult model may be devastating. In general, the use of models is inappropriate with preschool and kindergarten children.

A valuable experience for children may be a visit from an artist. This visit is not for the purpose of talking to the class, but for the purpose of sketching or modeling with a group of children. The artist and children may draw a picture of the classroom's aesthetic display or may go outdoors to sketch a landscape or the school's pet. In such a visit, the artist is asked to work alongside the children, acting as consultant to them. Participation in this is, of course, purely optional; not all children will want to do this nor is it appropriate for children below the primary grades.

When there are enough adults in the room to provide the necessary supervision, participating in art work oneself is a rich experience for both teacher and child. There is comraderie as teacher and children engage in an art activity which occupies hands and eyes. Teacher participation, however, does not mean that the teacher demonstrates to children how to draw a picture or create a model of an object.

ENCOURAGING EFFORTS AND HELPING CHILDREN EVALUATE. Hoping to encourage a child's artistic efforts, some teachers praise children's work indiscriminately with such phrases as "That's lovely, Johnny; my you always do such nice work!" Such praise is seldom helpful. Children know that not all of their products are equally good.

It is dishonest to say that a child who has used many different colors of paint which have all run together to produce a muddy brown has produced a lovely picture if you do not really feel that it is. The comment, "Susy, you used a lot of different colors today," provides honest feedback and encouragement. When praise is given a child's work, tell why you like it. Point to something specific and comment on it in an approving way. Conversations between teacher and child which elicit the child's own judgments will help the teacher suggest directions for future work.

DISPLAYING ART PRODUCTS. When children have put their best efforts into an art product, they deserve to have their work displayed in a worthy manner. Flatwork may or may not be mounted, but should be attractively displayed. Three-dimensional work should also be displayed attractively and not just left in a jumble on a shelf. Suggestions for displaying products can be found in the illustrations in Figure 8.

Although there should be an opportunity for each child's work to be displayed, not every work a child does need be displayed. If space permits, a wall space may be alloted for hanging a picture of each child's choice. It is important to foster discrimination in selecting a work to be displayed. The rare work of a child who seldom uses the art center, however, should be selected no matter what the quality. The child who uses the center daily should be asked to choose the best product for display.

Materials for the Visual Arts Center

BASIC MATERIALS

Crayons—both large primary size and regular
Pencils
Library paste
White glue
Scissors—include some for left hand
Powdered paint—red, blue, and yellow; and other colors later
Plasticene (sometimes called plastolene)

Figure 8. Displaying flatwork.

BASIC MATERIALS (*cont.*)

Colored construction paper

Manila or white paper—larger sizes for younger children

Newsprint—24″ × 36″

Brushes—long handles, half-inch; and other sizes later

OTHER COMMERCIAL MATERIALS

Ceramic clay

Pipe cleaners

Colored tissue paper

Colored chalks or pastels

Paper plates

Balls of string

Craft materials—glitter, sequins, raffia, balsam, etc.

Wire—different thicknesses for different purposes: mobiles, papier mache, etc.

Wire snippers

Wallpaper paste

Yarn

Gummed tape—various types, sizes, colors: transparent, masking, plastic

Watercolors

WOODWORKING MATERIALS

Carpenter bench and peg-board for tool storage

Vise or clamps

Hammer

Nails—variety of the larger sizes

Saw

Screwdriver

Nails and screws

Pliers

Hand drill

Nuts and bolts

Wrench

Wood—soft wood scraps from lumber yard

INGREDIENTS FOR HOMEMADE MATERIALS

Linit starch

Soap flakes

Flour

Sugar

Powdered alum

Salt—non-iodized

INGRIEDIENTS FOR HOMEMADE MATERIALS (*cont.*)

Food coloring

Salad oil

Cream of tartar

Oil of clove

BEAUTIFUL JUNK

Cans—various sizes: 1- 2- 3-lb. coffee cans, shortening cans, orange juice
    cans

Cartons and boxes—various sizes: shoe boxes, round oatmeal boxes, pack-
    ing boxes

Plastic bottles—various shapes and sizes

Egg cartons—for storing scissors and pencils as well as for crafts

Magazines

Scraps of material

Scraps of yarn and string

Scraps of construction paper

Seashells, pebbles, bits of colored glass

Aluminum foil pie plates, frozen dinner plates, etc.

Plastic bags for storage of materials—plasticene, clay, etc.

Baby food jars

RECIPES FOR HOMEMADE ART MATERIALS

Finger paint base (1 gallon)

3 cups Linit starch (dry)

Slightly more than 2 cups cold water

        (Mix above together)

Add 9 cups boiling water and bring just to boiling point. Remove from
heat and add 2 cups soap flakes (Ivory, Lux, or other).

Beat while hot, approximately 5 minutes.

Food coloring (1 large tablespoon per pint container) or tempera paint
(dry) may be sprinkled on mixture as children use it.

Tweedle Paste

Stir in top of double boiler:	½ cup sifted flour
	½ cup white sugar
	½ tbsp. powdered alum
	1½ cups cold water
Add to above stirring constantly:	1½ cups boiling water.

Cook over hot water until clear. Add 15 drops of oil of cloves. Beat well.
Store in wide-mouth jars with lids.

Hints: Powdered alum is available in the spice section of the grocery store.
Oil of cloves may be purchased at a drugstore. A one-ounce bottle may
cost $1.00 but will last through many batches of paste.

Play dough #1

½ cup salt (non-iodized)
2 cups cold water
Food coloring (optional)

Bring above ingredients to bubbling on medium heat.
Remove from heat. Add 2 tbsps. powdered alum.
Add 3 scant cups of flour slowly, stirring well.
Pour onto board and knead well. It will still be hot. If it seems sticky, add flour until desired texture is reached.
Note: It is best not to add the three cups of flour all at once. Start with about 2½ cups and add more if needed.

Play dough #2 (New Tartar)

1 cup flour
½ cup salt
1 cup water
1 tbsp. salad oil
2 tbsp. cream of tartar

Mix above ingredients together with food coloring (optional) in a large sauce pan. Place over high heat, stirring constantly. As the mixture heats, it will thicken and form a ball leaving the sides of the pan. When this happens, remove from heat and allow to cool until it can be handled. Knead until smooth.

Cornstarch clay

1 cup cornstarch
2 cups baking soda
1¼ cups cold water

Mix together, cook over medium heat stirring constantly for about 4 minutes until mixture thickens to moist mashed-potato consistency. Cover with damp cloth to cool. Knead. Figures made with this clay will harden overnight.

Activities for Instruction in the Visual Arts

ACTIVITIES TO DEVELOP COMPETENCIES FOR SELF-EXPRESSION IN THE VISUAL ARTS

1. Activity: Brush painting (PP-P)

Materials: Easels, tables, or floor space; aprons, smocks, or old shirts to protect clothing; large (24″ × 36″) sheets of newsprint, butcher paper, manila or other paper; powdered tempera paints and water; a variety of brushes with long handles; sponges, rags, water, paper towels for clean-up.

Procedure: Prepare an area near a source of water. Cover floor with oilcloth, heavy plastic, or linoleum rug. Set up easels and clip on paper (or have it nearby for children to obtain).

Mix paint in clear plastic or glass containers such as large baby-food jars. Cans may be used, but colors are not as easily seen. Choose containers which will not tip over when brushes are left in them. Paints may be set on a table next to the easels or in the trays of the easels.

For best results, place powdered paint in the containers first and add water in small amounts until desired consistency is obtained. For beginners, a brush may be placed in each color. Clean brushes may be stored in a can, brush-end up. Children can select brushes as needed. Teach children to wash out brushes between dippings and when finished painting.

When children desire to paint, the teacher should print or have the children print their names in the left corner of the paper. Names may be printed on the reverse side to avoid obscuring the name with paint.

When painting is finished, help the child place painting in a safe place for drying. A clothesline is useful for this purpose, and if it is hung low enough, children can hang their own pictures.

Suggestions and Variations: A selection of colors in containers on a table adjacent to the easel area allows children to choose the colors they want. From time to time teachers should comment on specific features of a child's work, such as colors used. For older children, provide brushes in a variety of shapes and sizes.

Start children with the primary colors: blue, red, and yellow. Add secondary colors: orange, green, and purple. Black, white, and brown may complete the collection. Use good quality, true colors. After children have had some experience with painting, they may like to mix their own colors. Provide the primary colors and black and white. Small palettes may be used for mixing, or muffin tins may be used. Children will need a cup of water to wash their brush each time they wish to use it in a different color.

A mural may be a group painting activity. Spread out a long sheet of butcher paper on the floor or a long table. Plan with the children for a mural depicting an experience or interest which is held in common.

2. **Activity:** Finger painting (PP-P)

Materials: Flat washable surface (table or floor), shallow pan (larger than 12″ × 18″) with water, glazed finger painting paper, finger-paint base (recipe on page 66), powdered tempera paint. Clothing protectors and clean-up and picture drying-materials as for brush painting.

Procedure: Print child's name on a sheet of glazed paper. Draw the paper through the water in the shallow pan. Put dollops of fingerpaint on several areas of the paper.

Fingerpaint may be pre-colored or fingerpaint base may be put on the paper and powdered tempera sprinkled in it. For each dollop of fingerpaint base, a different color may be used.

Suggestions and Variations: Encourage children to use whole sweep of palms and arms up to the elbows and to experiment with various ways of using hands and arms.

For beginners more interested in the feel of finger-painting, painting may be done directly on a table which has a hard finish or on trays. Prints may be made by pressing paper on top of fingerpainted table or tray if desired.

Finished finger paintings may be used as covers for five-gallon ice-cream-carton wastebaskets, scrapbook covers, gift-wrapping paper, or storage-box covers.

It is essential to have water for clean-up within easy reach.

3. *Activity:*   Rubbings (P)

Materials: Paper; crayons, chalks, pastels, or charcoal; leaves, embossed flat metal, burlap, or other textured materials.

Procedure: Lay textured material on table and cover with paper. Using the side of the crayon (paper removed), piece of colored chalk, pastel, or charcoal, rub firmly over entire surface of the paper. Outlines of materials underneath the paper should appear. If chalk, charcoal, or pastels, are used, spray with fixative (in well-ventilated area or outside).

Suggestions and Variations: Use a variety of textures as base for one rubbing. As it will take practice to use just the right touch—neither too hard nor too soft—this variation should be reserved for children who have developed a degree of motor skill.

4. *Activity:*   Straw painting (PP–P)

Materials: Plastic drinking straws, paper, poster paint.

Procedures: Dribble paint in several colors on paper. Blow the paint through the straws to create designs.

Suggestions and Variations: Paint should be fairly thin to flow easily. Use primary colors for beginners.

5. *Activity:*   Crayon–water color etching (P)

Materials: Water-base paint, crayons, sharpened stick or nail file, paper, brush.

Procedures: Cover the paper completely with one or more colors of thin paint; water color is best. Allow to dry. Color over the paint thickly with a dark colored crayon (black is commonly used). Scratch designs with a pointed stick or nail file.

Suggestions and Variations: This is not recommended for beginners, for it requires patience for a series of processes. In addition to pointed tools, a flat-edged tool may be used to scrape off a width of crayon as may be desired for drawing a building.

6. *Activity:* Crayon-water-color resist (P)

Materials: Tempera paint, crayons, paper, brushes.

Procedure: Draw a picture with crayons. Paint over the entire picture with tempera paint. Paint will not adhere to areas covered with crayon wax.

Suggestions and Variations: A light-colored paint will allow the crayon drawing to stand out. Tempera paint should be thin.

7. *Activity:* Collage (PP–P)

Materials: Paper plates; medication cups, egg-carton cups, or jar lids; white glue; scissors; miscellaneous materials such as scraps of cloth, yarn, colored construction paper, colored tissue paper, colored glass, pebbles, beans, macaroni, sea-shells, old magazines, old greeting cards.

Procedure: On a table, spread out trays of selected scraps of material: paper plates, egg-carton tops, shoe-box lids, or paper for a base; small containers of glue. Demonstrate ways of applying glue to objects to be used in the collage. Small objects may be dipped in glue, while popsicle sticks may be used to spread glue on paper. When finished, set aside to dry.

Suggestions and Variations: Have children select items wanted for their pictures and arrange them on the dry paper before starting to glue. (This sort of planning should not be expected from young preprimary children who are more interested in manipulating the materials than in making a picture.) Holes may be punched in the edges of paper plates, egg cartons, or heavy paper for lacing with yarn to give a framed effect.

For tissue-paper collage, paint the base with a thin coat of diluted glue. Then place the pieces of tissue on top and press.

Combine a neighborhood walk with this activity by having children pick up materials for collage. "Just what you can hold in your two hands" is a good rule.

8. *Activity:* Design printing (PP–P)

Materials: Poster paints, cut onion, carrot, and potato carved in designs, slices of orange, etc.; orange-juice cans may be used, as may other objects; paper; containers for poster paint, meat-pie tins, wide jar lids, or small bowls or saucers; pieces of old sponges to place in bottom of paint containers; bowls of water.

Procedure: Mix poster paint until it is very thick. Place each color in separate container by pouring it over sponge until sponge is soaked with paint. Dip objects into paint on top of sponge and press on paper. When desiring a design in several colors, wash object in bowl of water after use with each color. (See Figure 9.)

Suggestions and Variations: Use colored construction paper as base for interesting contrasts. Printed paper may be used as wrapping paper or for covering wastepaper baskets, cartons, or scrapbooks. Paint may be applied by brush rather than dipping if desired.

9. *Activity:*   Modeling (PP–P)

Materials: Salt-and-flour dough, plasticene, or ceramic clay; popsicle sticks, orangewood manicure sticks, toy rolling pins, cookie cutter, etc.

Procedure: Have clay readily available for children to work with as they wish. If clay is stored in 2- or 3-inch diameter balls in a crock, children can easily get it on their own. Ceramic clay and

Figure 9. Design printing.

salt-and-flour dough clay will harden if exposed to air for more than a short period of time. Older children who have developed some skill may wish to make objects, let them harden, and then paint them. Plasticene and salt-and-flour dough made with oil will not harden readily if kept properly covered.

Suggestions and Variations: Cut out shapes from rolled clay. Cover with textured material and press evenly with rolling pin for textured medallions. If made with ceramic clay and fired, these may be Christmas-tree ornaments, wind chimes, or pendants. Remember that for young children who have had little experience with modeling, the clay itself is enough for the first few weeks. Add tools gradually. Also remember that the younger children will not set out to make "something" with the clay. They are more interested in how it feels and what it does.

10. *Activity:* Carpentry (PP–P)

Materials: Workbench, hammer, saw, nails, vise, glue, hand drill, screwdriver, screws, nuts and bolts, wrench, pliers, plane. Soft wood in a variety of sizes.

Procedure: Start a woodworking center with just a few tools, such as hammer, screwdriver, and hand drill. Add other tools later after children become accustomed to the center. Demonstrate safe use and care of tools in a planning period or to small groups as they use the area.

Suggestions and Variations: Children's first woodworking will probprobably consist only of driving nails into wood. An example of this kind of work can be seen in the photo of two three-year-old girls on page 73. Children are very proud of this accomplishment and value these creations very much. When first introduced to the saw, they will probably only cut wood into pieces and not attempt to put these together to make anything. It would be a very serious error in judgment to assume that these pieces mean nothing to the child and attempt to place them back in the stockpile of wood. These are precious pieces and the child will want to take them home. Again, it should be remembered that young children are far more interested in manipulating and controlling the materials than in making "something." As children gain experience working with wood, they will want to begin making things. It is important that materials are available for their work. Nails should be provided in a variety of sizes. Wood of all shapes and sizes should also be available. Materials such as soda pop bottle caps or discs cut from dowel rods may be used for wheels. Popsicle sticks resemble airplane propellers.

Early woodworking creations may consist only of a few nails in a piece of wood.

Paper and fabric scraps are often useful as boat sails, and uphol-
stery can be used for a car seat or chair. Felt-tip pens can be used
to add details to wood constructions.

All tools should be real, not toy, and should be kept in top working
order.

11. *Activity:*   Mobiles (K–P)

    Materials: Quarter-inch dowel cut in varying lengths (less than
    12″); strong black string or picture wire; miscellaneous materials
    such as scraps of cloth, yarn, pipe cleaners, construction paper, old
    magazines, old greeting cards.

    Procedure: Show a variety of mobiles and talk about how they
    are made. This "showing" and "talking" may be initiated by the
    teacher by hanging several mobiles about the classroom. Children
    are sure to notice them and ask questions.

    The teacher can demonstrate tying or other means for fastening
    strings or wire and testing for balance. Pictures from magazines or
    greeting cards may be mounted on tagboard before being attached
    to the mobile. Ceramic clay medallions may be used.

Suggestions and Variations: A wire coat hanger may be used as top bar and objects suspended from it. Show children how to cut spirals for spring effect and to fold paper for snowflake effect. The wire frame of a small lampshade would make an interesting variation.

13. *Activity:* String and yarn art (PP–P)

Materials: Colored yarns or string, manilla or construction paper, dilute mixture of tweedle paste or white glue, shallow pans.

Procedure: Pour the glue or paste into shallow pans. Set on a table with lengths of yarn and provide paper or paper plates for base. Demonstrate arranging yarns of different colors on the base as a plan. Immerse yarn in glue. Arrange in design on paper. Allow to dry.

Suggestions and Variations: Blow up balloons. Using a continuous strand of yarn or string, wrap paste-soaked yarn around the balloon leaving spaces for a lacy effect. Use sausage shaped balloons to make cages for toy animals or animals modeled from clay. Make a shade for a hanging lamp by using a large round balloon. As balloons are to be popped and removed, do not use white glue (for older children).

Substitute paint for paste. Cut string into 8″ × 12″ pieces. Draw string through the paint, lay on paper, and lift off. Repeat as desired. For wheel-spoke effect, hold one end firmly to paper; holding the other end taut, lay string on paper. Continuing to hold the end on the paper, lift string, move it a short distance and lay it down again. Repeat as many times as desired. For spatter effect, hold one end securely in one spot on the paper, and holding the string taut with thumb and forefinger of the other hand at an angle off the paper, flick the string with your middle finger.

14. *Activity:* Papier mâché (PP–P)

Materials: Newspapers, flour paste (commercial wallpaper or tweedle paste), a shallow basin or pan, water, string or picture wire, miscellaneous cartons and tubes (rollers from paper towels, wrapping paper, toilet paper, etc.). After figures are completed, you will need: poster paints, brushes, scraps of construction paper, yarn, fabric, and other scraps for decorating; white glue.

Procedure: Working with children, help them bunch and tie newspaper or used tubes for legs. To attach these, use strips of paper dipped in paste or use wide masking tape. Wrap tape or paper strip around end to be attached and up over body.

Prepare flour paste in shallow pan to about consistency of thick pea soup. Tear newspapers into long one- or two-inch strips. Pull through paste and apply to base figure. Apply strips around joints first for extra strength. Continue until figure is completely covered and smooth. Paper toweling torn in strips forms a good final coat. Set aside to dry. Drying may take several days depending on size of figures, number of coats of papier mâché, and weather conditions. When figures are fully dry, provide materials for painting and other finishing touches. (See Figure 10.)

Suggestions and Variations: Encourage children to work on their own, offering to help when requested or when frustration level appears beyond tolerance.

Younger children may not be ready for a project such as this, which requires an extended period of time. A papier mâché project should not be initiated unless additional adult help is available or children can work with minimal supervision.

Use a shared experience such as a well-liked story or a trip to the zoo or a farm as a starter for a papier mâché as a medium for making models in connection with social studies or science.

15. *Activity:* Puppet (papier mâché) (P)

Materials: Plasticene; materials for papier mâché.

Procedure: Form a small head from plasticene. Be sure to make a good neck about the size of the middle finger. Cover with small strips about one-half inch wide of newspaper soaked in paste as described above. Cover around neck but leave bottom uncovered. When dry, cut the papier-mâché head in half by incising with a sharp knife from bottom of side of neck in front of the ears and over the top. Remove plasticene and put two halves together, covering the joint with strips of paste-dipped paper. When dry, decorate as desired.

To make clothes, cut a piece of fabric twice the length of the hand from tip of middle finger to tip of thumb when hand is outstretched. Fold the length and cut a hole in the middle of the fold the size of the puppet's neck. Sew sides together forming sleeves which will fit over thumb and fourth finger. Trim. Turn right side out and attach to head. Add collar and trimming as desired. (See Figure 11.)

Suggestions and Variations: Copenhagen puppets: Use round balloons as base for molding head. Cover with papier mâché as for hand puppets and add features. Attach to broomsticks. A piece of

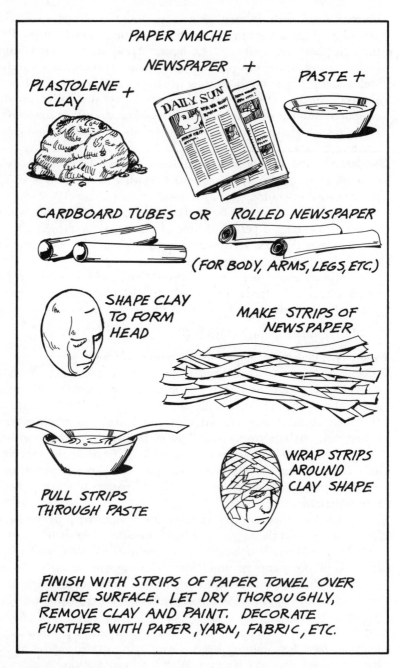

PAPER MACHE

PLASTOLENE + CLAY

NEWSPAPER +

DAILY SUN

PASTE +

CARDBOARD TUBES OR ROLLED NEWSPAPER

(FOR BODY, ARMS, LEGS, ETC.)

SHAPE CLAY TO FORM HEAD

MAKE STRIPS OF NEWSPAPER

PULL STRIPS THROUGH PASTE

WRAP STRIPS AROUND CLAY SHAPE

FINISH WITH STRIPS OF PAPER TOWEL OVER ENTIRE SURFACE. LET DRY THOROUGHLY, REMOVE CLAY AND PAINT. DECORATE FURTHER WITH PAPER, YARN, FABRIC, ETC.

Figure 10. Papier mâché.

COPENHAGEN PUPPET

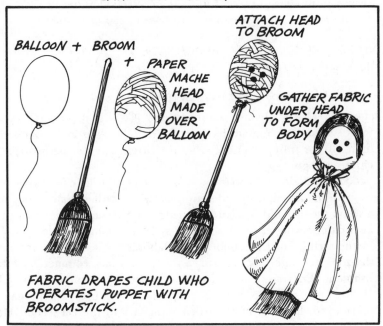

Figure 11. Copenhagen puppets.

fabric decorated as desired may be gathered and attached at joint of broomstick and head so that fabric drapes child who operates puppet with broomsticks.

16. *Activity:* Paper bag art (PP–P)

Materials: Paper bags of various sizes, scissors, white glue or tweedle paste, construction paper scraps, yarn, and fabric scraps.

Procedure: *For masks*—Choose large bags which will fit over head and shoulders of children. Show children how to help each other find proper places for cutting holes for eyes, nose, mouth, and arms. Demonstrate ways to decorate with construction paper cut in strips and rolled on pencils for curls, or with yarn and fabric for eyebrows, hair, etc. Masks may be painted if preferred.

For hand puppets—Choose bags a little larger than the hand. The bag should be just large enough that the bottom fold can be easily moved up and down with fingers inserted. Demonstrate placement of facial features on bottom of bag.

Suggestions and Variations: Avoid leaving models; show child a variety of models to present ideas then put models out of sight after children have had opportunities to handle and examine them.

ACTIVITIES FOR DEVELOPING APPRECIATION OF THE VISUAL ARTS

1. Activity: Field trips (PP–P)

Materials: Make advance arrangements (1) with personnel at site to be visited, (2) for adults—parents or others—to accompany children, (3) for transportation. Obtain written parental permission for children to go.

Procedure: Field trips may be taken to provide a core experience from which art and other learning activities will radiate. They may also be used to add needed knowledge to a project under way or to be a culminating experience. Field trips may be as simple as a walk in the vicinity of the school or as elaborate as a trip to a museum, the zoo, the state fair, a farm, a dairy, or other commercial establishment. En route and on arrival encourage comments on what children see and direct their attention to features which may be overlooked. Elicit reactions when returning to the classroom. Have children describe their experiences verbally or draw pictures of things they saw.

Suggestions and Variations: Take a walk in the neighborhood specifically to see an animal, tree, or building. Ask children to tell and show with gestures how things look.

It is not necessary for the entire class to go on every field trip. An adult, volunteer, or aide, may take a small group to visit something of special interest.

Do not require all students to engage in a follow-up activity; this should be optional.

When making arrangements, ask for a guide who is skilled in talking with young children and in eliciting their questions, comments, and reactions.

When visiting a museum, decide in advance which exhibits you wish to visit. Setting limits in advance may prevent very active youngsters from darting from room to room. It is more important for children to enjoy thoroughly one or two works of art than to have the buzzing confusion of sensory images resulting from trying to see everything in the same day.

For children who have shown a special interest in an exhibit ar-

Field trips extend children's experiences.

range a return trip. A parent who has an interest in art may take them.

2. *Activity:*   Masterpiece of the week (PP–P)

Materials: A file of prints of masterpieces. Cover the prints with clear plastic or laminate to preserve them for longer use. Prints that are pre-laminated are available from the National Gallery. Some works to include are:
- Works of Cimabue and Giotto (particularly around Christmas, as these are primarily of religious themes).
- Works from the Dutch school of genre artists: Brueghel, Vermeer, Hals, Steen, Rembrandt for their portrayal of Dutch life.
- Paintings from the French impressionists: Renoir, Monet, Manet, Cezanne.
- Landscapes by Turner and Constable.
- Picasso—particularly his blue period. (*Le Gourmet*, which depicts a small boy eating from a bowl, is a favorite).
- Van Gogh's landscapes and still-lifes for their brilliant color.
- Murillo's painting of a peasant boy leaning on a sill.
- Rosa Bonheur's painting of a horse fair.
- Renoir's and Degas's paintings of children as well as the latter's paintings of ballet dancers.

- Gainsborough's portraits of children.
- Velasquez's paintings for color contrast and shapes.
- Photographs of statues—Greek classics, African, Michelangelo.
- Works of Braque and Dufy for sharp, clear abstract design.
- Oriental prints for delicacy and grace.
- American Indian prints.
- The Americana of Thomas Hart Benton, Grant Wood, Norman Rockwell, Stephen Dohanos, Frederic Remington.
- African paintings and designs.
- The Mexican masterpieces of Rivera, Sequeiros, and Tomayo.

Prints of masterpieces may be obtained from your local art gallery. Some libraries have collections which may be checked out in the same manner as books. If these resources are not available to you, write to the Metropolitan Museum of Art in New York City; the Art Institute in Chicago, or the National Gallery in Washington, D.C., for catalogs of prints.

Procedure: Pictures displayed in classrooms should go beyond children's art and pictures designed to teach a concept. Trite, cute pictures of doubtful artistic value should be avoided. Art work selected from a wide range of periods and styles should be presented if children are to develop aesthetic appreciation.

Select prints for interest to children because of subject matter or for bright colors and vigorous design. Paintings of children, family groups, landscapes, and still-life and also colorful abstracts (non-representational art) may be included. Photographs or reproductions of statues should also be included. Photography is also a means of artistic expression and artistic photographs should be displayed also.

Ask children to select "the masterpiece of the week" and hang it in a spot chosen for this purpose. Such a spot should be low enough for children to examine the picture closely, yet open to unobstructed long range view. (See Figure 12.)

Suggestions and Variations: Keep the file of masterpieces in the quiet corner for leisurely viewing.

On a trip to the art museum, select and purchase a print of some work seen there.

3. *Activity:* Aesthetic display (PP–P)

Materials: A small area in the classroom set aside for the purpose; shelf space, a small table, a chair; fabric, colored corrugated cardboard, or other materials to provide background; any of the following: colored bottles, musical instruments, flowers, leaves, fruit, in-

Figure 12. Aesthetic display.

teresting rocks, plants, seashells, statuettes, costumed dolls, bowls,
vases, attractive dishes, model cars, etc.

Procedure: Setting up a display which has no other function than
   to be aesthetically pleasing helps a child develop a sense of design
   and balance and may be a stimulus for drawing or painting. There
   are many forms such a display may take. A chair draped with fabric
   falling in soft folds over the back and around objects of good design
   is one. Blocks may be used to form small shelves or pedestals and
   placed in front of standing rolls of colored corrugated cardboard.
   A piece of fabric may be tacked to a bulletin board and fall in folds
   which accent a display on a shelf below. Any of these three and
   more are possibilities for aesthetic displays. Teachers will usually
   make the first display. As the year progresses, encourage children
   to change the display and to make one of their own.

Suggestions and Variations: Avoid sameness in composition. Some
   displays should be symmetrical and others asymmetrical. Curved
   lines may prevail one time and angular lines another.

METHODS AND ACTIVITIES FOR INSTRUCTION IN MUSIC AND MOVEMENT

Guiding Work in Music and Movement

Music is a large part of our lives. It soothes, inspires, entertains and generally enriches us. Children should have many and varied musical experiences.

PROVIDING EXPERIENCES.   Experience should be provided for the entire class as a group, for small groups, and for individuals. Having well-equipped centers allows children to have independent experiences with music. Although children need freedom to experiment with music on their own, they also need the guidance that can only come from teacher-child face-to-face interaction. It is doubtful if children can learn to identify and discriminate among pitches, tones, rhythms, harmonies, melodies, and other musical concepts without the aid of the teacher.

In the early years, teachers will frequently include music as part of a class meeting. Sometimes it may be singing as a pleasant way to start the meeting. This also serves as a transition from individual to group work. Other musical experiences such as listening to records or musicians can also be activities for the entire group.

Individuals and small groups of children who have special interest in music also need opportunities to work independently. Much of the music competence a child acquires can only occur from exploring and practicing independently. Organization in a center is useful for this type of learning. Because the activities which take place in a center may be distracting, rules may be needed. Perhaps work in some of the centers will be permitted at certain times of the day and not others. Perhaps appointments for teacher assistance with certain projects will be needed. When clearly understood by teacher and children, such limits provide freedom for more creativity than when they do not exist.

ENCOURAGING EFFORTS.   The fascination inherent in music is enough to get most children interested in exploring music. Participation by the teacher in musical activities at group time or other times of the day can also encourage children to become involved in music. In addition, knowing that a dance, an instrumental piece, or a song will be presented to an audience provides incentive for sustained involvement. When a small group of children become involved of their own choice in working on such a presentation, the teacher may suggest a time when they may perform for their classmates. A wider audience may be desired for a program that the whole class has worked on. The audience may be another class or parents.

It is wise to remember that the important part of the musical production is not the final product, but the process. Performing for an audience should also be the children's decision. The teacher may reflect the wish, expressed by one or two children, or the teacher may suggest it if it seems the child needs this kind of encouragement. Such performances, however, must be for the benefit of the children, not the teacher.

EVALUATING WORK.   Noting changes in quality of performance over time provides evaluation of progress in music. For younger children, the teacher may make an anecdotal record of observations. For example, having played a recording of "Raindrops Keep Falling on My Window," a child was heard singing the song softly at naptime. The teacher's recording of this incident provides evidence of the child's learning.

Older children might keep written records of their work in the center for exploring sound. For example, a child who experiments with filling glasses with water to different levels to duplicate the notes of a five-tone scale may write an account of procedure and findings.

Still another way to evaluate progress is to make tape recordings of children's performance at intervals throughout the year.

Music Centers

A LISTENING CENTER.   Near a record player, in addition to story records, there should be a selection of musical recordings. A wide variety of music including nursery rhymes, jingles, folksongs, popular pieces, and classical music should be found there. Children are never too young to enjoy the finest music, and symphonic and operatic selections should be included. For a description of the enthusiastic response of four-year-olds to classical music, see *Discovering Music with Young Children* by Eunice Bailey.[9]

A FREE-MOVEMENT AREA.   Some children may be content to listen to music with only small body movements such as rocking, gently tapping a foot, or waving a hand, but movement should not be limited to that. Another area is needed where children can move freely in response to music; where they can run and skip, gallop and glide, swing and sway,

---

[9]E. Bailey, *Discovering Music With Young Children* (New York: Philosophical Library, 1958), pp. 39–42.

swoop and slither. Here they experience the mood of the music, the tempo, and the rhythm. They respond to these with their whole bodies.

In most public schools, the free-movement area would be a gym or auditorium which is available at periods of the day when unused by other classes. If the classroom is large enough, the teacher might consider designating an area for movement activities. Such an area may also be used for dramatic play. In this area small groups of children may independently explore music and movement. Larger, teacher-led groups would engage in music and movement activities in the gym when it is available.

AN AREA FOR EXPLORING SOUND.   One center in the classroom should be an area where children are free to explore sound. It should be located at the farthest distance possible from the quiet corner and at sufficient distance from woodworking and other noisy activities so that the sounds of these activities will not interfere with children's listening to and discriminating among sounds.

In the area for exploring sound there should be a variety of simple rhythm and musical instruments, both commercial and homemade. Materials for making musical instruments should also be available, but may be more appropriately housed in the art center.

Instruments which will be placed in the center may be introduced to the class in a planning session first. As each instrument is introduced, the children should be invited to compare it with other instruments. For example, children might be asked to compare bells with oriental temple blocks. The temple blocks have a non-reverberating hollow sound, whereas the bells have a clear, ringing tone. If the children respond in terms of pitch instead of tone, the question of pitch might be explored.

Music Materials

In the area of exploring sound there should be a wide variety of musical instruments. Such equipment should include instruments which produce sound through being hit or shaken—percussion—through being blown—winds—and through being plucked or scraped—strings. Examples of instruments which may be purchased are:

PERCUSSION

Drums	Xylophone
Cymbals	Oriental temple blocks
Rattles	Blocks
Triangle	Tone bars or resonator bells
Bells	Piano
Glockenspiel	Tambourine

WINDS	STRINGS
Recorders	Guitar
Flageolet	Autoharp
Ocarinas	Ukulele
Harmonicas	Violin
Flutophones	
Tonettes	

Instruments which have been made from inexpensive and scrap materials should also be available in the center for exploring sound. Some suggestions will be found among the activities in this chapter, but for further suggestions the reader is referred to Hawkinson and Faulhaber.[10]

Percussion instruments are those most commonly used in the early years. They have relatively constant pitch and are not difficult to play. They can also be simulated readily with homemade instruments.

Though most percussion instruments must be considered rhythmic and not melodic, bells, xylophones, tone bars, the glockenspiel, and the piano are both. A variety of these instruments should be found in the center for exploring sound. There are many types and sizes of bells which should be included. Bells selected for this purpose should parallel the tones of the familiar C-major scale.

There are a variety of stringed instruments from various peoples and times, some of which are quite simple and may provide models for instruments that may be made in the classroom. In connection with studies of history and geography, instruments such as the sitar, psaltery, and viola da gamba may be introduced. Musicians often collect such ancient instruments, and the alert teacher looks for such resources.

Wind instruments are often omitted from classrooms for hygienic reasons. In a classroom which fosters self-reliance as well as good health habits, provisions can be made for avoiding the transmittal of disease through the use of a common mouthpiece. A soap-and-water solution which includes a small amount of chlorine bleach may be used to clean the mouthpiece after each use. A small tray with cotton balls, the cleansing solution in one small bowl and clear water in another, and a supply of paper towels may be placed next to the wind instruments. The children may be taught to cleanse the mouthpiece effectively without damage to the instruments.

A piano may be a valuable asset to a program for young children but it is not an essential item. Should one be offered you free for the

[10]J. Hawkinson and M. Faulhaber, *Music and Instruments for Children to Make* (Chicago: Albert Whitman, 1970).

taking, check it out first. Be sure the piano can be tuned. The space a piano takes in the classroom is more valuable than a piano which cannot be properly tuned. An out-of-tune piano is damaging to the development of a sense of pitch.

Children should be allowed to experiment with playing the piano. Although there is a need for clearly understood, reasonable rules, learning may be inhibited by too-stringent unexplained rules. When, within limits, children can freely explore sounds, they are building a firm background for musical expression.

Activities for Instruction in Music and Movement

ACTIVITIES TO HELP CHILDREN DEVELOP COMPETENCIES FOR SELF-EXPRESSION IN MUSIC AND MOVEMENT

1. Activity: Singing songs (PP–P)

Materials: Teacher's ability to sing a simple melody and repertoire of songs. Piano, autoharp, or guitar accompaniment is helpful but not essential. Recordings may be used when learning a song if necessary.

Procedure: Select relatively short songs with simple, repetitious words and melody and strong rhythm. Four to six lines is a reasonable length. Single-word or phrase variations provide new verses in many well-loved songs.

For example: "Where is thumbkin?" names a new finger in each verse while the rest of the words remain the same. Once children are familiar with the base song, word changes are easily introduced. When teaching new songs, do not introduce too many verses at once. Teach one until children are reasonably familiar with it before going on to the next. One way to teach a verse is to go all the way through it several times and then ask the children to go through it with you.

To emphasize the melody of a song, lead the children's singing by indicating with your hand when the melody goes up, down, or stays the same. More complicated rhythms can be emphasized by clapping your hands.

Suggestions and Variations: After children are familiar with a song and with the sounds of a variety of instruments, they may be asked what instruments they think would sound good in a particular place in a song. A child who suggests one should be allowed to try it. Other instruments may be added in the same way. Because children will probably play with any instruments in their hands, it is wise to keep them next to yourself and hand them out only as needed. Have some children sing the melody while others sing rhythmic accompaniment, as in *The Little Drummer Boy*, in which "vroom, vroom" is sung underneath the melody on a key-note in a low register on the accented beats. Older children may enjoy singing rounds. For example, *Brother John* has four parts. The class may be divided into halves or, for some advanced children, into four sections. Other adults may be needed to lead each section unless the children are able to sing the round independently.

2. *Activity:* Mini-opera (PP–P)

   Materials: The teacher's good spirits, ingenuity, and pleasant voice. Scales, one or more familiar tunes, or improvised tunes.

   Procedure: Carry on a singing conversation with a child by asking a question on an ascending scale and having the child answer on a descending scale. A familiar tune such as *Frère Jacques* may be used, and the dialogue takes place like this:
   Teacher and class: "Where is Susy? Where is Susy?"
   Susy: "Here I am. Here I am."
   Teacher and class: "How are you today, Miss?"
   Susy: "Very fine, I thank you."
   All: "Glad you're here. Glad you're here."

   Suggestions and Variations: Teacher and aide may demonstrate by singing questions and responses to each other. Call children together by singing your request or answer a child's question with singing.

3. *Activity:* Exploring sound (PP–P)

   Materials: A variety of rhythm and melody instruments as they are available to you: drum, rattles, bells, blocks, tambourines, triangles, glockenspiels, oriental temple blocks, harmonicas, recorders, guitar, autoharp, ukulele, tone bars, xylophone, etc.
   Homemade equivalents of the above or other scrounged materials. Clay pots in graduated sizes hung from a horizontal bar by knotted ropes pulled through the holes; pop bottles filled with varying amounts of water; matched glass tumblers and a pitcher of water; pipe in varying lengths and thicknesses suspended from a bar as in the photo on page 88.
   Metal or plastic shakers containing such materials as rice, pebbles, beans, seeds.

   Procedure: Arrange a selection of the above on a table in the center for exploring sound. Allow children to explore freely. Encourage them to guess what is inside the shakers. Play guessing games by having them shut their eyes and guess what instrument is played. Talk about differences in sound.

Pipes can be used to make chimes.

For children who can read, provide activity cards with suggestions
for further exploration. Examples:
Next to the xylophone or any instrument with a full major scale:
"Can you find out how to play *Mary Had a Little Lamb*? Hum the
tune to yourself, then match the notes you play to your singing."
Next to an assortment of percussion instruments: "Can you make
a sound like rain falling? a horse galloping? children skipping?"
Next to five glasses and a pitcher of water: "Fill these glasses with
water so they sound like C, D, E, F, and G on the piano or xylophone. When you find the right pitch, put a label on the glass."
Suggestions and Variations: Have children shut their eyes and listen
for sounds. When children are out of doors is an ideal time. Ask
them to identify sounds they hear. Encourage them to imitate
sounds and to use descriptive words. Talk about the effect and
quality of sounds. Encourage children to have listening adventures
independently. They may record what they hear by drawing pictures, writing a story, or telling about it on a tape recorder. Have
more advanced children guess which bell was rung from a set of
bells, which key of the piano was struck, which tone bar was hit.
Tape record different everyday sounds and have children guess
what they are.

4. *Activity:*   Rhythm instruments (PP–P)

Materials: Drums, maracas, tambourines, triangles, gongs, sticks; blocks, cymbals, bells.

Procedure: Using recordings or playing the piano, play music with well-defined rhythms. Lead the children in moving to the music, marching, skipping, hopping, or running as the rhythm suggests. Have children sit on the floor. Introduce a piece of music with a strong rhythm. Have children clap in time to the music. As individuals show that they are responding well to the rhythm, hand out instruments to substitute for clapping. Introduce only a few instruments at a time. Have an instrument such as the tambourine struck only on the accented beats. Have children set instruments aside and listen to the music. Ask them to listen for points at which different instruments might be used: a triangle at the end of a phrase, sandblocks marking the rhythm of one section, etc.

Suggestions and Variations: March around room in time to music and use rhythm instruments to accent beat. Use rhythm instruments as accompaniment for singing also.

5. *Activity:*   Music notation (P)

Materials: Chart of musical staff and letter names of notes, stick-on labels, felt pen.

Procedure: Place chart of the musical staff and letter names in back of keys on the piano. Put labels showing staff position and letter name on tone bars or xylophone. Write letter names with felt pen on piano keys. Refer to keys struck by name.

Introduce games suggested under exploring sound using letter names for different tones. Place beginners' piano pieces on the piano or next to other instruments for children to try.

Suggestions and Variations: Transcribe tunes made up by children. Play them for their composers. Encourage them to pick their tunes out on the piano or xylophone. Utilize word recognition games substituting musical notes for words. Examples: Paint notes in staff positions on $8\frac{1}{2}''$ by $11''$ pieces of cardboard covered with plastic. Scatter them on the floor. As one child or an adult calls the letter names, the other children scramble to put hands or feet on the correct note. Matching games of the lotto type may also be made.

6. *Activity:*   Composing original songs (P)

Materials: Tape recorder, lined music paper, pencils, resonator bells, xylophone or piano.

Procedure: With a group of children, introduce a short new song, leaving off the last line. Ask children to finish the song by making up their own tune. If children show ability to do this, they are ready to make up a tune for a favorite poem. Select a four-line poem and have children say it with you and clap the rhythm of the words. When you are sure they have the rhythm, ask if they think the song should start on a high note or a low note, and then whether it should go up or down. Having reached a decision on this, sing the first phrase together. Continue to elicit ideas for the remainder of the song. To record the tune, a tape recorder may be used as each line is composed or the tune may be written on the blackboard. To notate, short lines relative to position of pitches in a scale may be used. For an example of a familiar tune written this way, see Figure 13. The tune is "Twinkle, Twinkle, Little Star."

Suggestions and Variations: After children have shown ability to do the above, encourage children to write their own verses and make up tunes for them. Although a few children may think of a tune first and then words, making up a tune for words which have been written is generally easier.

Individuals who make up their own songs may use the tape recorder during the process of creation. Later, the song may be transcribed. If you do not have the ability to do this, ask a musical friend to do it for you. After transcription, have the composer add words (if not

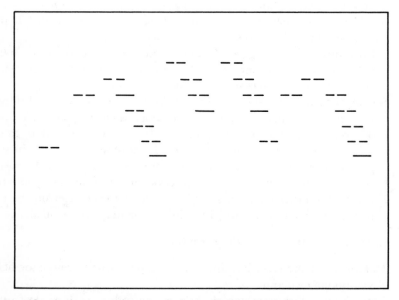

Figure 13. A simple notation for *Twinkle, Twinkle, Little Star.*

written earlier) and illustrations. Then add the song to the class library.

Suggest children try to compose their tunes on resonator bells or xylophone. This will be more successful if the F and B bars are omitted, leaving only the pentatonic scale—C,D,E,G,A. Persevering, talented children may be able to transcribe their own tunes with the help of charts and labels.

Teach songs children have composed to other children in the class.

ACTIVITIES TO HELP CHILDREN DEVELOP
AESTHETIC APPRECIATION OF MUSIC AND MOVEMENT

1. Activity: Using recordings (PP–P)

Materials: Record player, earphones, selection of recordings. Recordings should be of good quality and include:

Children's songs
Folksongs
Jazz
Symphonies
Operatic selections such as "The Children's Prayer" from Humperdinck's *Hansel and Gretel*, "Barcarolle" from Offenbach's *Tales of Hoffman*, "Toreador Song" from Bizet's *Carmen*, Menotti's *Amahl and the Night Visitors.*

Procedure: Play records at various times during the day. Show children how to select, play, and return records to storage. Encourage children to listen independently using earphones. Use recordings as accompaniment for movement and dance. Introduce a recording at a group meeting. Use records which introduce instruments. Recordings such as Britten's *Introduction to the Orchestra* or Prokofiev's *Peter and the Wolf* are especially good.

The narration for the latter introduces the instruments used to portray the various characters. Have pictures of instruments available and show at appropriate times indicated in the recording. Encourage children to identify instruments in other recordings by sound.

Suggestions and Variations: Have a comfortable attractive listening area where children may curl up on soft cushions to listen to music.

2. Activity: Visits from musicians (PP–P)

Materials: Invite musicians to visit class. Brief them on what new kinds of experience you want children to have, your expected outcomes, and the kinds of questions and curiosity they will encounter. Prepare the children by having them think of questions to ask and by discussing appropriate behavior. Listen to records which feature the instruments the visiting musician will bring.

Procedure: When the musicians arrive, children should greet them and show them the area where the class will meet. Gather all children together and enjoy the musicians.

Suggestions and Variations: Ask the musician to demonstrate the way the instrument is played and to play scales as well as pieces. Ask a group of musicians to demonstrate the way in which different melodies fit together into a harmonious whole.

For older children, arrange with an organist for a field trip to hear and see an organ.

3. *Activity:* Concerts for children (PP–P)

Procedure: In many urban areas symphony orchestras play special concerts for children. As for any field trip, arrange for parental consent and assistance to attend the concert. Before going to the concert, obtain the program to be played and play recordings of some of the numbers. Discuss these with the children. When preparations are carefully made, the concert should be enjoyed by all who attend.

Suggestions and Variations: Follow-up activities might include drawing or painting pictures, writing stories, or learning songs based on melodies heard. If there have been many musical experiences in the classroom, even four-year-olds may enjoy a concert.

4. *Activity:* Music in field trips (PP–P)

Procedure: Make usual arrangements for a field trip. Discuss with children sounds they might listen for. Obtain recordings of programmatic music in which the sounds of animals, the city, or the sea may be heard; for example, Saint-Saëns' *Carnival of Animals*, Gershwin's *An American in Paris*, or Debussy's *La Mer*. Recordings of musical expression of visual impressions such as Moussorky's *Pictures at an Exhibition* and Holst's *The Planets* may be used when appropriate. On the field trip, suggest that children listen for sounds. Questions or suggestions which may be used are:

"Close your eyes; what do you hear?"
"Tell me how it sounds; imitate it."
"Is the bird call higher or lower than the dog's barking?"
"How does a truck sound different from an automobile?"
"How does a truck going up hill sound different from one going down?"
"How does the rustling of leaves make you feel?"
"Can you hear the wind in the trees? What kind of sound is it?"

If appropriate, when returning to the classroom, listen to recordings of programmatic music.

Suggestions and Variations: After a field trip, have children reproduce with homemade and commercial instruments the sounds they heard.

METHODS AND ACTIVITIES
FOR INSTRUCTION IN DANCE

Guiding Work in the Dance

TYPES OF DANCE. Dance for young children may be divided into two types: **movement,** which is related to ballet, and **folk dancing.** The two bear much the same relationship to each other that visual art does to crafts. In movement the dancer is free to express feelings and thoughts, whereas in folk dancing the dancer performs the prescribed steps. Yet both may claim a legitimate place in the early years.

Although both kinds of dance should be experienced by young children, movement is particularly important. Movement requires intense involvement of body and mind. It increases awareness of self and others and of the form and motion of things in the environment. At one and the same time, movement is an individual and a group activity; individuals respond to the words of the teacher or to music in their own ways yet are in the company of and may interact with others.

The receptive experiences which form the basis for expressive movement encompass virtually all the sensory experiences in life. The teacher's role is to raise these experiences to awareness by asking children to express their perceptions both verbally and motorically.

PROVIDING DANCE EXPERIENCES. Experiences with expression in movement will usually be instigated by the teacher as a group activity, but opportunities may be provided for children to continue to explore movement as individuals or in small groups. If there is no room for a free movement area in the classroom, the record player might be taken outside for this purpose.

Folk dancing, which for younger children takes the form of singing games, is a social experience. In order to participate, children are expected to follow specified patterns of behavior—the rules. Some games are useful to promote skill in distinguishing between left and right and in using one side of the body and then the other. Folk dancing may serve to aid in the development of gross motor coordination.

A dance or a singing game may be introduced as an alternative to other activities during an active period of the day, the time when children usually go to the playground. No child should be coerced into participation in such singing games or folk dancing; it should be completely optional.

PROVIDING DANCE VOCABULARY.   Dimondstein[11] states that the components of movement are space, time, and force. The teacher's guidance of movement should direct children to explore the dimensions of each of these. The following outline indicates some concepts associated with each of these dimensions:

Space
Direction—backward, forward, diagonally, through
Level—high, low, middle
Range—size, shape

Time
Rhythm—pulse, beat, stress
Pace—mood, steady, changing
Tempo—fast, slow, moderate

Force
Tension—resistance to pull of gravity or momentum
Balance—extending arms or legs, reaching, hopping
Dynamics—heavy, light, stronger, relaxed, fast, slow

While teachers direct movement through descriptive words and music, they should avoid modeling or giving precise how-to directions. For true artistic expression the dancers must be encouraged to make their own interpretations and responses. Group expression may evolve from children's agreeing to use similar motions as part of their interpretation.

Folk dancing, on the other hand, requires direct teaching and modeling. The steps and motions of each dance have been handed down from generation to generation and can only be transmitted in this way.

ENCOURAGING EFFORTS.   As suggested earlier, generalized praise is seldom helpful, whereas commenting approvingly on specific actions gives useful feedback. As children participate in movement activities, the teacher should make specific comments such as 'John, you're taking slow heavy steps; you make me think of an elephant," when the suggestion

11G. Dimondstein, *Exploring the Arts with Children* (New York: Macmillan, 1974), pp. 173–187.

was to think of something very heavy and walk as heavily as it might move.

Older children may wish to present their interpretation of a poem or a piece of music in dance or mime, and arrangements for such a performance may be made. Folk dancing may be part of a school social event. Such occasions provide an incentive for improvement but should not be an end in themselves.

EVALUATING WORK. Observing children and making anecdotal records over time provide a means of evaluating progress. The children's own feelings about increased competence—what they could do at the beginning of the year and what they can do now—may be elicited in conversation.

Progress in movement is marked by such things as improved coordination, greater expressiveness of movements, greater variety of movements, and greater ease in participation in movement. In folk dancing, ability to distinguish right from left, ability to hop, skip, and run in step with the other dancers, and ability to keep in step with the music are marks of improved competence.

Activities for Instruction in the Dance

ACTIVITIES TO DEVELOP COMPETENCIES
IN SELF-EXPRESSION IN DANCE

1. Activity: Expressing concepts of time, space, and mood (PP–P)

Materials: The teacher's knowledge of level of development, and a plan for concepts to be expressed; adequate space; children dressed for ease of movement.

Procedure: Start by asking children to find "their own space." This is a place where even with outstretched arms, they do not touch anyone else. Then ask children to explore their space without moving from where they are: "Down to the floor; up as high as they can reach; over to the side; to the front; to the back." While remaining in the same spot, children may be asked to: "Make yourself as small as you can," "Make yourself as big as you can," "Take up all your space."

Ask children to move in a variety of ways, always keeping their space. Movements might include swinging parts of the body, or bending parts. Work for awareness of space, time, and force in all their dimensions. Work on contrasts: fast and slow, tall and short, jerky and smooth, big and little.

Suggestions and Variations: To be made to children:

"Go around the room moving very slowly. Try to move at the same speed, but on a different level (higher or lower)." "Move around the room using just one part of your body touching the floor."

"Let one part of your body lead as you move slowly across the room. Change to another part of your body."

"Begin to run across the room. When you hear the bell, freeze."

2. *Activity:* Movement to music (PP–P)

Materials: Record player; selection of records including music that is fast and even (running), slow and even (walking) accented and even (marching), and uneven (galloping; skipping); lengths of nylon rope—seven feet for children, nine feet for adults; large chiffon scarves.

Procedure: Give children freedom to respond to music as they wish. At first, do not give children ropes or scarves; let them just use their bodies. Children may need some guidance to respond appropriately to rhythm, tempo, and mood of the music. Ask questions which will help. "Is the music fast or slow?" "Is the music high or low?" "Does the music sound like marching or skipping?" "Oh, it changed there. Did you hear that?"

Suggestions and Variations: Nylon ropes may be used to swing, twirl, skip with, or to draw a circle around each child. To do this, have children hold ends of the rope in each hand and drop it in back of them. Stooping, the child may put the two ends in front and arrange a good circle. Scarves may be used by children to trail in the breeze as they run, to lift high to the sky and down to the ground, to wrap around themselves, to become wings.

3. *Activity:* Folk dance (PP–P)

Materials: Recorded music, piano or guitar if desired. For the youngest children folk dancing usually consists of singing games such as *Ring-around-the Rosy, Here We Go Looby Loo, Doing the Hoky-Poky, A-Tisket A-Tasket, Little Sally Walker, London Bridge, The Farmer in the Dell.* Record albums and books which include these and others are easily found.

Older children may enjoy learning such folk dances as *Chiapanecas (The Mexican Hat Dance),* The *hora, varsuvienne, polkas,* or the *Virginia Reel.*

Procedure: Select the dance to be taught on the basis of your observations of children's ability to follow directions and to respond to rhythm. Gather children in a line or semicircle so that you are facing the same direction as they. Distribute older children or adults who know the dance among the children. Demonstrate steps for children to imitate.

When the children have mastered the basic steps, put on the music. Step, evaluate, and re-teach as necessary.

Suggestions and Variations: The teacher should be aware of less popular and less coordinated children, making sure they are frequently chosen in such games as *Little Sally Walker* and *The Farmer in the Dell* and that they tactfully and discreetly be given help to master the steps. Some may prefer to play rhythm instruments for dancing. If you do not have a repertoire of dances, arrange for a physical education teacher or a dancer to teach some simple dances to you and others on the staff.

ACTIVITIES FOR DEVELOPING AESTHETIC APPRECIATION OF THE DANCE

1. *Activity:* Visit from dancers (PP–P)

   Materials: Gym or other large space where the dancer and children may work.

   Procedure: Ask a dancer to visit the class and to demonstrate steps for the children. The dancer may be a ballet dancer, a mime artist, or one having a specialty such as Spanish dancing. The visit will be more meaningful if the dancer will also work with the class, helping them to improve their dancing.

   Assemble children for watching the dancer and dancing with him or her if this has been the arrangement.

   Suggestions and Variations: See suggestions in sections on art and music for similar activities.

   Take the class or a group of children to see a ballet, mime show, or dance presentation.

2. *Activity:* Rhythms (PP–P)

   Materials: Records of rhythmic music if desired. The gym or other large free space.

   Procedure: Divide the class into two groups. Have one group clap different rhythms with or without music while the other group moves to the rhythms.

   Suggestions and Variations: Substitute rhythm instruments for clapping. Switch groups so that all have an opportunity for each activity.

3. Activity: Awareness of movement (PP–P)

   Procedure: Call attention to the way trees move or the way wind
   or different animals move. Time-lapse movies of plants growing
   may be shown to show the slow movement in nature. Call attention
   to the way dancers move and the moods they express. For example:
   "Chrissy makes me think she's happy because she is whirling so
   lightly; Jon looks angry when he stomps his feet and shakes his fist."
   Suggestions and Variations: Have some children dance and ask other
   children to comment on the moods expressed.

METHODS AND ACTIVITIES
FOR INSTRUCTION IN DRAMA

Guiding Work in Drama

   TYPES OF DRAMA.   There are three forms of drama for the early
years: **dramatic** or **role play, creative dramatics,** and **formal drama.**
Dramatic play is common to all young children. At school it will be
found not only in the dramatic play area, but also in the block area and
on the playground. Whenever one child says to another, "You be the
mother and I'll be the baby" or "You be the garage man and I'll be the
man who needs gas" or "You be Robin and I'll be Batman," dramatic
play starts.

   Creative dramatics is a conscious and usually teacher-directed effort
to retell a story in dramatic form. The story may be one which has been
read and reread, or it may be one children have made up. In creative
dramatics, the children may assume the roles or they may use puppets.
Creative dramatics is particularly valuable in encouraging and extending
oral language.

   Formal drama is the presentation of a play using the lines as the
author has written them. As a form of dramatic expression, it has little
place in the young child's classroom. Filmed or live drama, however, may
be used for instruction and entertainment. The wise teacher will use
drama to bring life and meaning to social studies and literature, capital-
izing both on the children's tendency to dramatize their experiences and
on their enjoyment of filmed and live drama.

   THE DRAMATIC PLAY CENTER.   An area of the room should be designated for dramatic play. The props in the area should be changed from
time to time as children have new experiences. The basic equipment of
the center may include child-size models of kitchen, dining-room, living-

Dramatic play is common to all young children.

room, and bedroom furnishings. When such furnishings are chosen, models which are not realistically detailed will offer more versatility.

The backs of self units may form the walls of this center. On one of these walls, a picture of a landscape may be taped. Framed with strips of paper and draped with fabric, the picture simulates a window. When the center is used as a store or post office instead of home, the shelf units may be turned to face the center.

With rearrangement of furniture and addition of props, such a center may become in turn home, doctor's office, store, fire station, bank, airport. If it is possible to retain an area as home and add another area, the play is enriched as some family member goes from home to work or whatever activity is suggested by children.

Somewhere within the center should be racks on which are hung various kinds of men's and women's clothes, including uniforms, shoes, hats, trousers, shirts, and party clothes. Dolls and clothing for dolls should also be available.

The source material for dramatic expression is found in children's lives. When children are involved in dramatic play, it is often the case that very little direct guidance is needed. Occasionally the teacher enters into the play with a comment or question which may add a new dimension. For example, seeing a group of children playing train, she may join the play. Buying a ticket, walking down the aisle, and taking a seat on the imaginary train, she may inquire about a dining car. If the children had not thought of this and are receptive, the play may be interrupted long enough to add the necessary equipment, a dining car steward, and waiters. As the play resumes with the additional children in the new roles, the teacher quietly leaves the scene to work with other children.

USING LITERATURE FOR CREATIVE DRAMATICS. Stories, poems, and nursery rhymes provide material for creative dramatics. It is easier to guide the dramatization of a story if it is told rather than read. Children should be encouraged to retell a story they have read or heard, too. The recall and relating of the events of a story in sequence must occur before it can be dramatized. The retelling of a story and succeeding dramatization is valuable not only as artistic expression but as an aid to developing language competence.

ENCOURAGING EFFORTS. The teacher's interest in dramatic play, shown by adding props or entering the play as suggested above, encourages participation and enriches the experience.

In creative dramatics, specific approving comments on children's performances will encourage efforts. If children show sustained involvement with dramatizing a story, they may wish to produce it for an audience. The addition of scenery, musical settings, and costumes will enrich the production and involve children with varying interests and talents.

EVALUATING THE WORK. The younger child shows egocentricity in dramatic play. As children develop competence, they become aware of their own roles in relation to others and so work together more cooperatively, building on each other's ideas. The scenes they play become more coherent; a logical sequence of events and a recognizable story line appears. They talk it out first, and then play out what they have agreed on.

The same developmental trend appears in creative dramatics. Observation and anecdotal records provide material for assessing progress. An integral part of dramatizing stories is the children's evaluation of their own work. The teacher guides this evaluation by asking questions about the believability of the characterizations and the actions taken.

As in all expressive art for the early years, the process is of utmost importance. Yet it is the product which is the ultimate evaluation of the work. A sensitive teacher recognizes that the product which is the norm for one child is a great achievement for another. The acceptable performance in a major role for a verbal child does not give the teacher as much satisfaction as the speaking of one line for a nonverbal child.

Activities for Instruction in Drama

ACTIVITIES TO HELP CHILDREN DEVELOP COMPETENCIES IN SELF-EXPRESSION THROUGH DRAMA

1. Activity: Doctor's office dramatic play (PP–K)

Materials: Chairs, tables, magazines, nurses and doctors uniforms and caps, flashlights, tongue depressors, soap, water, paper towels, thermometer, stethoscope, cot, sheets, band-aids, cotton, hypodermic syringes (minus the needle). A play doctor's kit will provide models of some of these things but usually not enough for good dramatic play.

Procedure: Show children materials which are introduced to dramatic play area. Talk about their experiences with doctors. Provide labels and demonstrate use of such things as stethoscope, thermometer, hypodermic syringe. Recall roles and activities of receptionist, nurse, doctor, and patients. Help children decide who will play each role. After children are involved, intervene when asked, in order to enrich the play or to prevent injury.

Suggestions and Variations: The skill of knowing when to intervene and when not to is developed through sensitive observation and practice. The best single sign may be level of involvement; if it is deep and children are working well together, do not intervene. If involvement is light, children are beginning to quarrel, or an objectionable practice creeps in, intervene tactfully.

2. Activity: Puppets (PP–P)

Materials: Puppets (see visual arts page 75 for a variety of ways to make puppets), puppet stage (may be made from a packing case), material for making scenery.

Procedure: In dramatic play gather children about you, introduce the puppet by name as you would a guest, and as the puppet speaks to the children and asks questions, the children will respond to the puppet as if it were a real person. The teacher also should converse with the puppet. When children show signs of readiness to use puppets, give puppets to them and help children think of things the puppet could do (wave bye, jump up and down, walk, shake its head "no," turn around, talk, etc.). Leave puppets on a shelf available to the children for their independent dramatic play.

In creative dramatics using puppets, select a favorite story or poem. Decisions children will need to make include:

> characters needed
> sequence of events
> scenery needed

Children may need assistance from time to time as they develop the puppet play. To the extent of their ability to do so, they should be encouraged to work independently.

Suggestions and Variations: Make a mock television set from a packing box. A hole the size and shape of a television screen may be cut and covered with clear plastic if desired. Paint on knobs and dials. A sequence of scenes may be drawn on long sheets of paper and rolled from side to side using dowels pasted on either end of the paper. As a story is read or told, the picture to illustrate each event is shown on the screen. Puppets may be used instead of the drawings.

3. *Activity:* Creative dramatics (PP–P)

Materials: A story or poem which has a clear sequence of events, action and simple dialogue. Props, scenery, and costumes enrich creative dramatics but are not essential.

Procedure: Guide the children's recall of the sequence of events or episodes. Name the characters which appear in each episode and the actions that occur. Review the content of the dialogue for each episode. Exact words and the form the action takes are the prerogatives of the children as they set out the story. For example, the first two episodes of *The Three Bears* may be plotted as follows:

Episode 1. Characters: The three bears.
     Actions: Sit down to breakfast, taste porridge, go for a walk.
     Dialogue: Mother tells when breakfast is ready; Baby says the porridge is too hot; Father suggests they go for a walk.
Episode 2. Character: Goldilocks
     Action: Walks in woods, sings, sees house, enters, sees porridge, tastes porridge in each bowl, finishes porridge in one.
     Dialogue: Talks about what she sees, the temperature of each bowl.

This planning should be elicited from the children through skillful questioning. Once the story has been recalled and the action plotted, the cast of characters is selected. Following the selection, children should be called by the names of the character they will play. Before action is started, a few more decisions must be made. The locations of the scenes and the entrances of the characters will be determined. When all plans are made, children enact the story with as little direct guidance as possible. After finishing, hold an evaluation session. Questions such as, "Did Darryl really sound gruff like Father Bear?" "Do you think the way Baby bear walks should be different from Father Bear?" "How can we make it better?"—should be asked. Children should replay the story using the suggestions made.

Suggestions and Variations: Activity cards suggesting that children make a play or puppet show may be placed next to a display of a favorite book, appropriate props, and costumes. This technique for initiating creative dramatics would not be appropriate for children younger than primary age.

A nursery rhyme which involves action may be used with the youngest children. For example, provide a candlestick and have each child jump over it as other children recite "Jack be nimble; Jack be quick. Jack jump over the candlestick." Allow children to make their own variations. For example, several small boys added several mice and a cat to their dramatization of *Hickory, Dickory, Dock*.

A story may be read and as a character, e.g., a fox, is introduced, the teacher interrupts the story, looks at the children and asks if there are any "foxes" in the room. A child who volunteers is brought up front and assumes the role. As the story continues, the teacher turns to the player and repeats what the character is doing, if necessary, to encourage the child to perform the action. Characters are added as the story continues. This is a very effective method with a "new" class when the story is read dramatically and with enthusiasm.

ACTIVITIES FOR DEVELOPING AESTHETIC APPRECIATION OF DRAMA

1. Activity: Television (PP–P)

Materials: Television set, cushion or rugs to sit on while watching.
Procedure: Select good quality programs which deal with human relationships. For example, *Mr. Rogers' Neighborhood* invites viewers to become part of the story and deals with feelings and human relationships. The puppets used in *Mr. Rogers' Neighborhood* help

to distinguish between fantasy and reality. After viewing, elicit children's reactions to the programs, conversing with them about the events and characters.

Suggestions and Variations: Converse with children about home television watching. Solicit parents' cooperation in reducing the watching of live and cartoon programs involving violence. When special programs for children are scheduled for early evening, send notes home with the children reminding parents of these programs.

2. *Activity:*   Attending a dramatic production (PP–P)

Procedure: Arrange a field trip to see a dramatic production, or arrange for the children to watch a play or puppet show that older students in the school may be putting on. With young preprimary and kindergarten children it is often helpful to familiarize them with the story line and characters before they attend the production. They delight in being able to recognize characters and predict what is going to happen next. Primary children can appreciate productions without having prior knowledge of the story line or characters.

Suggestions and Variations: Many theater groups have special productions for children. Many puppet groups will come to the school to give a production.

Do not overlook the possibility of asking students from nearby colleges to come perform for children. If they are enrolled in puppetry, creative dramatics, or children's theater classes, they are usually required to become involved in a certain number of performances as projects. If they know you are interested in having them come, they are often delighted to do so.

Remember that young children (under five) think that puppets are real. If the puppets pose questions, or find themselves in a problem-solving situation of which the audience has knowledge that would help solve it, young children often talk to the puppets to answer their questions or give them information. Children who respond in this way are not being "naughty" or "rude"; they are involved. This behavior does present some problems if all the children from a school are brought together in one room for the performance and there is a wide age range in the children attending. Older children can be quiet during the performance and should be asked to do so. But this is difficult to enforce if younger children who are talking are present. Perhaps the best solution is to try to arrange a separate performance for the younger children. Many children's theater groups are very sensitive to the way young children respond and have developed productions that actively seek to involve children both verbally and physically in the puppet plays.

ADDITIONAL RESOURCES

Records to Use With Children

Follet Educational Corporation
Discovering Music Together record series (records for singing, listening, and moving.)

Bowmar Records
#51 *Animals and Circus*
#52 *Nature and Make-Believe*
#53 *Pictures and Patterns*
#62 *Masters of Music*
#65 *Music, USA*
#66 *Oriental Scenes*
#68 *Classroom Concert*
#70 *Music of the Sea and Sky*
#83 *Ensembles, Large and Small*

Capital Records
Instruments of the Orchestra

RCA Victor Educational Department
Adventures in Music series (2 albums per grade)
Instruments of the Orchestra

Educational Activities, Inc.
Hap Palmer Song Albums

References for Teachers

ANDREWS, G., *Creative Rhythmic Music for Children.* Englewood Cliffs, N.J.: Prentice-Hall, Inc., 1954.

ARONOFF, F., *Music and Young Children.* New York: Holt, Rinehart and Winston, Inc., 1969.

BAILEY, C., *Sing a Song With Charity Bailey.* New York: Plymouth Music Co., 1955.

BAILEY, E. *Discovering Music With Young Children.* New York: Philosophical Library, 1958.

BENDER, J., "Have You Ever Thought of a Prop Box?" in Katherine Read, ed., *Ideas That Work With Young Children.* Washington, D.C.: National Association for the Education of Young Children, 1972.

BRIEN, S., "Music To My Eyes," *School Arts,* 70 (1971), pp. 30–31.

CHERRY, C., *Creative Art for the Developing Child.* Belmont, Calif.: Fearon Publishers, 1972.

———, *Creative Movement for the Developing Child.* Belmont, Calif.: Fearon Publishers, 1971.

DANIELS, E. C., "Creating Musical Sounds," *Instructor,* 81 (1972), pp. 64–65.

DIMONDSTEIN, G., *Exploring the Arts With Children.* New York: The Macmillan Company, 1974.

HAWKINSON, J., and M. FAULHABER, *Music and Instruments for Children to Make.* Chicago: Albert Whitman Co., 1970.

HOOD, M., *Teaching Rhythm and Using Classroom Instruments.* Englewood Cliffs, N.J.: Prentice-Hall, Inc., 1970.

HOOVER, T. L., *Art Activities for the Very Young.* Worcester: Davis Publishing Co., 1961.

LANSING, K., *Art, Artists, and Art Education.* New York: McGraw-Hill Book Company, 1971.

NELSON, L., "Maximizing Creativity in the Classroom," *Young Children,* 21, no. 3 (1966), pp. 131–135.

RICHARDSON, E. S., *In the Early World: Discovering Art Through Crafts.* New York: Pantheon Books, 1964.

ROWEN, B., *Learning Through Movement.* New York: Teachers College Press, Columbia University, 1963.

RUSSELL, J., *Creative Dance in the Primary School.* New York: Frederick H. Praeger, 1963.

SHEEHY, E., *Children Discover Music and Dance.* New York: Teachers College Press, Columbia University, 1968.

SMITH, R. B., and C. LEONARD, *Music in the Child's Education.* New York: Ronald Press Co., 1970.

STEICHER, M., "Concept Learning Through Movement Improvisation: The Teacher's Role as Catalyst," in Katherine Read, ed., *Ideas That Work With Young Children.* Washington, D.C.: National Association for the Education of Young Children, 1972.

4
language
arts

THE use of language is what makes humans unique. The ability to put information and understanding into symbolized form enables us to communicate with each other in a very special way. Ability with language affects the child's learning in all other areas, and because of this, teachers need to be especially competent in teaching language arts. The purpose of this chapter is: (1) to help teachers understand the nature of language, (2) to help teachers understand how children learn and use language, (3) to help teachers understand language skills appropriate for young children, and (4) to provide suggestions for activities and materials that teachers can use for language instruction.

THE NATURE OF LANGUAGE

Language is Abstract

Tracks left by animals in mud or snow, the beep of a car horn, and a periscope above the surface of the water are all symbols. Art forms involve the use of symbols too. In visual arts, materials are used to represent objects. In movement and dance, the body is used to symbolize objects, events, and feelings. The symbols used in each of these cases are not abstract, however, for each bears some direct relationship to that which it represents. Because of this lack of abstraction, linguists refer to such symbols as signs.[1]

Language makes use of special symbols. Words are assigned to objects, ideas, and feelings in an arbitrary way. We could assign words differently as long as we all agreed to do so. This arbitrariness is what makes language abstract. It is also what makes it social. Assuming that we would experience animals, mud, and snow, we would probably be able to determine for ourselves that certain markings indicate the presence of animals. In contrast, we could look at an object forever and not be able to determine what it is called unless we hear someone else call it by its name.

In addition to the abstractness of language that results from the lack of physical relationships between words and what they represent, there is an additional level of abstraction that is obtained by combining words in different ways, by varying inflection, and by varying the forms

---

[1] J. Piaget and B. Inhelder, *The Psychology of the Child* (New York: Basic Books, Inc., 1969), p. 51.

of a word. We do not use individual words strung together at random in a monotone. We speak in organized sentences, and the way we form these, as well as the way we speak these, carries meaning. To say, "Ruth hit the big twig," is quite different from saying, "Big Ruth hit the twig," and both of these differ from saying, "Hit the twig, big Ruth." The arrangement of language symbols according to rules is known as **syntax.**

Language Takes Many Forms

Language symbols can be produced or interpreted, and they may be spoken or written. When we talk we are producing spoken language. When we listen we are interpreting spoken language. When we write we are producing written language. When we read we are interpreting written language. All forms are closely related so that skill in one area influences skill in another, and yet each requires skills that are unique.

Language Varies and Changes

One might expect that different groups of people would use different words to represent the same things. This is true. In addition, because people's experiences differ, one might also expect that some groups would have words for which there are no comparable words in other languages. This is also true. When groups of people are isolated from one another and when their experiences differ, their languages develop differently too. When these differences are so great that people cannot understand each other, people are said to speak different languages. When the differences are slight, people are said to speak different dialects of the same language.[2]

As people move from one region of the world to another or as groups come into more frequent contact through commerce, they often begin to incorporate aspects of each other's language into their own. This is one way languages change. Languages also change internally as names are created for new places, products, and events.[3]

CHILDREN AND LANGUAGE

Children and Talking

Any adult who has tried to learn a foreign language would probably argue that the task is very difficult. Indeed, a language is a complicated

---

[2]R. W. Langacker, *Language and Its Structure* (New York: Harcourt, Brace & World, Inc., 1968), pp. 175–198.
[3]Langacker, *Language and Its Structure,* pp. 175–194.

system. Surprisingly, though, language learning takes place in children.[4] Merely by being around language, children learn language with little or no instruction in the usual sense. Language does not appear full blown, however; it emerges during a child's first six years of life. During this period of time there are discernible levels of development, and these have implications for how language goals can be achieved.

Infants are born with the ability to vocalize. At first their vocalizations are confined to crying, but it is not long before noncrying vocalizations are added. The earliest speech sounds are largely open vowel sounds, but consonants soon appear. By eight months of age children are combining a consonant and vowel sound in syllables which they repeat. Examples include "ma-ma-ma-ma," and "ga-ga-ga-ga."[5]

Genuine language, as distinct from speech sounds, begins with the association of specific verbal sounds with specific people and objects. Most children say their first word during the last part of their first year and gradually add other words from then on.[6] Though their articulation may not be perfect, it is clear they understand the function of language; a word can be used to indicate something else.

For a short period around fourteen to sixteen months, many children speak in what appear to be nonsense sentences. This behavior is called expressive jargon, and children seem to be imitating the rhythm and flow of sentences although they are using nonsense words.[7]

Sometime prior to their second birthday, most children begin to combine two words into sentences. They do not combine words at random; rather, low-information words are omitted and high information words are retained. For example, whereas an adult might say, "I want some oatmeal right now," a child would say, "Oatmeal now."[8] The message gets across not just with the excellent selection of key words, but also with the use of inflection. The voice of a child who had wanted to ask the question "Are we having oatmeal now?" would have been raised instead of lowered at the end of the statement. Already then, the child is using syntax. Words are selected, ordered, and spoken with differential emphases.

Between two-and-one-half and six the child increases in language ability. Children learn more and more words for objects, actions, ideas,

[4]D. McNeill, "Developmental Psycholinguistics," in F. Smith and G. A. Miller, eds., *The Genesis of Language* (Cambridge: MIT Press, 1966), pp. 15–16.

[5]O. C. Irwin, "Infant Speech: Consonantal Position," *Journal of Speech and Hearing Disorders*, 16 (1951), pp. 159–161.

[6]R. Brown and U. Bellugi, "Three Processes in the Child's Acquisition of Syntax," *Harvard Educational Review*, 34, no. 2 (1964), p. 133.

[7]L. J. Stone and J. Church, *Childhood and Adolescence*, 3rd ed. (New York: Random House, 1973), p. 219.

[8]Brown and Bellugi, *Harvard Educational Review*, 34, p. 133.

and feelings. For example, a young child may call a knife a "cutter" because that's the action it performs, and the child does not know the word for the object we call a knife. As children are exposed to the language of others, however, they will learn that various objects that cut have different names, including knife, scissors, and saw. This is vocabulary development. There is evidence from research to suggest that vocabulary development can be rather directly influenced by direct adult assistance.[9]

In addition to vocabulary development, syntactical development is also progressing. Children are combining more and more words to make sentences, and they have internalized many language rules. One of the characteristics of the language of children between three and six is the overgeneralization of rules for forming verb tenses and for forming plurals. They seem to learn the general rule first and then apply it to the exceptions too. For example, rather than saying, "My daddy taught me to cook," a child may say, "My daddy teached me to cook." Similarly, a child might say, "My dog has four foots," rather than, "My dog has four feet."

Sometimes these errors upset teachers and parents and they attempt to correct children by trying to have them repeat the correct form of the word. These attempts at correction usually confuse young children even more, and they often change the words, but make other errors. For example, they may change "foots" to "feets," or "teached" to "taughted."[10] This contrasts sharply with the response an adult might receive from a child after a correction of vocabulary. For example, if a child calls a cat a dog and the adult responds by saying, "That's not a dog; that's a cat," the child is likely to say, "cat." These differences would suggest that while direct correction is a good strategy for helping children learn vocabulary, it is not such a good strategy for helping them learn other aspects of language.

Throughout the period from two to seven or eight, the ability to produce speech sounds is also increasing. Some speech sounds appear before others.[11] No doubt, physical as well as cognitive factors influence the emergence of speech sounds. The lower face, including the mouth and jaw, is one of the least developed areas of the head in the newborn child. These structures stay relatively undeveloped throughout infancy. There is considerable growth during the late preschool and early middle

[9]C. B. Cazden, "Suggestions From Studies of Early Language Acquisition," in C. B. Cazden, ed., *Language in Early Childhood Education* (Washington, D.C.: National Association for the Education of Young Children, 1972), p. 4.
[10]McNeill, "Developmental Psycholinguistics," p. 69.
[11]M. C. Templin, "Certain Language Skills in Children: Their Development and Interrelationships," *Institute of Child Welfare Monograph*, no. 26. (Minneapolis: University of Minnesota Press, 1957).

childhood years and again during adolescence. The reader should also recall that, beginning around six months of age and lasting until about the tenth year, there is a steady progression of tooth eruption, tooth loss, and tooth replacement. These changes also affect the child's ability to produce sounds. [12]

So far, we have focused on structural aspects of verbal language. For the child, however, verbal language behavior is not motivated solely or even primarily by the desire to perfect specific language skills, but rather by the desire to communicate.

Infants cry to signal their distress. Often, as soon as the adult is in view the infant stops crying. The hunger or wetness that the infant wished to tell others about may remain for several more minutes, indicating that they alone do not result in the crying. The infant's crying is apparently a means of communication, and once it has been effective in drawing an adult near, the infant will often stop. Parents say that an infant even cries differently to communicate different kinds of distress, and there is probably some truth to this assertion.

Infants communicate with coos and babbles too. As if to express their satisfaction, babies just a few months old will increase their vocalization if played with and talked to. Later, they often use specific vocalizations to indicate specific needs. The author once observed an eight-month-old infant who made a loud and constant "ah ah ah ah" sound when he saw something out of his reach that he wanted. Such things were often too high on a shelf or too far back on an end table to be able to reach, and the infant would stand holding on to the furniture with one hand and reach with the other while saying, "ah ah ah ah." When given the object, the child would stop making this sound, but often giggled or made other sounds, as if to express delight.

When children start using real language, much of their talking is still motivated by a desire to communicate their needs and wishes. They use a word to express what they want to eat, where they want to go, what they want to do, or what they want to know. "Up!" "Milk!" "Bye-bye." "Ball?" "No!" All are said with a purpose.

Preschool children use language for the same purposes as younger children and for some additional purposes too. Children of this age now use language to talk about past and future things and things make-believe, not just immediate things. They tell us about what they did the day or night before, about the trip to a movie several weeks earlier, and about the toy they are going to receive for their birthday next week. They make up tall tales about themselves, others, and make-believe characters. They create scripts as they engage in dramatic play or use puppets.

[12]Stone and Church, *Childhood and Adolescence*, pp. 4; 350–51.

At first the language preschool children use is somewhat limited because they lack extensive vocabulary, facility in putting words together, and ability to organize their thoughts and put these into verbal form. These abilities improve tremendously during the years from three to five, however, so that by the end of this period most children are extremely competent in their use of language.

Children and Listening

Listening is a skill beyond the physical ability to hear. It implies a motivational component that might be described as "the desire to hear." In other words, even when hearing is completely normal, we can somehow not "hear" things around us. Actually, we are not listening in these situations. We do not hear because our attention is focused somewhere else.

Hearing and listening are so keen in the young child that infants no more than one month old have been found to re-alert to a "puh" sound after having been habituated to a "buh" sound.[13] This change in behavior indicates that the babies can hear the difference between the two sounds.

In speaking of the development of listening skills, then, we are really talking about developing children's ability to choose selectively the sounds they will orient to, not about developing basic capacities to hear and listen. Because we are surrounded by so many competing sounds, we all must learn to ignore some and not ignore others. Because of our experiences, some topics come to have more value for us than others; some types of voices and language come to be more pleasant than others; some sounds relax and soothe us while others do the opposite. Our task is somehow to help children learn to listen to those things we think worth listening to, at the level required for comprehension.

Children and Reading

Educators do not always agree about how children learn to read. Some of the disagreement can probably be traced to differences over what should be considered as reading. To some, it may mean being able to recognize and say a written word which the child has seen a number of times and to which some meaning is attached. To others, it may mean being able to pronounce at first sight a written word which stands for an unfamiliar object or idea. For still others, it means being able to com-

---

[13]P. D. Eimas, E. R. Siqueland, and J. Vigorito, "Speech Perceptions in Infants," *Science*, 171, 1971, pp. 303–6.

prehend, as well as pronounce, words that have never been seen before by the reader.

In this book reading is viewed broadly to include all of the above. One or another type of reading, however, may be more appropriate for children at different developmental levels. For example, in the beginning stages of learning to read, it makes sense to use words that stand for familiar objects and ideas. Exposure to these words might come from labels in the classroom (helpers' chart; area labels; names on art work) or other words in the child's environment (stop signs; exit signs; labels on food containers). This type of reading involves only skills of visual discrimination, paired-associative learning, and memory, rather than complex analysis and integration skills.

Even three- and four-year-olds can and do learn to read many words by "sight" and are delighted that they can. An adult tells the child what the words say when the child asks, and the child learns them. Many children learn to read some words this way before they even know the names of all the letters that make a word. Usually, these are words that are important to children, such as their names, the names of friends, the words in the title of a familiar story book, or the name of a favorite cereal.

Although this whole-word approach is a good place to start, it does not give the child what might be called "reading power." In other words, it would take a very long time to accumulate even a reasonably large reading vocabulary in this way. There comes a time when children can benefit from learning to read words on their own without relying on adults in the beginning to say each new word.

When children can read new words, they are said to be able to **decode.** Reading methods that stress this ability are known as **decoding approaches,** as opposed to sight or whole-word approaches. Actually, children can learn to decode through a sight approach. To say to a child who knows the words "boy" and "bat" by sight, "They start with the same sound. Can you think of another word that starts with that sound too?" is teaching decoding skills. To say each letter out loud while writing a child's name on art work is also teaching decoding skills. To comment that Stephen's name begins with the same sound as Stephanie's and that they begin with the same two letters is also teaching decoding skills. The difference between the two approaches, then, is one of emphasis. Decoding approaches stress decoding skills first and lead to reading words, whereas sight approaches start with words and use these to teach decoding skills. When children's ongoing experiences are used as the source for the sight words, the approach is known as **language experience.**

In order to decode new words, a child must have auditory discrimination skills and know letter names and letter-sound associations. When

Children's names are often among the first sight words learned.

Children's names can provide opportunities for teaching reading skills.

hearing a word, a child must be able to detect the letters it contains, and when reading a word, a child needs to be able to change written letters into sounds. Though this may all sound very straightforward and simple, it is not. One of the difficulties is that some letters do not represent just one sound, but several. Sounds represented by letters change depending on their position in words. To determine which particular sound to give a letter in a written word, children must analyze the letter in relation to other letters in the word. They must then pull from a repertoire of rules the correct rule for this situation. This behavior requires cognitive processes such as analysis and integration.

Children of four and five years of age can learn letter names and can begin to detect some specific sounds in words they hear or speak. However, though many four- and five-year-olds do learn some decoding skills and begin to use these to read, they usually can not handle formal instruction in letter-sound associations. It is just too difficult for them to master from a rule-and-analysis point of view. There is a general characteristic of children's learning that the reader will encounter again in the discussions of children and science (page 215) and children and mathematics (page 163). It is that the thinking of preprimary and kindergarten children is not governed by rules. Though they can learn many of the specifics that go into rules and operate with these on an intuitive basis, they cannot integrate the specifics into an organized system. Somewhere around six or seven years of age there is a qualitative change in children's thinking, and rule-oriented behavior becomes possible.[14] At this time, introduction of phonics rules may be helpful.

Fluent reading does not depend solely on the ability to read individual words, whether it be by sight or decoding. We anticipate many words, so read them neither by sight nor by sounding them out. If all the readers of this book were to fill in the blanks in the following passage, we would probably find striking similarities among the words chosen.

> The sky grew dark. It thundered and _____. Soon it began to _____ and _____ wind started to _____. My brothers started _____ cry. I told them not _____ worry. We were safe. Nothing could hurt _____ down here in Grandmother's fruit _____.

Certain words make sense in the blanks because of their meanings. Lightning and thunder go together. We learn these associations through experience. Other words make sense because they fit our language patterns. What this illustration points out is that reading is influenced by

---

[14]S. H. White, "Evidence for a Hierarchial Arrangement of Learning Processes," in L. P. Lipsitt and C. C. Spiker, eds., *Advances in Child Development and Behavior* (New York: Academic Press, 1965).

general experience with the world and by experience with spoken language. The young child who does not yet have a well-developed vocabulary or reasonably mature language patterns is not ready to learn to read sentences and passages. Good basic experiences and many opportunities to talk about them will do far more to help the child learn to read than hours spent learning specific decoding skills. Of course, the use of familiar words for sight reading and the learning of letter names and letter-sound associations as they emerge informally can be included too.

It does us very little good to read if we do not understand what we have read. This aspect of reading is referred to as **reading comprehension.** When young children first begin to read, they must focus considerable concentration on saying the words. Because of this, it is wise to have them read about things that are quite familiar. We always comprehend better if we read of things about which we already know something. Later, children can learn about unfamiliar things by reading about them, but such reading should be kept to a minimum when children are just beginning to read.

Children who have had rich experiences will be able to handle a wider selection of reading materials because they will be familiar with the content. For children who have not had such experiences, teachers should arrange as many as possible. Though such experiences may seem to be totally unrelated to the development of reading abilities, they are actually quite closely related.

Perhaps the most important element in the development of reading ability is the desire to learn to read. Most children want to learn to read. They see the power this gives the adults in their world. It is typical for four- and five-year-olds to ask "What does it say?" in reference to menus, signs, books and letters. Kids want to know what words say and they want to be able to say them themselves. When reading is learned in a way which helps children unlock some of the puzzles in their world, this type of interest will be maintained. If reading is learned in a way which is not related to children's worlds, or in a way that requires extraordinary effort, they are likely to think it useless or not worth the effort. Monotonous lessons and rote drill have no place in the teaching of reading to young children.

Children and Writing

There are several quite different aspects to writing. There is the physical skill required to draw the letters and connect these to make words. Then there is the skill required to formulate ideas and organize these into a coherent whole. Finally, there is grammatical skill.

The physical aspect of writing assumes a certain degree of physical readiness. The child must have good use of hands and fingers in order to form the lettters. Children who are still using a whole-hand grasp to manipulate crayons or brushes, are probably not going to benefit much from instruction in forming letters because their hand movements are still controlled by the large muscles of the upper arm. Movements controlled in this way are large and gross and do not translate well into the specific and precise movements needed to form letters. Children who are at this level need opportunities to paint, use crayons and draw with chalk. They do not need lessons in pencil-holding and letter formation.

When children have adopted a finger grasp for using crayons, pencils, or brushes and have begun to rest their arm on the table top when using these tools, it is quite clear that the control of the movements is coming from the hand and fingers. When these behaviors appear, children are physically ready to learn to form letters. Many children exhibit these behaviors by late in their fourth year and some exhibit them earlier. Children who *want to know how* to make letters can benefit from instruction at this time.

Even so, movements will still be imprecise, and children's attempts will appear awkward. The point is, though, that from here on, specific practice in writing letters may do more to improve letter-writing skill than waiting for a higher degree of physical maturation. We are all rather awkward when learning any new physical skill, whether it be skating, skiing, or knitting. Physical maturity alone does not make us skillful. We must have a chance for instruction and practice too.

As in most areas of learning, learning to form letters takes time. It is a lengthy process for several reasons. First, the movements are not easy to make. Second, there are many letters. Third, some letters are very similar to other letters, making it easy to confuse one with another. Fourth, the child must learn that with these special two-dimensional symbols, orientation is a significant attribute. It is not just the configuration of the lines that makes one letter different from another, but the left-right or up-down orientation as well.

Young children do not attend to orientation at first, and reversals appear in their writing.[15] This is nothing to be alarmed about. In fact, it should be expected. The child has spent the first four or five years of life learning that with three-dimensional objects, orientation is not important. A cup is a cup is a cup, whether it is placed right-side-up or up-side-down, handle to the left or handle to the right. Objects do not

15E. J. Gibson, "Development of Perception: Discrimination of Depth Compared with Discrimination of Graphic Symbols," in J. C. Wright and J. Kagan, eds., *Basic Cognitive Processes in Children, Monographs Society for Research in Child Development*, 28, no. 2 (1962), 5–32.

acquire a different name when they are changed from one position to another. When an S is made by a child so that it looks backward to an adult, the child—paying attention only to configuration—thinks it looks the same as any S.[16]

Adults can help children learn that orientation is a significant attribute by asking them to compare a letter they have made with a model of the letter. The adult should simply ask, "Does the letter you made look like this one?" The child, even when having made a letter with reversed orientation, will probably say that letter is the same as the one the adult is pointing out. The adult can then say, "Oh, yours looks different to me because it goes this way and the other letter goes this way." The adult should point out the difference with a finger when describing it verbally. Without such an explicit explanation of the difference between the letter made by the child and the model shown, children are likely not to understand what the difference is between their letters and the models.

It will still take considerable time after the child understands that orientation is a significant attribute before reversals can be expected to disappear completely from the child's writing. Even though children know that letters go a certain way, they must remember what the right way is. Models of letters displayed in the classroom can serve as a handy reference for the children until they have built up strong enough mental pictures of their own. If allowed to proceed at their own pace and in their own way, without pressure and fanfare, children will often approach learning to write letters with mastery behavior similar to that used when working puzzles or building with blocks.

The ability to organize ideas for writing is closely related to general experiential background and language ability. Children develop ideas by being in an environment that helps them ask questions, think about what they have seen, talk about what they see, and think about and listen to what others think. One of the most important skills required in writing is the ability to present ideas in ways that the reader can understand. This requires that one be able to see things from another's point of view. Because children are egocentric, they have special difficulty both in talking and in writing in a way that a person who has not had their particular experience can understand what it is they are trying to say. They often leave out necessary information and details because they assume everyone else knows what they know. Opportunities to interact with people, both adults and peers, provide situations in which children are re-

[16]A. D. Pick, "Some Basic Perceptual Processes in Reading," in W. Hartup, ed., *The Young Child: Reviews of Research* (Washington, D.C.: National Association for the Education of Young Children, 1972), vol. 2, p. 145.

quired to consider other people's feelings and ideas. People will ask questions when they do not understand what a child says. Through these experiences children will gain a clearer idea of what they must tell others if they wish to be understood. These experiences will help children express themselves clearly when they try to communicate through writing.

Even very young children can "write" in the sense that they can express ideas and feelings that can be put into written words. In fact, their ability to write in this sense precedes their ability to write physically. If teachers will take dictation for the children or provide a tape recorder, their early writing can be preserved. Gradually, children can learn to write their own stories. At first, this may involve the physical writing of just a few words that the teacher helps spell. Later, children can write most of the words by referring to the words they have accumulated in a personal dictionary or word bank.

The first dictated stories of preschool children will be short and may not form a very coherent whole. They may consist of a few statements that bear little relationship to each other, and there may be no clear beginning or end. With more experience, their stories will become more organized. During the fifth or sixth year many children begin writing extensive stories. Though the number of characters may be confined to a minimum, their activities are sometimes endless. In addition the stories are quite organized. Events are related to one another and a clear beginning and ending are apparent. As with many other skills, proficiency in writing depends on the opportunity for experiences in writing as well as experiences that provide children with exposure to the writings of others.

Children in the primary grades continue to develop skill in writing if they are given opportunities to write. The organization of what they write is now even more complete, and the entire work may be divided into chapters or acts.

One of the technical skills required in writing is that of punctuation. When children begin to tell their stories to adults who write them down, they can begin to develop some understanding of punctuation. If adults point out the periods, commas, question marks or exclamation points they use, even preschool children begin to grasp these. Adults should also point out that they are using a capital letter to begin each word that starts a sentence.

When children begin to write down things for themselves, teachers should help them use punctuation marks. It has been this author's observation that children respond quickly to instruction in the use of punctuation marks. This observation indicates that punctuation involves a different type of learning, and apparently less complex, than does grammar, for example. The period seems to be the punctuation mark used and learned first, perhaps because of the frequency with which it occurs.

Commas seem to be the most difficult, and question marks and exclamation points fall somewhere in between.

Around five or six years of age, some children seem to become especially interested in punctuation marks and even seem to fashion their stories for the purpose of using certain marks. I once took dictation for a kindergarten child's story about a wicked queen and her beautiful daughter. When I wrote the queen's harsh statements and orders to her daughter, I followed them with an exclamation point which I explained to the child. As the story proceeded, harsh statements and orders became ever more frequent, and the child began to say, "exclamation point," at the end of each, to indicate that I was to use that mark. When the story was complete, she insisted on counting the number of exclamation points that had been used before I was permitted to read the story back to her.

LANGUAGE SKILLS FOR YOUNG CHILDREN

It should be apparent from the discussion in the preceding section that young children develop language skills very rapidly. Even the three- or four-year-old comes to school with a great deal of language competence. It is the teacher's job to support the skills children have and help them extend these.

In the section which follows, language skills are separated into categories which include talking, listening, reading, and writing. Since language skills are so interdependent, it is probably misleading to present them in separate sections. Even though all language skills interact and influence each other within a child, however, it may be helpful to teachers if skills are differentiated into specific areas. This differentiation should not be viewed as a guide for how children should experience learning in the language arts, but rather as a checklist for teachers to use in planning experiences. An experience may promote the development of many skills simultaneously, but without some knowledge of specific skills, teachers may miss an opportunity for learning that could be provided by a given experience.

Talking Skills

Skill in using verbal language involves several components. First, there is **vocabulary development.** Children must learn what words to use to stand for objects, actions and feelings that they want to talk about. Second, there is **speech** accuracy. Third, there is the development of the ability to speak in sentences according to rules of language. This is known as **syntactical development.** Fourth, for children who speak a dialect or a language other than **Standard English,** there is the learning of standard speech. (Refer to page 125 for a discussion concerning the teaching of Standard English.) Children must also develop skill in **organizing and expressing thoughts** so that others can understand what they mean. We are not referring here to good articulation, but rather to the ability to select and organize the information necessary for other people to know what it is the child is trying to tell them. Finally, children need to develop skill in **communicating information to a group.** In addition to fostering the skills required to organize information around an idea and present it verbally in a somewhat coherent way, teachers should be concerned that children approach with ease and confidence situations involving verbal communication.

Listening Skills

Listening is a necessary language skill that must be supported. Varying degrees of attention are required for different kinds of listening. The reasons for listening, the listening context, and the complexity of materials influence listening behavior.

There are basically four categories of listening: marginal, appre-

A listening post helps children focus their listening.

ciative, attentive, and analytical.[17] Goals should support all of these. **Marginal listening** is the casual listening a child does when involved in two activities simultaneously such as when a child listens to a song or record while he experiments with clay. **Appreciative listening** occurs when a child concentrates on a listening activity because it is fun or pleasurable. Concentration is required, but with little or no effort such as when a child listens to a play or music. **Attentive listening** requires that all possible distractions be eliminated or at least curtailed so that the child can focus completely on the source of communication. In schools, attentive listening is often required when children are being given directions.

The most complex form of listening is **analytical listening,** which not only demands the most concentrated effort on the part of the listener, but also requires a response. Children may have begun by listening marginally, appreciatively, or attentively, but now become completely involved in the listening as they weigh the information, seek supporting or conflicting evidence, and make judgments and inferences.

Reading Skills

Perhaps the first goal in teaching reading is to nurture children's desire to read and help them **identify with the role of the reader.** Another goal should be to help children understand that the **written word is just talk written down.** Language ability is also important to the development of reading ability. **Language development,** therefore, should be a reading goal too. Children must also develop reading **comprehension** skills. At first this will involve being able to understand what is read to them by someone else. Children show evidence of such comprehension when they can relate events in the story to personal experiences, answer simple questions about a story and can retell it in sequence. Later, comprehension skills must involve being able to answer questions or tell about or apply the material children have read to themselves.

Actual ability to read words will depend on the development of a **sight vocabulary** and upon decoding skills such as **knowing letter names** and **forming letter-sound associations.** Children must also learn that print is placed on the page in a **left-to-right** and **top-to-bottom progression.** Children also need to learn how to interpret **punctuation** marks.

Writing Skills

Writing involves several skills. First, there is **handwriting,** which refers to the actual forming of letters. When they are ready children

---

17National Council of Teachers of English, *Language Arts for Today's Children* (New York: Appleton-Century-Crofts, 1954), pp. 80–81.

should be shown how to form the letters. A guide for forming letters in manuscript form is shown in Figure 14.

Spelling is another writing skill that children need to learn. It is closely related to skill with letter-sound associations. Because children continue to learn these associations throughout most of the primary years, it should be expected that many words will not be spelled accurately by pre-school and early primary-age children. While teachers should be tolerant of such errors, especially when they occur in children's creative writing, they should have goals related to spelling and should provide activities that will help children improve their ability to spell.

The teacher should also have goals for developing children's **creative writing skills.** Finally, children must begin to develop **grammatical** skills and skill in using **punctuation.**

METHODS FOR TEACHING LANGUAGE ARTS TO YOUNG CHILDREN

An Environment Which Encourages Expression

From the moment children enter the classroom, language surrounds them. They exchange greetings with the teacher and other children. They plan the day's activities by reviewing the previous day's work and agreeing on things to be done. At all times they use language to solve problems, to share ideas, and to support ego development. Rich and stimulating experiences, encouragement in conversation with peers, and warm verbal adults who talk with them promote the development of language.

In an atmosphere of acceptance there will be talk, lots and lots of talk: child with child, child with small groups, child with large groups, child with teacher, child with other adults, and child with materials. The silent classroom where friends cannot sit next to each other because they talk is not a room that supports language development. Most of our talk is with friends.

When children must have something to share verbally, it must be something the listener wants to hear. Sometimes show-and-tell periods are one-way communications with aggressive, verbal children often making shallow comments about experiences that are largely irrelevant for listeners. Discussions for making decisions about what the class has done or will be doing that day would be more relevant to each child.

Relating Language and Content Goals

Traditionally, schools have separated talking, writing, and reading even though psycholinguists have repeatedly demonstrated the interrela-

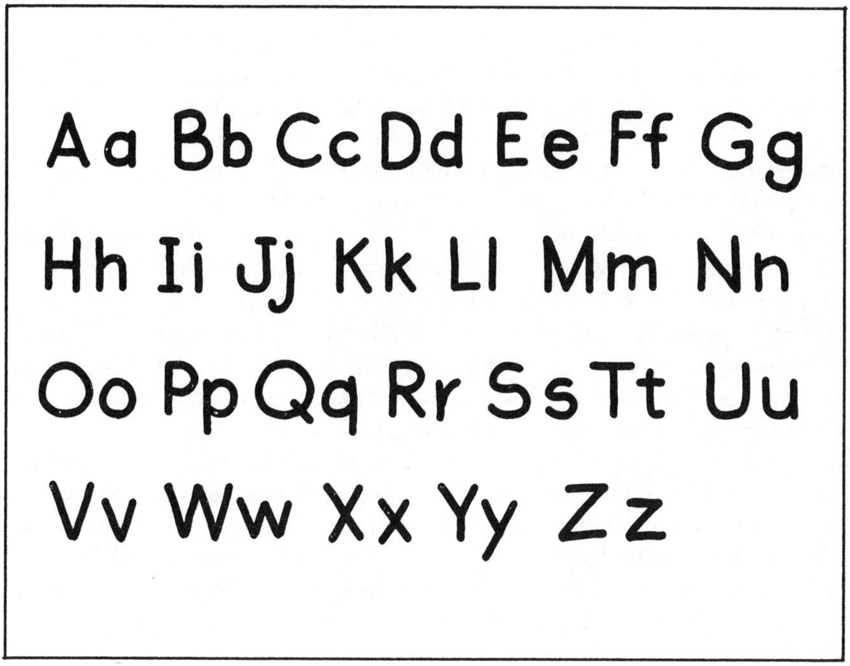

Aa Bb Cc Dd Ee Ff Gg
Hh Ii Jj Kk Ll Mm Nn
Oo Pp Qq Rr Ss Tt Uu
Vv Ww Xx Yy Zz

Figure 14. Manuscript letter guide.

tionships of these areas of language. In the past, the emphasis in the lower grades was on development of skills; the upper grades focused on the learning of content. The learning of skills cannot be separated from meaning, however. Skills can perhaps be taught best within the context of meaningful experiences. These experiences may include science, social studies, and mathematics, as well as personal experiences. In talking, listening, thinking, writing, and reading about these experiences, language skills are being learned.

Teaching Bilingualism

The language children bring to school is their only means of communication. At this point, it does not matter *what* language it is—Standard English. Black English, or Spanish. Language differences are not language deficiencies. In fact, different languages are appropriate in different contexts.

A good language program begins with the children's language. Any attempt to modify directly the child's native language upon that child's *entrance* into school is not only inappropriate, but may also prevent further growth.

Cazden[18] suggests that preschool teachers should focus on expanding the child's first language and not try to change non-standard forms beyond the provision of Standard English models. She suggests that alteration runs the risk of extinguishing not only the non-standard forms, but verbal behavior in general. Because language for learning is much more important with young children than language for social mobility, the danger of extinguishing verbal behavior outweighs any possible gains. Saville-Troike[19] recommends that if the young child lives in a monolingual non-English-speaking community and attends a bilingual school, it is perhaps best to focus on this first language. If, however, no bilingual school is available, such children will experience frustration and failure with Standard English unless high priority is placed from the beginning on teaching them English *as a second language.* Teachers, however, must show that they value the child's first language.

To provide for the learning of Standard English, it is necessary that the teacher know enough about the children's language to be able to give the specific help needed in the transition from the language or dialect to Standard English. Teachers of Spanish-speaking children will need to be able to speak Spanish and understand its structure; teachers of Black children will need to know the similarities and differences between Black English and Standard English.

ACTIVITIES FOR LANGUAGE ARTS INSTRUCTION

The balance of this chapter consists of practical ideas for teaching language arts to young children. They are organized to follow closely the outline of goals presented on pages 121–124.

Talking

ACTIVITIES TO HELP CHILDREN EXTEND VOCABULARY

1. *Activity:* Mystery box (PP–K)

   Materials: Attractively decorated box and assorted objects such as paper clip, yarn, cork, fabric, sandpaper, etc.
   Procedure: A box with an assortment of objects within it. Place

---

[18]C. Cazden, "Some Implications of Research on Language Development for Preschool Education" (Paper presented at Social Science Research Council Conference on Preschool Education, Chicago, 1966).
[19]M. Saville-Troike, *Bilingual Children* (Arlington, Va.: Center for Applied Linguistics, 1973).

box in an appropriate learning center. The children reach in, feel one object and describe it to a peer or the teacher. Teachers can supply descriptive words to help children. They may ask, "Is it soft or hard?" "Is it stiff or does it bend?" "Is it fuzzy or smooth?" In this way, children learn vocabulary.

Suggestions and Variations: Rather than describe the objects hidden in the mystery box, children may be asked to identify the objects. A pincer clothespin, an acorn, a paper clip, a nut and bolt, a piece of velvet or corduroy, a piece of styrofoam, etc., may be placed in the box. Children can try to identify the items by touch, but may not know what they are called. Teachers or other children can supply the new words.

2. *Activity:* Picture file (PP–P)

Materials: Pictures of all kinds of objects, plants, animals, and people, including those that indicate different feelings.

Procedure: Place pictures where children can look at them. A picture album made from an old card album may be a good way to make them available to children. They can look through the album and learn to identify the pictures by name. Teachers or other adults, or children who are familiar with some of the things depicted will have to supply the words to children who do not know them.

Suggestions and Variations: Pictures may also be used on bulletin boards or in other display areas. Pictures found in old magazines may be used by the children to make books. Teachers can then label the pictures for the child or take other dictation children want to give.

3. *Activity:* Field trips (PP–P)

Materials: Various materials depending on the field trip taken.

Procedure: Refer to field trip discussions on pages 78 and 79. These experiences contribute much to vocabulary development. Teachers should familiarize themselves with special machinery, tools, and processes that might be used at the place the children visit so children can be provided with the names.

4. *Activity:* Snack (PP–P)

Materials: Snack items.

Procedure: When sharing snack with children, discuss the food informally. Refer to food in specific and precise ways, such as "fresh" or "frozen" strawberries, "French-fried" potatoes, peach "halves" or "slices," etc.

Suggestions and Variations: Talking about the food at snack time can be a bit overdone. Be certain to use accurate and descriptive terminology when referring to the food, but do not bore children with endless food discussions.

5. *Activity:* Color names (PP–K)

   Materials: A box of objects of various colors; a collection of paint chips from a hardware store; a set of commercial color plaques; a color wheel.
   Procedure: Place one of the materials listed above in a learning center. When children use the materials, help them use the appropriate names for the colors.
   Suggestions and Variations: Do not place all the materials in a center at the same time. Use one set for awhile, and then replace it with another set of materials.

6. *Activity:* Singing (PP–K)

   Materials: Simple instruments to accompany songs, or tapes and records. The teacher's voice can also be used.
   Procedure: Sing all kinds of songs appropriate for young children. Songs in which children can substitute words are especially good for language development. *Wheels on the Bus* and *Where Oh Where is Dear Little Mary?* are two songs that are of this type. (For suggestions on how to teach songs, see pages 86 and 87.)

7. *Activity:* Stories (PP–P)

   Materials: Story books.
   Procedure: Read books to children both during story time and, when you can, during activity time. Talk with children about words in the book. For example, if the book is about a ferocious lion, ask children if they know what "ferocious" means.
   Suggestions and Variations: When discussing words in stories, sometimes ask children to think of another word that could be used in place of the one appearing in the story. For example, if the story refers to a "ferocious" lion the teacher might ask, "What other words could we use to describe that lion?"

8. *Activity:* Informal talk (PP–P)

   Materials: Nothing special.
   Procedure: Talk with children informally about anything and everything. For example, name the patterns (stripes, plaids, polka dots), weaves (corduroy, gingham, flannel, seersucker) and fabric (wool, cotton, polyester) of their clothes. Help them learn the names for parts of school equipment (brush bristles, paint palette, fish-tank

Children learn vocabulary and language patterns from listening to stories.

filter and pump, record-player arm and turntable, etc.) by using these terms yourself.

9. *Activity:* Cooking (PP–P)

Materials: Ingredients for the recipes; utensils necessary for their preparation.

Procedure: When children cook, use technical terms with them to describe cooking processes. They will learn words such as "knead," "chop," "dice," "whip," and "scald." Also, name the ingredients that are used.

ACTIVITIES TO HELP CHILDREN
DEVELOP ACCURATE SPEECH

All of the activities listed in any of the other areas of talking may also be used to help children develop accuracy in speech, for

A good story captures almost
every child's attention.

when children talk, they are practicing speech sounds too. The
most important influence on the development of good speech is
having good adult models to listen to.

1. Activity: I said this, not that (K–P)

Materials: Tape recorder, tape, and words that are difficult for a
child to pronounce. This list will vary from child to child and
from class to class.

Procedure: Children can practice pronunciation by recording words
on which they have been working. Have children listen to their
own tapes. Young children, for example, confuse "pin" and "pen."
Spanish speakers find the word "yellow" difficult to produce.

Suggestions and Variations: Ask a child to do this activity with a
friend who will give help in hearing new or difficult sounds. If a
child has a great deal of difficulty making some sounds, and it appears not to be typical immature speech, this child should be seen
by a speech specialist. Ask the specialist for ideas to use in the classroom to help the child.

2. Activity: Tongue-twisters (PP–K)

Materials: None.

Procedure: At group time, teach children tongue-twisters such as

Peter Piper Picked a Peck of Pickled Peppers. These give children practice in forming different sounds and sensitize them to correct pronunciation.

ACTIVITIES TO SUPPORT
CHILDREN'S SYNTACTICAL DEVELOPMENT

1. Activity: Dramatic play (PP–K)

Materials: Props for house or store play.
Procedure: Encourage several children to play together in the dramatic play area. Children usually talk to each other as they play. In fact, the dramatic play setting has been found to elicit more talk from young children than most other settings.[20]

When appropriate, the teacher may join the children's play and interact verbally with them. It seems most helpful if this verbal interaction is directed towards the child's activities and interests. For example, if a child is "cooking" dinner when the adult enters and offers the adult a plate and says, "eat," the adult might respond by saying, "Oh, you want me to eat lunch with you? Okay, I'll sit down over here." The adult might go on to inquire about what it is that everyone is eating. The child may answer, "Soup." The teacher might then say, "Good, it's cold outside. It's a good day to have soup for lunch."

2. Activity: Reading books (PP–K)

Materials: Story books.
Procedure: Try to find time to read to individual children or small groups of children during activity time. Encourage children to talk about the story and the pictures. These conversations provide children with a chance to talk about things of interest and expose them to mature language from the teacher as well as from the book.

3. Activity: Informal talk (PP–K)

Materials: Nothing special.
Procedure: Talk with individual children or small groups of children in all kinds of situations during the day. Such times might include arrival time in the morning, snack time, lunch time, and much of activity time too. These conversations should be about

[20]H. P. Marshall, "Relations Between Home Experience and Children's Use of Language in Play Interactions With Peers," *Psychological Monographs,* 75, no. 509 (1961), pp. 9–15.

children's ongoing activities or other topics that are of interest to them.

4. *Activity:* Songs and poems (PP–K)

Materials: None.
Procedure: Teach songs and poems to children during group time. These experiences expose children to mature language patterns.

ACTIVITIES TO HELP CHILDREN DEVELOP COMPETENCE IN THE USE OF STANDARD ENGLISH

1. *Activity:* Stories and songs (PP–P)

Materials: Records and a listening post or record player.
Procedure: Provide records of stories and songs in Standard English for children to listen to during activity time. Children will enjoy the stories and songs, and will at the same time be gaining familiarity with Standard English.
Suggestions and Variations: Provide an attractive assortment of books and encourage adult speakers of Standard English—volunteers, aides, parents—to read to the children. If there are children who speak a different language, e.g., Navajo or Spanish, provide books in these languages also and encourage native speakers to read from them. Hearing books read in both Standard English and the native language will help children learn English as a second language while retaining their own. Care should be taken to see that there is a good balance between the two.

2. *Activity:* Language master listening (K–P)

Materials: Language masters and blank language master cards.
Procedure: Language masters provide children with good language models and allow them to record their own words and sentences. In running through the cards, children can compare their language to the teacher's model. The teacher can prepare cards to teach children their addresses. For example, on a card with John's picture clipped to it, the teacher can tape, "My name is John Taylor, and I live at 200 Main Street."
Suggestions and Variations: Make up some language master cards which demonstrate Standard English forms of common phrases. Then ask a question which calls for a response using the same form. "My name is Mary. What is your name?" (Spanish speakers tend to say, "I am called Mary."—"*Me llamo Mary*.") "I am six years old. How old are you?" (Spanish speakers tend to say, "I have six years."

"*Yo tengo seis años.*" Black children may say, "I be six.") When the child records his answer to the question he can hear his voice as well as the taped one.

3. *Activity:* Conversations (PP–P)

   Materials: None.
   Procedure: Carry on conversations with children on the playground or inside about their block building, jungle-gym climbing, painting, sand building, or some experience they have in common. The teacher should be able to carry on these conversations in the child's native language. The teacher can provide translations into Standard English for statements the teacher knows the child has mastered in his own language.

4. *Activity:* Dramatic play (PP–K)

   Materials: Props for house or store play.
   Procedure: Encourage children to engage in dramatic play. If the class contains children who speak a language other than English as well as children who do speak English, the non-English-speaking children will pick up a great deal of language from the other children. (The English-speaking children will learn some of the other language too, although the influence tends not to be very great when the non-English-speaking children are few in number.)

ACTIVITIES TO HELP CHILDREN DEVELOP SKILL IN ORGANIZING AND EXPRESSING THOUGHTS

1. *Activity:* Block building (PP–P)

   Materials: Unit blocks; appropriate props, such as small people or transportation toys.
   Procedure: Make materials available to children during activity time. As children play together with these materials, they will inevitably talk with each other about what should be built and how they should go about building it. These situations are excellent ones for giving children practice in organizing and expressing their ideas and feelings.

2. *Activity:* Dramatic play (PP–P)

   Materials: Those described for dramatic play on pages 101 and 270.
   Procedure: Promote dramatic play by providing space and props. As children engage in dramatic play, they will talk with each other. They will often have differing ideas about how the play should

proceed and these differences provide an excellent opportunity for children to organize and express their ideas and feelings.

Dramatic play provides an opportunity for children to organize and express complex ideas and feelings.

3. *Activity:* Discussion time (PP–P)

Materials: None.

Procedure: Often at group time at the end of an activity period, individual children offer to explain or are asked to explain how they did or made something or how something happened. These occasions provide excellent opportunities for children to organize and express ideas and feelings.

4. *Activity:* Activities suggested in the Social Science chapter that involve classroom visitors (pages 276 and 284).

Materials: None.

Procedure: Follow the procedure suggested for the activities. Experience listening to others who present complex ideas and feelings helps children develop skills too. Children also need to be given many opportunities to present their own ideas and feelings.

ACTIVITIES TO HELP CHILDREN DEVELOP SKILLS IN RELATING INFORMATION TO A GROUP

1. Activity: Discussion or evaluation time (PP–P)

Materials: Materials will vary depending on the topic.

Procedure: Children may describe to the whole group how they made something or what they found out about something during activity time earlier in the day.

Suggestions and Variations: Teachers should avoid making these presentations routine and boring. Not every child needs to relay information to others in this way every day or even every week. When children have mastered a process or learned about something that is of interest to them and which they would like to share, then it is appropriate to encourage them to present the information to the group.

The teacher may be able to arrange a visit by one of the students to a class next door to explain a process or give a talk on a special topic of interest. As children progress in the primary grades, it is perfectly appropriate for a teacher to help them organize such presentations, to encourage the child to practice the presentation before actually delivering it, and to help the child think of ways to make the presentation more interesting and clearer to an audience.

Listening

ACTIVITIES TO HELP CHILDREN DEVELOP MARGINAL LISTENING ABILITIES

1. Activity: Easy listening (PP–P)

Materials: Learning centers or individual projects.

Procedure: As children work on projects, encourage them to talk with each other about these, play records, etc. Occasionally, call attention to a sound such as the ticking of the clock, the chirp of a bird, or the beep of a car horn.

Suggestions and Variations: While a story is being read, a child may listen quietly working a puzzle. While children are resting or preparing for their naps, quiet music may be playing in the background. Children may paint while listening to music. Field trips provide many opportunities for children to hear unplanned sounds and noises.

ACTIVITIES TO DEVELOP
APPRECIATIVE LISTENING ABILITIES

1. Activity: Listening and discussing (PP–P)

Materials: A designated place for group meetings.

Procedure: Children and adults should be seated so that each one can easily and comfortably see everyone else. Children should be encouraged to share ideas, achievements, and feelings. Individual children may tell about projects they have completed. Children can learn appreciative listening behavior by the teacher's model of looking at the speaker attentively, asking questions, reflecting about what the speaker has said, and communicating to the speaker an interest in what is being said. Children should be encouraged to enter into the conversation by asking questions and suggesting possible uses for the project or possible solutions for a common concern.

Suggestions and Variations: In order to come to any feasible conclusions and make a judgment, children must listen to each other. If children enjoy listening to a child describe a just-completed boat, it would be appreciative listening. If children listen in order to make a boat of their own, attentive listening has occurred. Analytical listening is accomplished when the ideas presented are evaluated in terms of feasibility.

ACTIVITIES TO HELP CHILDREN DEVELOP
ATTENTIVE LISTENING ABILITIES

1. Activity: Interesting sounds (PP–P)

Materials: Tape recorder.

Procedure: In order to help children develop sensitivity to common sounds, take children on a walk around the school or block and ask them to listen to outdoor sounds. Sometimes no more instructions are given; other times the teacher may ask children to listen to the quality, distance, volume, or similarities and differences of sounds that are heard. Other times, the teacher may ask the children to listen to specific sounds such as cars, work machines, or crickets. Guide children by asking, "Can you identify the sound?" "Can you make the sound?" "Was it nearby or far away?" "Was it a high sound or a low one?"

Suggestions and Variations: Listen to classroom sounds such as those of musical instruments. Read stories that emphasize sounds. Have children make up their own sounds, record them, and illustrate what they think could have made the sounds. These could be animals or machines.

2. *Activity:* Do as I do (PP–P)

Materials: Noise-producing object such as a drum or tambourine. Children's hands may·be used instead.
Procedure: One child beats a drum a specific number of times, the other children clap or tap the same number.
Suggestions and Variations: Begin with simple beats, progressing to complex patterns such as two fast and one slow beat. The loudness of the beats can also be varied. Children's names may be used and children asked to identify which name is being clapped; e.g., Elizabeth is four beats: two accented and two not.

3. *Activity:* Sound boxes (PP–K)

Materials: Commercial sound boxes or substitutes made from boxes, plastic bottles, or cans. Make two of each kind.
Procedure: As children shake the containers they identify the ones that are identical. They can also point out those that make loud sounds and those that make soft sounds as well as other differences.

4. *Activity:* Name my sounds (PP–K)

Materials: Children's bodies and classroom equipment.
Procedure: This activity works best as a group activity.
Select one child to make a sound out of the other children's view. This may require that they close their eyes. Sounds may be that of shutting a door, tapping with a pencil, dropping a block, rumpling some paper, or pouring water from one glass to another. The other children guess what is creating the sound.

ACTIVITIES TO HELP CHILDREN DEVELOP ANALYTICAL LISTENING ABILITIES

1. *Activity:* Simon Says (PP–P)

Materials: None.
Procedure: The leader, the teacher or a child, gives a command to each child by name to move in some fashion from a starting line toward a finish line. The called-on child is to perform the command if it begins with "Simon says." For example, if the leader says,

"Mary, take a giant step," Mary should not move. But if the command is "Simon says: take a giant step," Mary takes the largest step that she can.

Suggestions and Variations: Children should be encouraged to give commands for a variety of unusual steps—scissor steps, skating steps, tip-toe steps—so that children learn to listen both for the words "Simon says" and the kinds of steps they are to take.

2. *Activity:* Following directions (PP–P)

Materials: None.

Procedure: A leader (teacher may demonstrate and then pick a child) issues three consecutive directions to a child by name. For example, "José, go to the window, tap on the pane three times, then turn to the class and say 'good morning' in Spanish." If José does these in the correct order, he becomes the leader.

Suggestions and Variations: Besides making a game of following directions, as above, the teacher should look for opportunities during the day to give a series of directions and note the ways in which children follow them.

Reading

ACTIVITIES TO HELP CHILDREN IDENTIFY WITH THE ROLE OF READER

1. *Activity:* Valuing reading (PP–P)

Materials: Reading materials, including books, newspapers, magazines.

Procedure: Share with the children interesting information which you acquired from a printed source. It may be about a familiar animal at the local zoo, a reference book with new information for the social science center, or a note from guests telling how much they enjoyed their visit. The model provided by the teacher's example is essential in guiding children to care about learning to read, and teachers should let children know that reading is the source of much information that is useful.

2. *Activity:* Cooking (PP–P)

Materials: Ingredients and utensils for food being prepared.

Procedure: Write out the recipe for the food being prepared even if it has only two or three simple steps. In this way, children will see that learning to read is valuable. (See example of assignment cards on page 33.)

3. *Activity:* Reading together (PP–P)

   Materials: Many different kinds of reading materials.

   Procedure: Read to children often. In reading to them, try to make the experience as intimate and personal as possible. Ask children to help you read a familiar story. Leave out key words that children are able to supply. Ask a child to help you turn the pages.

4. *Activity:* Pretend reading (PP–K)

   Materials: Familiar story books.

   Procedure: Provide many opportunities for children to be the readers. Children can often read picture books to friends. After hearing a story read many times, children enjoy "reading" the story to others. It must be available in the book area so children can get it.

   Suggestions and Variations: Often, preschool children bring books with them to a group story time. Sometimes they want the teacher to read their books, but at other times they just want to look at or hold their book while the teacher reads the story. Children who behave in this manner are probably showing that they value reading and that they want to do what the adult does. While it is reasonable to expect that children will not read their own books out loud while the teacher is reading, it is probably a mistake to criticize the child's behavior. If the teacher feels that children should listen more attentively to the teacher's story than they seem able to do when permitted to hold their own books, the teacher should make certain that informal opportunities are provided at other times throughout the day for children to engage in this activity.

ACTIVITIES TO HELP CHILDREN UNDERSTAND
THAT WORDS IN PRINT ARE TALK WRITTEN DOWN

1. *Activity:* Experience chart (PP–K)

   Materials: Large piece of paper and magic marker.

   Procedure: The teacher writes down what the children say about an experience they have shared. The teacher may write the chart with the whole group or with a small group of children who have been engaged in a project together. By seeing that what they say can be written down, children begin to appreciate the relationship between spoken and written language.

2. *Activity:* Shopping lists (PP–K)

   Materials: Paper and pencil.

   Procedure: When a trip is to be made to a store to buy ingredients for cooking, supplies for pets, etc., help children make a list before they go. The teacher writes down the items that everyone agrees are needed.

3. *Activity:* Writing children's stories (PP–K)

Materials: Paper and pencil.
Procedure: The teacher writes down the story as told by the child. Often, the story is told to accompany a picture the child has made.

ACTIVITIES TO HELP CHILDREN DEVELOP
READING COMPREHENSION SKILLS

1. *Activity:* Questions about stories (PP–K)

Materials: Story books.
Procedure: After reading a story to children, the teacher should ask them questions about it; these should include specific questions about the characters, what they did, and what happened to them. In some stories, such as *Where the Wild Things Are*,[21] it is not made explicit that the story is largely the child's dream. When using such a book, the teacher may want to ask questions to help children reach an understanding about what really has happened. For example, the teacher might ask, "Do you think the boy's room really turned into a forest with wild things in it?"
Suggestions and Variations: Teachers can extend questioning about stories to help children apply what occurred in the story to their personal lives. In addition, teachers can help children think beyond the specific story to a situation in the future. For example, the teacher might ask, "Do you think the boy will be afraid of the doctor the next time he must go see her?"
When children are reading for themselves, they can be given questions to answer. Older primary children may be interested in writing short reports about books in the classroom or school library. These can be kept in a book for other children in the class to refer to in deciding which books they would like to read.
When primary children have done extensive reading on a topic of interest, they may want to organize a short oral presentation to give to the whole class.

[21]M. Sendak, *Where the Wild Things Are* (New York: Harper & Row, Publishers, 1963).

2. *Activity:* Reading directions (PP–K)

Materials: Directions for assembling a terrarium, making cookies or bread, making a crystal garden, caring for a pet, etc.; supplies for the specific project.

Procedure: Read the appropriate directions to the child or children who are involved in the project. Then let the child carry out the project, giving help as needed (such as repeating the directions).

Suggestions and Variations: As soon as children are able, let them read the directions themselves. It is a good idea for the teacher to ask the children to explain what the directions say should be done before they begin the actual project. This would be especially true if the process is complicated or when materials to be used are expensive or scarce and could not be replaced if ruined.

3. *Activity:* Story dramatizations (PP–P)
(Refer to the drama activities on pages 101–103 in Chapter 3.)

ACTIVITIES TO DEVELOP SIGHT VOCABULARY

1. *Activity:* Labels (PP–P)

Materials: Felt pen, cards, masking tape.

Procedure: Print the names of various objects in the room on cards and attach to appropriate objects (window, door, chair). Label storage areas for materials that are to be stored there. Label walls and corners to indicate directions—north, south, east, west.

Suggestions and Variations: On the playground set up an area with road signs giving directions for tricycles and pedestrians. One child may act as officer holding up signs for tricycles to *stop* and children to *walk*.

2. *Activity:* Puzzle cards (K–P)

Materials: Construction paper or tagboard, pictures cut from magazines, felt pen, paste, laminating materials or clear contact paper.

Procedure: Cut construction paper or tagboard in uniform sizes; e.g., $3'' \times 5''$, $5'' \times 7''$, or $8\frac{1}{2}'' \times 11''$. On one half of each card attach or draw a picture. On the other half, print the name of the object shown. Laminate or cover with clear contact. Cut card in half unevenly. Each card should be cut differently—sawtooth, curved lines, etc. (See Figure 15.) Place in language center.

Suggestions and Variations: Start with very simple words and add words as children show an interest and ability.

Figure 15. Picture word puzzle cards.

3. Activity: Using children's names (PP–K)

Materials: Paper, tagboard, magic markers.

Procedure: Use children's names at every possible opportunity. Place children's names on their lockers, cubbies, or tote boxes. If children are organized into more than one story group at story time, make a list of names for each group and post these on the wall in the area of the room where the groups meet. Prepare name cards for a helpers' chart as described on page 16. Write children's names on their artwork. Prepare a set of name cards to place in a container on the shelf in the language arts area of the room. Children like to search through the cards and find their own names and the names of friends.

4. Activity: Experience charts (PP–K)

Materials: Paper and magic markers.

Procedure: The procedure has been described in activity #1 on page 139. In addition to learning that words in print are just talk written down, children will learn to read words that frequently appear in the charts. Learning of words is increased when teachers read the chart back to children when it is finished, and when teachers leave it available in the room and help children read it individually or with a friend during activity time.

5. Activity: Picture lotto with words (PP–K)

Materials: Tagboard, picture seals or pictures cut from magazines, fine-tip magic marker. Make several tagboard lotto playing cards by marking off a 6″ × 6″ card into nine 2″ × 2″ squares. Paste a picture in each square. Cut nine tagboard squares, each 2″ × 2″ for each playing card, and paste on them pictures identical to those appearing on the playing cards. Write the name of the object in each picture underneath the picture on the playing card and on the matching squares.

Procedure: Make the lotto materials available in a container on a shelf in the language arts area. Children use the materials to play lotto as usual, but the words provide added learning for children who are interested. Children know what the words say because of the pictures.

6. **Activity:** Writing children's stories (PP–P)

Materials: Paper and magic markers or pencils.

Procedure: The procedure has been described in activity #3 on page 140.

Suggestions and Variations: When children begin doing some of the writing for their stories, a personal dictionary or word bank can help them learn new words without the constant help of an adult. When the child first asks for the word to use in a story, the teacher can write it on a card which will go in the word bank, or on a page in the dictionary. The child can draw a picture next to the word as a reminder of what the word says. When the child needs the word for future stories, it can be obtained without the teacher's help. From time to time the teacher and child should go over the cards in the word bank to discard those that the child knows well. Too many words in the bank make finding needed words too difficult.

7. **Activity:** Making statements (PP–K)

Materials: Tagboard strips 2″ high and varying in length. On the longer strips, write parts of sentences such as "I like. . .," "My name is. . .," "Your name is. . .," "Today is. . . ." On shorter cards, write individual words that could be used to complete the sentences. For example, words such as "dogs," "cake," "school," and "hamburgers" could be made to go with "I like. . . ." Name cards for children in the class could go with "My name is. . . ." and "Your name is. . . ." Words for the days of the week as well as adjectives to describe the weather ("cold," "sunny," "hot," "cloudy") could be made to go with "Today is. . . ."

Procedure: Start with just one of the incomplete sentences at first until children understand how the materials are to be used. When children have mastered the first set of materials, replace it with another sentence strip and word cards. Continue this process through three or four sentences, Then place all three or four out together. Children will discover they can use words to complete more than one sentence. For example, "I like *Mary.*" "Your name is *Mary.*" "I like *Monday.*" "Today is *Monday.*"

ACTIVITIES TO HELP CHILDREN DEVELOP THE ABILITY TO RECOGNIZE AND NAME LETTERS

1. Activity: Feely letters (PP–K)

Materials: Sandpaper, pipe cleaner, sand, felt, rice, and bean letters glued on cards, wooden and magnetic letters.

Procedure: Young children need experiences with letters—just playing with, matching and trying to make their names. Make some of the above materials available where they may be freely used by children. Teachers or peers will need to provide letter names to those who do not know them.

Teachers help children learn letter names.

2. *Activity:* Letter Bingo (PP–K)

   Materials: Bingo cards using letters. Small cards with letters to be used by the caller. Bottle caps for the players to use to cover cards as letters are called.

   Procedure: Follow the usual bingo procedures. Give one playing card and nine bottle caps to each player. Have a child be the caller. Encourage the child to say the name of the letter being called rather than just showing it to the players.

   Suggestions and Variations: Make the first bingo game using upper-case letters. Later, make another bingo game that contains upper- and lower-case pairs together in a square (Aa, Bb, Cc, etc.). In this way, children will begin to learn both forms, and which letters go together.

3. *Activity:* Typewriting (PP–K)

   Materials: Typewriter and paper.

   Procedure: Make the typewriter and paper available to the children. In working with the typewriter, they will learn some of the letter names. The teacher can provide these by telling the child what letters he has typed when he shows him his paper. Children will learn names from each other too.

   Suggestions and Variations: The teacher might ask the child to type certain letters such as an "A," a "T," and an "M." This will let the teacher know if the child knows the written symbols that go with the names.

   In order to avoid problems due to memory, the teacher can record on tape some letter names that the child can then listen to as he types them. There should be a sufficiently long pause between letters to give the child time to find the lettter on the typewriter.

4. *Activity:* Letters in my name (PP–K)

   Materials: Magnetic letters and magnetic board or felt letters and felt board, or paper letters.

   Procedure: As children find letters for their names, help them say the letter names. Often, children can pick out the letters in their names but do not know the names of the individual letters.

5. *Activity:* Letter-card game (PP–K)

   Materials: Tagboard cards, 2″ × 3″, with a letter written on each one.

   Procedure: Children can either use these individually to practice naming letters, or two or three children may use the cards together to play a game. When playing a game, place all cards face down in deck between the players. The player whose turn it is turns over one card, and, after naming the letter on it correctly, the child may keep it. If the player cannot name the letter, the card must go to the bottom of the deck. The child with the most cards at the end of the game wins.

Suggestions and Variations: Games with rules are difficult for children under five years of age.

ACTIVITIES TO HELP CHILDREN LEARN LETTER-SOUND ASSOCIATIONS

1. *Activity:*   Consonant picture board (PP–P)

   Materials: Tagboard 16″ × 16″. Draw lines to make 2″ squares on the board. In each square paste pictures of objects whose names begin with consonant phonemes. Make tagboard letter cards 2″ square. Write a consonant on each, making two or three cards for each consonant.

   Procedure: Child says name of the item in each picture on the board and places over the picture the consonant that the name starts with. The teacher can look at the board when the child has completed covering all the pictures.

   Suggestions and Variations: The teacher can make a similar board using pictures of items whose names *end* in consonants.

2. *Activity:*   Picture spin (PP–K)

   Materials: Cardboard spinner board marked with four consonants (see Figure 16); picture cards of items whose names begin with phonemes for consonants shown on spinner board.

   Procedure: Two or three children may play. Place picture cards face down in the deck. Children spin and pick up a card. If the picture name begins with the phoneme represented by the lettter spun, the child keeps the picture. If it does not, it must be placed on the bottom of the deck. The child with the most picture cards when the deck is empty wins.

   Suggestions and Variations: Games with rules are difficult for children under five years of age.

3. *Activity:*   Picture card matching (PP–K)

   Materials: Tagboard cards with pictures pasted on them. Pictures should be of items whose names start with consonants. Make sure you have at least three pictures for each consonant (house, hoe, hay; top, tie, timer; man, mouse, menu).

Figure 16. Consonant spinner board.

Procedure: Child sorts pictures into sets which all begin with the same letter.

4. *Activity:*   Consonant-picture bingo (PP–K)

Materials: Playing cards drawn so there are nine spaces in which to paste on pictures (objects pictured should begin with single consonants); loose cards with one consonant written on each (to be used by the caller); blank pieces of paper or bottle caps for players to use as markers on playing cards.
Procedure: Caller calls letters from the consonant deck. Players must cover pictures whose names begin with the consonants called.

5. *Activity:*   Same first phonemes (PP–K)

Materials: None.
Procedure: In situations where you might want children to start doing something in small groups rather than all at once (e.g., getting coats on to go home; moving from the large group to a smaller story group), indicate which children are to go first by calling a phoneme and asking only those children whose name begins with that phoneme to go. For example, all children whose names begin

with "B" may be asked to put their coats on first. This group may be followed by children whose names start with phonemes represented by "S" or "T."

6. *Activity:* Thinking of words (PP–K)

   Materials: None, or paper and pencil.
   Procedure: Encourage children to think of words that begin with similar sounds whenever possible. For example, when you write children's names, ask whether they can think of other words that start with the same sound as their names. Sometimes it is fun to try to think of words during group time. The teacher can write the words on a large sheet of paper so the children can see the relationship between verbal sounds and written letters. It is interesting to keep a list of words for one sound for a week or so and each day check to see if anyone has thought of a new word to add. Children will often ask their parents for words and come to school with them. These lists can then be hung on the wall of the classroom. Many children try to read these, and some succeed.

7. *Activity:* Letter sound books (K–P)

   Materials: Paper, pencils, paste, pictures.
   Procedure: Have children label pages with a consonant and collect the pages into a booklet. Children can cut out pictures of items whose names begin with the phoneme represented by the letter and paste them on the correct page. Children can also write the names of the items below the pictures or ask the teacher to write them.

8. *Activity:* Names that rhyme (PP–K)

   Materials: A collection of objects so there are pairs whose names rhyme (shell–bell; book–hook; can–pan), or pictures of objects whose names rhyme.
   Procedure: Help children pair the items or pictures whose names rhyme.

9. *Activity:* Poems and songs (PP–K)

   Materials: A collection of finger plays, poems, and songs that utilize rhyming words. Nursery rhymes are also very good.
   Procedure: At story or group time, teach children simple finger plays, nursery rhymes, and songs that utilize verse that rhymes. Children enjoy repetition with these so they should be recited and sung over and over for many days. Encourage children to substitute other rhyming words for the words they have learned in the verse.

10. *Activity:* Riddles (K–P)

Materials: Simple riddles.

Procedure: After learning a few riddles, have children guess answers to other riddles. For example, "I rhyme with rake. You eat me. What am I?"

Suggestions and Variations: Older children may enjoy making up their own riddles and writing them down to make a riddle book.

11. *Activity:* Taking dictation (PP–P)

Materials: Paper and pencil.

Procedure: When taking dictation for children's stories the teacher can involve the child in determining the letters that should be used to spell words. This helps children learn letter-sound associations.

Suggestions and Variations: The extent to which the children can determine the correct letters in a word will depend on their experience with letters and sounds. With a young child who has had little experience, the teacher should assume most of the responsibility for spelling the words, but should verbalize while writing the letters for each word.

12. *Activity:* Which words rhyme? (PP–P)

Materials: None.

Procedure: This activity should be used in a group setting, perhaps when there are a few minutes to spare from one activity to the next. The teacher says three words, only two of which rhyme. The children must call out the word that does not rhyme with the other two. Children can also take turns thinking of three words, only two of which rhyme.

13. *Activity:* Difficult sounds (P)

Materials: Any of those suggested above, but emphasizing the particular sound to be learned.

Procedure: Teachers can use all of the techniques suggested in the above activities to teach sounds of any level of difficulty. Teachers should refer to a good phonics book to determine all of the sounds children should become familiar with and then design materials and activities to help children learn these as they are ready.

ACTIVITIES TO HELP CHILDREN LEARN LEFT-TO-RIGHT AND TOP-TO-BOTTOM PROGRESSION

1. *Activity:* Reading to children (PP–P)

Materials: Story books.

Procedure: In reading to children occasionally point out where you are reading by running your finger under the print. You might also point out pictures as you go from page to page. This will help children get the idea that books are organized from left to right.

2. *Activity:*   Picture sequences (PP–K)

Materials: A collection of pictures that tell a story when placed in a sequence. Small cardboard frames to place each picture on. Frames should be attached to one another and the first one on the left should be colored to indicate the starting position.

Procedure: Children can arrange the pictures to tell the story. Color-coding the first frame on the left helps insure that the child will start there and go to the right.

3. *Activity:*   Writing (PP–K)

Materials: Children's work, paper, pencil.

Procedure: In any situation in which you write something for children whether it be their names on art work or dictation for a story, they will see you modeling the left-to-right progression. If you write more than one line, they will see the top-to-bottom progression also. After children have had sufficient opportunity to observe these procedures, you might begin asking them where to begin the writing. In this way, their attention will be called specifically to this idea.

4. *Activity:*   Experience chart (PP–P)

Materials: Large paper, magic marker.

Procedure: Experience charts are written by the teacher with a group of children. Children recall aspects of an experience such as a trip to the store, a visit from an artist, or cooking some soup. As the children recall the events or tell of their feelings about the events, the teacher writes down what they say. Because children see the words going onto the paper, they are again observing the left-to-right and top-to-bottom progression.

ACTIVITIES TO HELP CHILDREN UNDERSTAND PUNCTUATION

1. *Activity:*   Reading stories (K)

Materials: Story books.

Procedure: When reading a story to an individual child or a small group, point out the punctuation marks used in the story. Be sure to read the story with the proper inflection and expression indicated by the marks.

2. *Activity:*   Experience chart (PP–P)

   Materials: Paper, magic markers.

   Procedure: Refer to the general procedure in activity #4 on page 139. Name the punctuation marks that you use in the chart, and mention the use of a capital letter to begin words that start each new sentence.

3. *Activity:*   Marks on tape (K–P)

   Materials: Tape recorder, tapes, paper and pencil.

   Procedure: Tape simple sentences, have children listen to these, and determine what punctuation is needed. For example, tape "I want some help," and "I want some help!" or "You're crying," and "You're crying?" or "I am a boy," and "I'm a boy!"

   Suggestions and Variations: A key can be made by writing the marks in order on a card. When children finish listening to the tape and writing the marks they think are appropriate, they can check them with the key.

4. *Activity:*   Reading for punctuation (P)

   Materials: Books and magazines.

   Procedure: Have friends read to each other. One child reads a sentence and the listener must say what punctuation is needed. This helps a child learn not only how to punctuate, but also how to read expressively: a listener who makes errors in stating what the punctuation marks should be will often point out how the sentence should have been read.

   (Additional activities to develop punctuation skills can be found in the section on writing that follows.)

   ### *Writing*

   ## ACTIVITIES TO HELP CHILDREN DEVELOP HANDWRITING SKILLS

1. *Activity:*   Chalkboard writing (PP–K)

   Materials: Chalk, space at the chalkboard or a small portable board; eraser.

   Procedure: Encourage children to use the materials during activity time. They will at first probably just draw or scribble, but there will come a time when they want to "write." They may ask you to write their names or other words, and then try to copy them.

   Suggestions and Variations: Place some cards with manuscript letters written on them in the chalkboard chalk tray. Children will find these and be encouraged to try to make the letters. It is helpful to place a colored dot at the top of the letter card so children can hold the letters at the proper orientation.

Provide pieces of colored chalk for variation, or give the children paint brushes and a can of water for writing on the chalkboard.

2. *Activity:* Names on work (PP–K)

Materials: Individual work and pencil.

Procedure: When you observe children who have a pretty good idea of the letters that make up their names, suggest to them individually that they write their names on their work. A good way to start is to dot the letters in and then suggest that the child write over the dots.

3. *Activity:* Write and rub (PP–P)

Materials: Manuscript letter guides enclosed in acetate sheet; wax crayon and towel.

Procedure: Make materials available in writing center. Guidance would include observing to see if the child is able to follow the arrows on the guide. For those who cannot, a simple demonstration can be offered. Sometimes children attempt to do this activity before they are capable of doing it correctly. They should be allowed to use the materials in their own way if this is the case. Children may also need to be shown how to clean the acetate sheet with the towel.

4. *Activity:* Magic slate (PP–P)

Materials: Magic slates that can be found in the dime store.

Procedure: Make magic slates available in the writing centers so children can use them to write on. These are often excellent materials for children just beginning to write, because they can erase and start over so easily.

Suggestions and Variations: Because magic slates are somewhat fragile under hard use, it would be appropriate for the teacher to make it clear to the children that these are not to be used for drawing, but only for practicing writing letters. This rule may also act as an incentive to encourage some children to write letters.

5. *Activity:* Individual letter guides (PP–P)

Materials: Dittoed papers with letters outlined in dots; pencils.

Procedure: Prepare a variety of guides each with two or three letters to the page. Place them in a box or basket in the writing center. Encourage children to practice writing letters by using these.

6. *Activity:* Writing over or under (K–P)

Materials: Pencils and paper.
Procedure: When children dictate stories which their teacher writes down, they can be encouraged to write over the words the teacher has written. If children have adequate skill, the teacher can leave room under each sentence for the child to rewrite the words.
Suggestions and Variations: Children are often more interested in writing over the teacher's writing if the original is in pencil and they may write over in colored magic marker.

7. *Activity:* Real writing (PP–P)

Materials: Pencil and paper.
Procedure: At all levels of skill, children should be involved in situations in which purposeful writing is going on. This may be writing a birthday card for a parent or friend, writing a grocery list to use while shopping in the dramatic play store, writing a thank-you note to a classroom visitor, or writing signs and building labels for structures made with unit blocks. Children need to be involved in situations that require writing so they will realize that learning to write is a useful endeavor. At first, the teacher will do the writing. Later, children will be able to do it.

ACTIVITIES TO HELP CHILDREN
DEVELOP SKILL IN SPELLING

All of the activities in the section on letter-sound association (page 146) also affect skill in spelling.

1. *Activity:* Labels (PP–K)

Materials: Objects in the room; labels.
Procedure: As children use items in the room and notice the various labels, call their attention to the letters used to make the word.

2. *Activity:* Writing children's stories (PP–P)

Materials: Paper and pencils or magic markers.
Procedure: When teachers take down children's dictated stories, they can ask children to help spell the words. At first, for young preschool children, the teacher will need to do most of the spelling. Gradually, children will be able to contribute the letters for the first sound in many words (especially consonants). Finally, they will be able to spell many words almost completely.

3. *Activity:* Spell with letters (PP–K)

Materials: Magnetic or felt letters and magnetic or felt board.
Procedure: If materials are out in a center where children can work with them, they will often want to "make" certain words. These may be words that are on the label cards around the room, or their own names, or the name of a favorite toy or food.

4. *Activity:* Letter draw (K–P)

Materials: Tagboard cut into ½″ squares. Write one letter on each square. Small box with lid to store letters on shelf.
Procedure: Have materials available in the writing or language arts center. Encourage children to draw 5, 6, . . . 10 letters from the box and try to make a word. Children can play alone or together. If enough letters are available, children may keep the words they make during each turn, and just return unused letters to the box.

5. *Activity:* Spelling bingo (K–P)

Materials: Acetate-covered blank bingo cards, crayons, wiping cloth, four sets of alphabet cards for the caller.
Procedure: Each child is given a spelling-bingo card, crayon, and wiping cloth. As the caller reads a letter from the alphabet box, each child writes that letter in any square on his card. Once a letter is written, it cannot be changed. The first child to spell a word correctly—horizontally, vertically, or diagonally—calls out "bingo" and wins.
Suggestions and Variations: Making dittoed bingo cards out of paper allows children to keep their completed bingo cards.

6. *Activity:* Spelling dictionaries (K–P)

Materials: 3″ × 5″ cards and large ring holders.
Procedure: As children ask for help with the spelling of words for their stories, write the word or have the child write the word, and place it in the ring holder to make a personal dictionary. New words should be placed on the ring in alphabetical order. As old words become unnecessary, these can be removed. (Spelling words and sight vocabulary words can be included in the same dictionary or word bank. Refer to activity #6 on page 143.)
Suggestions and Variations: Children can quiz each other on their spelling words.

ACTIVITIES TO HELP CHILDREN DEVELOP
THE ABILITY TO WRITE CREATIVELY

1. *Activity:* Taping (PP–P)

   Materials: Tape recorder and tapes.

   Procedure: Children who cannot write can record their creative verse or stories. The tape can then be used later if the teacher wants to transcribe it for the child. Even older children who can write like to talk their creative writing into a tape first and then write it later.

   Suggestions and Variations: Children enjoy listening to their own or their friends' tapes.

2. *Activity:* Parts of stories (PP–K)

   Materials: Story books.

   Procedure: After reading a story to children, talk about it with the children. The talk may include a discussion of characters as well as a discussion of the sequence of events. Through discussing these aspects of the creative writing of others, children will be learning something about how to write creatively themselves.

3. *Activity:* Story writing (PP–P)

   Materials: Paper and pencil.

   Procedure: Even young preprimary children create stories and delight in telling them to someone, particularly their teacher. Often, these stories are told as an explanation of a picture the child has made, but this is not always the case. Teachers should occasionally ask if the children would like their stories to be written down. (If the story accompanies a picture, the writing should be done on a separate piece of paper which can later be attached to the picture. Writing in the spaces on a picture often spoils its appearance.) These stories can become quite lengthy after children have had some experience in creating them. There will come a time when it will be appropriate for the teacher to suggest that individuals organize their stories in booklet form. Children may also benefit from some pre-writing thinking about characters and sequence of events. With primary age children it will probably be most common for pictures illustrating the story to be drawn after the story is written, whereas with younger children the story often follows from the picture making.

Suggestions and Variations: Children learn to write creatively by writing and then sharing with others what they have written. Teachers should offer supportive and helpful suggestions which will help children express their thoughts more clearly. Sometimes this can be done through questioning: "What did the man look like?" "What were the boy's feelings about being lost?" "What do you think might happen to the dog when the family comes home and sees what he has done?"

It is not a good idea to ask children to rewrite stories which they say are finished. Children will incorporate new learnings into their next story. Often, children write many stories using the same characters and setting. They may be interested in organizing these into a book for the library corner.

4. *Activity:* Writing scripts (K–P)

Materials: Films or filmstrips without sound; tape recorder and tape.
Procedure: Encourage children individually to view the films and filmstrips and tell their own interpretations of the action. Children may be interested in listening to each other's tapes.

5. *Activity:* Writers to visit (PP–P)

Materials: Samples of the writer's work, which may include a story book or a story in a magazine.
Procedure: Arrange for the writer to visit the class. Make sure the children are familiar with what the writer has written. It may be interesting to have the writer read to the children a favorite story of his or hers. It would also be desirable for children to be able to share their writing with the writer during activity time.
Suggestions and Variations: Write to authors of some of the children's favorite stories. Children may be interested in where the authors live, what they do other than write, and how long it took to complete a particular story.

ACTIVITIES TO HELP CHILDREN DEVELOP GRAMMATICAL SKILLS

1. *Activity:* Matching words to pictures (K–P)

Materials: Sets of pictures depicting one object and more than one object; word cards to match each picture, i.e., ball, balls. (See Figure 17.)
Procedure: Make materials available in the writing or language arts center. Children must match the appropriate word to each picture.

Figure 17. Picture word card
puzzles for plural formation.

2. *Activity:* Scrambled words (P)

   Materials: Several sets of words that make up sentences. Each word
   should be written on an individual card. The complete sentence
   that can be made from the words should be written on an acetate-
   covered strip.

   Procedure: Two children working as partners get a set of words in
   scrambled order. Taking turns, each child takes the set of words
   and tries to arrange them into a sentence. The sentences made by
   the children can be compared with the sentence on the sentence
   strip. (There may be several sentences that can be made from one
   set of words. This will give children good experience in finding out
   that different arrangements of words result in different meanings.)

3. *Activity:* Missing verbs (P)

   Materials: Sentence pairs written on tagboard strips; omit the verb
   in each sentence by leaving a blank (i.e., The girl_____the tree.
   The girl is_____the tree.). Small cards on which the missing verbs
   are written (i.e., climbed, climbing).

   Procedure: Store sentence strips and verb cards in a small box in
   the language arts center. Guidance would include observing to see
   if children are completing the sentences correctly.

4. *Activity:* Class newspaper (P)

   Materials: Ditto master; paper, pencils, typewriter (optional).

   Procedure: It may be best to have a small group of children work
   on each newspaper, but change the composition of the group with
   each new issue of the paper. Children will need some guidance in
   deciding what should be included in the newspaper and how it can
   be organized. Since the newspaper will be read by everyone, grammatical structure should be correct. Drafts should be checked by
   the teacher and by the children, and any errors should be corrected

before the final copy is printed. This provides an excellent opportunity for children to appreciate and use each other's skills.

ACTIVITIES TO HELP CHILDREN
DEVELOP SKILL IN USING PUNCTUATION

1. Activity: Writing in punctuation marks (P)

Materials: A file of acetate-covered sentences needing punctuation; colored pencils, wiping cloth.

Procedure: Children may select sentences to punctuate. When they finish, their work can be checked by the teacher or a peer. Marks can be erased, and cards can be returned to their storage box.

2. Activity: Class newspaper (P)

Materials: Same as in activity #4 on page 157.

Procedure: Refer to the general procedure in activity #4 on page 157. In checking drafts, the teacher should help children use appropriate punctuation marks.

ADDITIONAL RESOURCES

ADAMS, H. M., "Learning to be Discriminating Listeners," *English,* 36 (1947) pp. 11–15.

ASHTON-WARNER, S., *Teacher.* New York: Simon and Schuster, 1963.

BERRY, A., "Listening Activities in the Elementary School," *Elementary English Review,* 23 (1946), pp. 69–79.

BROWN, R., and U. BELLUGI, "Three Processes in the Child's Acquisition of Syntax," *Harvard Education Review,* 34 (1964), pp. 33–51.

Bureau of Curriculum Development, *Language Arts Games.* New York: Board of Education of the City of New York, 1971.

BURROWS, A. R., J. D. FEREBEE, D. S. JACKSON, and D. O. SUNADER, *They All Want to Write.* Englewood Cliffs, N.J.: Prentice-Hall, Inc., 1952.

CARRILLO, L., *Informal Reading-Readiness Experiences.* San Francisco: Chandler Publishing Co., 1964.

CAZDEN, C., "Some Implications of Research on Language Development for Preschool Education." A paper prepared for the Social Science Research Council Conference on Preschool Education, Chicago, February 7–9, 1966.

CHOMSKY, C., "Write First, Read Later," *Childhood Education,* 47 (1971), pp. 296–299.

DARROW, H. F., and R. V. ALLEN, *Independent Activities for Creative Learning.* New York: Teachers College Press, Columbia University, 1967.

DURKIN, D., *Teaching Young Children to Read.* Boston: Allyn & Bacon, 1972.

ENGLE, P., *The Use of Vernacular Languages in Education.* Arlington, Va.: Center for Applied Linguistics, 1975.

HALL, M., *Teaching Reading as a Language Experience.* Columbus, Ohio: Charles E. Merrill, 1970.

HEILMAN, A. W., *Phonics in Proper Perspective,* 2nd ed. Columbus, Ohio: Charles E. Merrill, 1968.

HERRICK, V., and M. NERBOVIG, *Using Experience Charts With Children.* Columbus, Ohio: Charles E. Merrill, 1964.

LAMB, P., *Guiding Children's Language Learning.* Dubuque, Iowa: William C. Brown, 1972.

LAVATELLI, C. S., ed., *Language Training in Early Childhood Education.* Urbana, Ill.: University of Illinois Press, 1971.

LEE, D., and R. ALLEN, *Learning to Read Through Experience.* New York: Meredith Publishing Co., 1963.

LENNEBERG, E., "Understanding Language Without Ability to Speak," *Journal of Abnormal and Social Psychology,* 67 (1962), pp. 419–425.

McNEILL, D., "Developmental Psycholinguistics," in F. Smith and G. A. Miller, eds., *The Genesis of Language.* Cambridge, Mass.: MIT Press, 1966.

MITCHELL, E., "The Learning of Sex Roles Through Toys and Books," *Young Children,* 28, no. 4 (1973), pp. 226–232.

MOFFETT, J., *A Student-Centered Language Arts Curriculum Grades K–13: A Handbook for Teachers.* New York: Houghton Mifflin Co., 1968.

National Council of Teachers of English, *Language Arts for Today's Children.* New York: Appleton-Century-Crofts, 1954.

SAVILLE-TROIKE, M., *Bilingual Children.* Arlington, Va.: Center for Applied Linguistics, 1973.

SHANE, H., M. REDDIN, and M. GILLESPIE, *Beginning Language Arts Instruction With Children.* Columbus, Ohio: Charles E. Merrill, 1961.

STAUFFER, R., *The Language-Experience Approach to the Teaching of Reading.* New York: Harper & Row, Publishers, 1970.

TOUGH, J., *Talking, Thinking, Growing.* New York: Schocken Books, 1973.

VEATCH, J., F. SAWICKI, G. ELLIOT, E. BARNETT, and J. BLAKEY, *Key Words to Reading: The Language Experience Approach Begins.* Columbus, Ohio: Charles E. Merrill, 1973.

WILT, M. E., "Study of Teacher Awareness of Listening As a Factor in Elementary Education," *Journal of Educational Research,* 62 (1950), pp. 626–636.

5
mathematics

MATHEMATICS is a mystery to many adults. Situations which require mathematical solutions leave us frustrated or even panicked. These feelings are especially unfortunate for the teacher who is faced with the task of helping children learn and feel comfortable with mathematics.

This chapter is designed to help teachers teach mathematics to young children. The chapter has four goals: (1) to help teachers understand mathematics itself, (2) to help teachers understand how young children learn mathematics, (3) to help teachers understand the mathematical concepts which are appropriate for young children, and (4) to provide ideas for materials and activities for mathematics instruction.

THE NATURE OF MATHEMATICS

We live in a world of objects, time, and space. Mathematics provides an agreed-upon system for describing these in terms of quantity or magnitude. Just as people have agreed that "pencil" is to be the word used to describe a specific writing tool, people have agreed that different groups of objects will be said to possess certain number properties. Without such a system, it would be impossible to talk with others about this aspect of the world.

It is important to note that mathematics involves two levels of knowledge. On the one hand are quantitative attributes and relationships of objects in the world, and on the other are symbols used to represent these attributes and relationships. This dual nature of mathematics has important implications for *what* is taught as mathematics and *how* it is taught.

The first implication is that mathematics includes both a *physical reality* and a *symbol system* for representing the physical reality. Children do not know mathematics if they manipulate symbols for reasons they do not understand or if they have no symbol system for organizing the physical reality they do understand. Good instruction should include both, together.

A second implication of the dual nature of mathematics indicates from where the learner must obtain mathematical information. Knowledge of the physical reality of objects is directly accessible to the learner, whereas the symbol system is not. A learner might know the relationship between a set of objects with the number property of 7 and a set of objects with the number property of 4 and not know that sets have names at all. For example, a three-year-old who is encouraged to share a pack of gum with four friends quickly finds out the relationship between the five sticks of gum and the people to whom it must be distributed. One that I observed even knew how to alter the situation in order to have a larger share of gum. The child tore two sticks in half for distribution and kept three. It was not necessary to know the symbol system of mathematics to perform these manipulations. A child who had wished to communicate to someone about this feat might not have fared so well. The symbol system is made up of arbitrary names which represent the manipulations or attributes of objects or a segment of time, and this knowledge is not directly accessible to the learner. Social mediation is necessary for the child to obtain this information. Someone must provide information about the symbols and relate these to the physical reality the learner is experiencing.

At times in the past there has been a tendency to teach all of mathematics as if it were a symbol without referents in the world. Children were told about mathematics. Though it is necessary and appropriate to tell children about the symbol system of mathematics, it is quite inappropriate to tell them about the relationships the symbols represent. This does not mean that teachers should never guide students to explore relationships with objects which they might not think of on their own. Students might never pose questions about the addition of equal sets (multiplication). Therefore, it is necessary for the teacher to raise questions which will lead students to consider relationships which make up mathematics. Experiences should then be provided to allow students to abstract for themselves knowledge about relationships.

CHILDREN AND MATHEMATICS

The nature of mathematics is not the only important consideration in teaching mathematics. The characteristics of the learner are crucial too. The child between three and six is in what Piaget[1] calls the **preoperational stage** of cognitive development. The preoperational child's thought is governed by perception rather than by logical reasoning. Because of this, young children do not have at their disposal one of the main tools necessary for acquiring a mathematical system: constancy of quantity across arrangements. Adults know that if they start with seven cubes they will still have seven whether they are arranged in a line, a circle, a clump, or a tower. Adults know that arrangement does not alter number. For

[1]H. G. Furth, *Piaget and Knowledge* (Englewood Cliffs, N.J.: Prentice-Hall, Inc., 1969), pp. 57–58.

the preoperational child, however, quantity is tied to the arrangement of objects in space. When the arrangement changes, the child thinks the quantity changes also. It is only through actions performed by the child that there emerges a concept of number distinct from that of space.

Teachers must also realize that the preoperational child cannot see the relationship between two independent actions performed on objects. This means, for example, that the child does not see a relationship between actions that we know as addition and subtraction. Though possibly learning through independent actions that two sets of two objects make four altogether, and that two objects remain when a set of two objects is removed from a set of four, the child does not see the logical connection between the two actions.

The preoperational child can learn specific relationships of the kind above if given an opportunity to manipulate objects and if provided with adult input which focuses on such relationships. The child cannot abstract the principle and apply it to new situations, however. In this sense, young children are very inefficient learners of mathematics. They do not take advantage of the lawfulness and logic of the system. Instead of *using* the logic to obtain specific bits of information, young children *build* the logic from specific bits of information.

Children from six to nine are capable of reasoning logically about concrete situations. They no longer confuse number with space. They can understand the logical relationship between independent actions and can even begin to deduce information from one action and apply it to another which they need not actually perform. For example, after combining two sets of three objects to obtain six objects, a child would be able to figure mentally that a set of three objects would remain if a set of three objects were removed from the set of six. The actual physical reversal of the first action would not need to be performed now because the child is capable of reversibility of thought. Children can perform actions *in their heads*. Of course, these mental actions would have been performed physically many times by the child previously, but their relationship to other actions would until now have gone unappreciated.

It should be realized that a child in the **concrete operational**[2] stage needs to perform physical actions on objects in order to understand mathematical ideas, especially when they have just been introduced. The important point is that with concrete operations children can perform mental actions which take their understanding beyond independent physical actions. The *consequences* of physical actions and the *relationship* of one action to others are now understood.

2Furth, *Piaget and Knowledge*, pp. 57–58.

MATHEMATICAL CONCEPTS AND SKILLS
FOR YOUNG CHILDREN

Number and Numeration

Mathematical concepts can be grouped into several categories. The concepts which receive the most attention in the early years are those dealing with number and numeration. Such concepts answer questions related to "how many?" or "which one?" There are many specific skills related to these concepts. First, to be able to ascertain "how many" one must be able to organize objects into sets. In other words, "how many" is always "how many of what?" The most basic skill required to obtain skills of number and numeration is **classification.** If children cannot separate one type of object from another, they cannot begin to determine how many of each there are.

Classification is also important as a basis for children's understanding of part-whole relationships. For example, blue triangles and red triangles are both subsets of the general class of triangles. Addition, subtraction, and fractions all involve part-whole relationships which are logically similar to the triangle illustration.

As soon as children can classify objects they can obtain relative ideas of "how many" by matching objects from one set with objects from another set. This is called **matching one to one.** An absolute answer to the question of "how many" is not obtained, but answers to questions about which group has more and which less can be. Concepts of **equivalence** and **non-equivalence** enter in here. Such questions are very basic and do not require that children know names for numbers or that they be able to count.

The next skills involve **recognition and naming of number properties.** A child learns to recognize a set of 1, a set of 2, and so on. Recognizing and naming sets in order as they increase by one is called **counting.** Many four and five year old children can say the numerals from 1 to 10 in order, and they sometimes go around asking everyone to listen as they count. Usually, this is not rational counting. The child who says the numerals in order with ease may not be able to count accurately a group of four objects. In such cases children typically use all the numerals they know, often ten, even though there are but four objects. Their problem is that they cannot match the set of numerals with the set of objects. They need much experience in counting concrete objects if they are to learn to count accurately.

A child who has a grasp of sets with different number properties, and can count, can begin to **combine** and **separate** sets. These skills build a concrete basis for the operations on number which we know as addition and multiplication (combining), and subtraction and division (separating). Even children four or five years of age can gain an understanding of the relationships among numbers *if* they have concrete objects to manipulate. They can put sets together and determine how many there are altogether, and they can take sets apart to determine all the different ways any set can be made. Too often, young children are drilled in counting to 10, 20, 30, or some other number, while relationships among numbers are ignored.

These relationships among numbers are particularly important when one reaches 10 in counting. In our **base-ten** number system we regroup in tens. For example, eleven is one group of ten and one group of one. Children can develop an understanding of the composition of eleven, twelve, or thirteen right from the start. They might even learn the names "ten and one," "ten and two," "ten and three," and so on, along with their more common counting names.

All of the above skills are expanded and extended in two ways as children gain more experience with number. On the one hand, they become familiar with larger numbers. They count to 50 instead of 20 and know that 50 has 5 tens and 2 twenty-fives. On the other hand, children become familiar with ways to use written symbols to represent what they had formerly symbolized only verbally.

Written symbols are simply representations for verbal symbols. Young children should first manipulate concrete objects and use *verbal* symbols to represent relationships they discover. Children can understand the written symbols only if they understand the verbal symbols for which the written symbols stand; moreover, both types of symbols make sense only when children understand the physical relationships that they represent.

It is appropriate for children to learn to **read numerals** after a basis for these has been developed through actions and verbal labeling. When a child can recognize and construct sets of one, two, or three objects, and can name these, the written symbols that represent these sets would have some meaning for the child. When a child can count by ones to fifteen, and knows from experiences such as using a pegboard that "one whole row of pegs and five pegs in a second row are fifteen altogether," the written symbol to represent fifteen would also have some meaning.

Learning to **write numerals** should follow extensive experience in using and learning to read written symbols. Children who cannot recognize and name a set of ten objects, or who cannot read the written numeral, might gain some perceptual motor skill from exercises in writing the numeral 10, but would learn very little about mathematics.

Children will also need to learn to read written symbols other than numerals. These symbols do not represent number properties, but actions that are to be performed on numbers. At first, these will include the addition sign ($+$), subtraction sign ($-$), and the equal sign ($=$). None of these should be introduced until the child has had extensive practice with the manipulations which these signs represent. Practice with objects, for example, would utilize verbal descriptions such as "four *and* five *make* nine altogether."

Still another concept which will be encountered as children begin reading and writing numerals is **place value.** Place value is a technique for indicating the value of a numeral when it is written down. For example, a "2" might have a value of 2 tens or 2 hundreds or 2 ones depending on its position or place. Since our number system is based on groups of ten, the value of any numeral is either itself (ones), ten times itself (tens), or multiples of ten times itself (hundreds, thousands, etc.). Children will need to be told which is the ones' place, the tens' place, and so on. They should have a good background for understanding the relationship of one place to another if grouping in tens and ones has been stressed from the beginning when dealing with numbers greater than 10. For example, if a child knows that 11 can also be called "10 and 1," it is an easy transition to understand that when it is written, a 1 is placed in the tens' place and another 1 is placed in the ones' place.

Other skill areas go hand in hand with the child's expanding grasp of number. First, there are the skills that have been known as **facts.** There are facts of addition, subtraction, multiplication, and division. These are all the possible combinations of each of the numbers from 0 to 9 for each of the four operations. Addition facts include 1 and 1, 1 and 2, 1 and 3, etc. Subtraction facts include 3 take away 1, 2 take away 1, 1 take away 1, etc. Multiplication facts include one group of 1, two groups of 1, three groups of 1, and so on, while division facts include how many groups of 1 there are in 3, how many groups of 1 there are in 2, how many groups of 1 there are in 1, etc. All of the facts result from and have their basis in the manipulation of objects (see discussion about combining and separating objects on page 164). What we usually think of as facts, however, are these manipulations in symbolized form such as $5 + 2 = 7, 4 - 2 = 2$. One goal of a mathematics program in the primary grades should be to help children gain facility with the facts in symbolized form. They should understand *in action*, however, what the different operations are. They should know that addition involves combining sets, that subtraction involves separating sets, that multiplication involves combining *equal* sets, and that division involves separating a set into *equal* sub-sets. Without such understandings, facts will not have much meaning for children and a great deal of rote drill will be required to learn them. When children understand the basis for the facts, they have a framework from which to remember them, and though practice is still required, less will usually suffice.

A final skill which children must master as they begin to manipulate symbols on paper is the use of **algorithms**. These are rules specific to each of the four operations on number (addition, subtraction, multiplication, and division). Algorithms are based on the facts for each operation and on the concept of place value. For example, when we add two-digit numbers such as 28 and 15, there are rules about starting with the column on the right and about carrying the 10 ones that result from the addition of 8 and 5. Children who have received adequate experience in practicing facts and working with place value should adopt algorithms with relative ease. Teachers may wish to refer to any good text on elementary mathematics to review algorithms.

Measurement

A second concept area which is stressed in the mathematics instruction of young children is measurement. Measurement, like number and numeration, deals with questions of how many and how much. In measurement, however, the quantity to be assessed is continuous rather than discrete. In number and numeration one deals with separate (discrete) objects which are combined or separated in order to ascertain how many, whereas in measurement one deals with a whole something (continuous) which is then described in terms of smaller units.

DIRECT MEASUREMENT. There are four general areas of direct measurement with which young children should gain familiarity: (1) length, (2) weight, (3) volume, and (4) area. Through measurement activities children will gain concepts of length distinct from that of weight, a concept of weight distinct from that of volume, and a concept of area distinct from that of volume.

Children must also understand **units** if they are to understand measurement. The purpose of measurement is to describe something in terms of smaller parts of itself. In order to do this, smaller pieces, or units, must be used to talk about the larger pieces. Although the adult world uses **standard units** such as inches, feet, yards, or meters, anything can be used as a unit as long as it possesses the distinctive characteristic of the object being measured. For example, a piece of string, a pencil, or a popsicle stick could be used as units of measure for length. Marbles, golf tees, or washers could be used as units of measure of weight. Squares of paper, mosaic tile, or index cards could be used as units for the measurement of area.

Children need experience with **non-standard units** before they use standard units. This is important because children need to see the separate pieces that make up a measurement tool. This is often vague when standard units are used at the beginning. For example, children have a difficult time understanding what an inch is when their only exposure to inches is a 12-inch ruler.

The use of non-standard units also permits children to gain appreciation for the practicality of standard units. Children can see for themselves that it is difficult to talk about how long something is when measured with toothpicks by one person and with popsicle sticks by someone else. It is the use of standard units that enables us to communicate clearly with someone about the quantity of an object. After children have experiences with non-standard units, they can be introduced to standard units.

Another measurement concept involves the **selection of appropriate units** for the object being measured. This concept requires an understanding of the relationship between the size of the unit and the accuracy of the measurement, as well as the size of the unit and the effort required to obtain the measurement. For example, it is much more tedious to measure the length of a room with a toothpick than with a foot long dowel rod, although the toothpick would result in the more accurate measurement. This conflict between effort and accuracy could be resolved by measuring with the dowel rod until a complete length no longer fits, and then finishing up with toothpicks. This is how a system of measurement is designed to work. We can describe the length of a room by stating that it is two meters and three centimeters long. Typically, the measurement is done with a yard or meter stick and reported in feet and inches or meters and centimeters. When children use unit blocks to build a road across the room and you see that it is 7 long blocks and 2 short blocks long, teachers know they are getting the basis of this idea.

INDIRECT MEASUREMENT. The four areas of measurement discussed above deal with *direct* measurement of quantity of one thing in relation to another. There are other areas of measuresment which involve indirect assessments because the quantity to be measured is not concrete. Time and temperature are non-concrete quantities whose measurement is introduced to young children.

Most children learn to "tell" time and read a thermometer during the first few years of elementary school. These competencies do not, however, indicate that children understand the mathematics of measuring time and temperature. They indicate only that children have learned to read clocks and thermometers.

In order to understand the difference between reading and understanding the measurement of time and temperature, it might be helpful to discuss the development of children's concepts of time. This development has been illustrated in research conducted by Piaget.[3]

Piaget's research indicates that preprimary children think tools for measuring time are controlled by their own actions. They think that if they swing their arm fast sand will fall through a sand timer faster than if they swing their arm slowly. They have no concept of *objective* time separate from their own *subjective* time.

It is not surprising that the young child should view time subjectively. Time seems to vary depending on what we are doing. Even adults experience days when time seems to either drag or fly. Time is perceived psychologically, and these perceptions often do not match the objective measurements of clocks. Therefore, preschool children who have had little experience with tools for objectifying time view it as purely subjective.

Primary age children realize that the time it takes for a clock to move a certain distance or for the sand to run out of a sand timer is the same regardless of the speed of any actions they might perform. Their concept of time is still not entirely accurate, however. For example, if one were to place two race tracks (one short, one long) on a table and race two cars down these, making sure that they started and stopped at the same time, most primary children would probably declare that the car on the longer track took more time than the other car to move down the track. They would not understand that cars can move different distances in the same time. They lack a concept of speed which would resolve the conflict.

In terms of clocks, primary children think it takes longer for the hands of a clock with a large face to go from one numeral to another than it takes the hands of a clock with a smaller face. This indicates that even for the primary child, time is still not completely objective. Though it is no longer connected to the child's actions, it is thought to reside in the timepieces themselves, as if each were keeping its own time.

It is not until the children reach the age of nine or ten that they fully understand that time is objective and that timepieces all keep the same time. In a sense, children have to solve a conservation problem in order to understand time. They must come to understand that time is not altered by the speed of their own actions or by the distance an object (clock hands) must cover.

Until children have a stable concept of time, they will find it difficult to understand how time is divided. As long as time itself is thought to vary depending on irrelevant factors such as the space between the

[3]J. Piaget, *The Child's Conception of Time* (New York: Ballantine Books, 1971).

numbers of the clock face, seconds, minutes, and hours will have little accurate meaning.

Although the development of children's understanding of temperature has not been investigated, one would suspect that a sequence similar to that for time is operating. In order to help children develop concepts necessary for comprehending the measurement of time and temperature, teachers should concentrate on developing the following understandings:

1. Time and temperature are not controlled by one's own actions or feelings;
2. Time and temperature are independent of the size of the tools used to measure them;
3. Different devices for measuring time and temperature can be synchronized so that they measure the same time and temperature.

The above understandings should be viewed as additions to what children are already being taught about time and temperature, because children do need to learn to tell time and read a thermometer. The concepts discussed here, however, deal specifically with the mathematics of measuring time and temperature, and children should understand this mathematical aspect also.

Geometry

Concepts related to geometry are also recognized as appropriate learnings for young children. It should quickly be pointed out that the formal geometry known to most adults is not what is being suggested for inclusion in mathematics instruction of young children. The unique cognitive abilities of young children do not equip them for dealing with logical proofs. Young children can learn about geometric concepts on a concrete level, however.

Understandings related to geometry would include the ability to **identify geometric figures and solids.** Children can recognize and sort into like shapes circles, squares, and triangles as early as three years of age and will learn the names readily. By five, children will typically be able to describe these basic shapes—circles are round, squares have four sides, and triangles have three. Squares and rectangles may be confused, however, and while children may see that an equilateral triangle does not look like a scalene triangle, they will not typically understand exactly what the difference is.

Geometric solids are distinguishable on the basis of the characteristics of their surfaces. Surfaces of solids are either flat or curved. Some solids have only flat surfaces (cubes, pyramids, rectangular prisms) and some have both flat and curved surfaces (cones, cylinders) whereas a sphere has only one curved surface.

Geometry competencies for young children would also include the **ability to construct geometric figures and solids.** Through construction activities, children should also come to **understand how different geometric figures and solids are related.**

Money

Children should also develop an understanding of money. First, there is the **recognition and naming of common coins and bills.** Second, there is the understanding of the **value of each piece of money.** This involves an understanding of number and the association of specific number values with specific pieces of money. Third, there is the understanding of the **exchange rate of one coin for another** or of **coins for a bill,** or of **one bill for others.** These understandings require many skills in number and numeration, including counting, conservation of number, addition, subtraction, and base ten. This means that preschool children will do well to recognize and name common coins and bills and learn the value of the smaller coins. Few preschool children will understand that a quarter is more money than fifteen pennies, and wise teachers do not waste their time trying to convince them.

ACTIVITIES FOR MATHEMATICS INSTRUCTION

The remainder of this chapter deals with ideas for classroom mathematics instruction. The organization of the practical ideas follows the order in which the mathematical concepts and skills have been presented. The activities included are of two types. Some are those which would be planned and designed for the specific purpose of providing children with opportunities to learn or practice a particular skill. Other activities are ones which might be planned to meet goals which may not be concerned primarily with mathematics, but from which mathematical learnings can be abstracted if the teacher is aware of their potential.

Number and Numeration

ACTIVITIES TO HELP CHILDREN
DEVELOP COMPETENCE IN CLASSIFICATION

1. Activity: Button bin (PP)

Materials: A large container such as a plastic ice-cream carton; a large variety of buttons which vary on as many attributes as possible, such as size, shape, color, and material; a flat container with separated spaces. (Egg cartons or trays used to separate layers of apple or orange crates work well.)

Procedure: Make container of buttons and trays available for children to work with. Verbal guidance such as "put the ones you think are alike together," should be ample for most children. Sometimes more guidance is necessary to help a child start. To do this, ask the child to choose a button and place it in a space. Then you select a button which is similar and place it in the same space, stating how they are alike. This should get the child started.

2. *Activity:* Making necklaces (PP)

Materials: Wooden beads in various colors and shapes; shoestrings for stringing the beads.

Procedure: Have a container with a variety of beads available for children to work with. Guidance would include questions such as "Can you make a necklace with just three kinds of beads?" or "Can you make a necklace of beads that are all alike in one way, two ways, three ways?"

3. *Activity:* Junk box (PP)

Materials: Odds and ends of stuff which might include a clothespin, several bottle caps, a pencil, an empty pharmacy bottle, a paper clip, a safety pin, a golf tee, several corks, several pebbles, a hickory nut, a toothpick, etc.; several small containers to sort objects into.

Procedure: Guidance should include asking the children to "put together those objects which they think belong together." It is important that the children be allowed to select their own criteria for the classes, although the guiding adult should inquire from time to time what the criteria are by asking, "Why did you put these together?"

4. *Activity:* Seed box (PP)

Materials: A collection of different kinds of seeds, including popcorn, field corn, lima beans, apple, sunflower seeds, pumpkin seeds, kidney beans, yellow-eyed beans, peas etc.; a container for the seeds; container with separated spaces such as an egg carton, to sort seeds into.

Procedure: Have seeds and container for sorting available. Guidance should include asking children to put together the ones that are alike.

5. *Activity:* Fabric box (PP)

> **Materials:** Twenty or thirty 3″ × 3″ pieces of tagboard. Samples of fabric cut into 2½″ × 2½″ squares mounted on the tagboard squares with rubber cement. Fabric pieces should include stripes, plaids, polka dots, solids, etc. Mounted fabric squares should be stored in the classroom in a suitable box.
>
> **Procedure:** Suggest that children put together the ones they think are alike. There will be a variety of ways in which this can be done, depending, on whether a child uses color, pattern, or some other attribute as the basis for grouping. Guidance should include asking children why they placed certain pieces together.
>
> **Suggestions and Variations:** Wallpaper samples work as well as fabric samples. A set of each is useful. One can be used for awhile and put away when the other is brought out. This change of material can revitalize the activity and make it of interest to children who need more practice.

6. *Activity:* Paper shapes (PP–P)

Materials: Red, yellow, and blue construction paper to make the following:

> 2 large triangles of each color
> 2 middle-sized triangles of each color
> 2 small triangles of each color
> (same as above for circles)
> (same as above for squares)

> **Procedure:** Guidance would include asking children to put together the shapes they think are alike. After a child has classified the shapes one way, the teacher might suggest thinking of another way it could be done.

7. *Activity:* Dramatic play (PP)

> **Materials:** Equipment to simulate a kitchen setting, including a refrigerator, stove, cabinet, table, and small utensils; empty food containers with labels still on, including cereal boxes, cake-mix boxes, vegetable cans, fruit cans, spice containers, and baby-food jars.
>
> **Procedure:** Ask children to bring containers for kitchen play, Suggest children "put them away" in the kitchen play area when they bring them. Ask questions such as "What should we put the corn

can next to? or "Do we have any other cereal boxes yet that we might put that new one with?"

Suggestions and Variations: Guidance will occasionally be needed at clean-up time to make sure the food containers are organized. It can help to ask a specific child to check the kitchen to make sure the shelves or cabinets are straightened up. The teacher can achieve the same goal by stopping by for a minute or two during clean-up and "helping." The teacher can talk while helping and make comments such as "Let's see, that's a cereal box. It will go up here with the others." Thus, through the teacher's modeling, children learn to put the containers away in this manner also.

ACTIVITIES TO HELP CHILDREN
DEVELOP COMPETENCE IN MATCHING ONE TO ONE

1. *Activity:*   Felt board (PP)

   Materials: Several different felt cutouts with multiple copies of each; felt board.
   Procedure: Have felt boards and felt cutouts available for children's use. Guidance would include questions such as "Are there as many _____ as _____?"

2. *Activity:*   Getting dressed (PP)

   Materials: Boots, mittens, hats, coats, or whatever clothing is appropriate for weather and climatic conditions.
   Procedure: While helping children dress for outdoor play or for going home, comment about the fact there is one mitten for each hand, one boot for each foot, one hat for one head, one armhole for each arm, etc.

3. *Activity:*   Outdoor play (PP)

   Materials: Usual outdoor equipment such as swings, tricycles, old tires, sand toys, etc.
   Procedure: There is always a certain number of each piece of equipment, perhaps six swings, four tires, four tricycles, and three sand pails and shovels. The number of children who wish to use the equipment usually varies from day to day and from one time of day to another. Sometimes there are more children who want to play with a particular item than there are items available. At other times, there are more of the item than there are children demanding to use it, and at still other times the number of items and number of children are the same. Teachers can use these situations by verbaliz-

ing about them. "There are just enough sand pails to go around." "Do you suppose someone else would like a tricycle? I see we have an extra one right now with no one on it." "Well, let's see if we can't find something else to do for awhile. All of the swings are taken. We have more children than we have swings, so we'll have to take turns."

4. *Activity:* Matching jars and lids (PP)

   Materials: Various jars with lids to fit them. (Sometimes provide a lid for every jar; at other times provide more jars than lids or more lids than jars.)
   Procedure: Have materials available for children to use. Since they are familiar with jars and lids, they will usually begin matching them up by themselves. In the situation where the groups are not equivalent, teacher interaction to develop concepts of "more than," "less than," or equivalent and non-equivalent sets will be needed.

5. *Activity:* Fill the cups (PP)

   Materials: Egg cartons cut into pieces of one section, two sections, three sections, and so on; rocks, marbles, plastic discs, or other small objects to place in the sections; container to hold objects chosen.
   Procedure: Have materials available in math center. Guidance should include instruction to "give each cup an object." Because of the structure of the materials, the child will be matching a set of one cup with a set of one rock, a set of two cups with a set of two rocks, etc.

6. *Activity:* Dominoes (PP)

   Materials: Ordinary commercial dominoes, large dominoes made by educational equipment companies, or tagboard-card dominoes made by the teacher.
   Procedure: Have materials available for children to work with. Encourage children to place dominoes together so the ends with equal sets are matched. Such guidance can be given by stopping by while a child is working with dominoes and asking, "Can we find another domino which has as many dots on one end as this one has," or simply, "Can we find one like this?" as you point to what you mean. Often, children will select one domino which they think matches another, though in fact it has either more or fewer dots. This is a good opportunity to emphasize the concepts of equivalent and non-equivalent sets.
   Suggestions and Variations: Dominoes is a more difficult material

for matching one to one, because the dots from one set cannot actually be placed side by side or lined up with the dots of the second set. Children have to do the "lining up" with their eyes. Therefore, other materials might be used for awhile for this skill before dominoes are made available.

7. **Activity:** Beans and dots (PP)

    Materials: Eleven 3″ × 5″ tagboard cards. Have one card plain. Use a felt-tipped pen to place dots on the other cards so there is one card with one dot, one card with two dots, one card with three dots, on up to one card with ten dots. Provide a small covered container of dried beans. Provide a box which will hold the tagboard cards and container of beans.
    Procedure: Have materials available for children to work with. Guidance would include suggestions to put a bean on each dot of a card.

8. **Activity:** Set board (PP–P)

    Materials: Tagboard or poster board marked off into ten 1″ × 2″ sections. Draw sets of small triangles, circles, and squares in all of the sections. Cut ten 1″ × 2″ tagboard cards to fit over the sections on the set board. Draw sets on the cards to match those drawn on the set board.
    Procedure: The child matches the loose set cards with the sets drawn on the board.

9. **Activity:** Paper shapes (PP)

    Materials: The same materials described for this activity in the classification section (page 173).
    Procedure: Children can match objects from one set (i.e., red triangles, yellow squares, etc.) with objects of another set, (i.e., blue triangles, red squares, little circles etc.). To maximize learning, teacher interaction is necessary to initiate these comparisons of "more than," "less than," and "the same as."

10. **Activity:** Peg-boards (PP)

    Materials: Any of the commercial peg and peg-board sets.
    Procedure: Children almost invariably place pegs in the holes in the various rows. The teacher can interact with a child who is using these materials by asking questions such as "Can you make another line of pegs that has as many as this one?" or "Which of your lines has more?" or "Which of your lines has fewer?"

11. *Activity:* Snack time (PP)

Materials: Cups and napkins; napkins and straws with cartons if milk rather than juice is served.

Procedure: Select children to pass out napkins and cups, or napkins, milk, and straws. Allow children to obtain these supplies from their storage places rather than giving them pre-counted bunches. Young children will typically obtain a "bunch" and pass these out to children, then go back to obtain more and pass these out, until each child has all of the needed items. By using this procedure, children are matching the objects of one set (children) with objects of another set (straws, milk, or napkins) and come face to face with concepts of "less than," "more than," and "the same as."

12. *Activity:* Clean-up time (PP)

Materials: Any materials or objects in the room which have specific slots, holes, or spots for storage. For example, there is one pair of scissors for each section of the egg carton. There is a cap for each magic marker. There is a jar of paste for each contact-paper circle stuck on the shelf. There is one pencil for each hole in the pencil holder. These organization schemes provide children with experiences in matching one to one.

13. *Activity:* Find the shoes (PP)

Materials: A large box or basket; shoes from all the children in the class.

Procedure: At nap or a movement activity when shoes have been removed, put all shoes in a basket. Two or three children may match pairs and deliver pairs to owners.

Suggestions and Variations: This activity also involves practice in distinguishing right and left and in tying shoes. Comparison of size of shoe with size of foot is also involved.

ACTIVITIES TO HELP CHILDREN DEVELOP COMPETENCE IN RECOGNIZING AND NAMING SETS AND IN COUNTING

Any of the activities and experiences in the classification and matching-one-to-one sections can also be used for developing the competencies here. Guidance, however, would need to include different questions. For example, a classification question might be "Can you put all of the ones that are alike in some way together?" whereas a matching-one-to-one question might be "Can you make a row here that has as many as that row over there?" A question related to helping children recognize and name sets might be "How many are there here?" A similar question would encourage counting. The materials can be the same in each case, but the questions must vary if the child is to learn different skills.

1. *Activity:* Set cards (PP–P)

   Materials: One-inch cubes; 24 tagboard cards, each 7″ × 6″; one-inch graph paper run on ditto, cut into 6″ × 5″ rectangles. (Glue graph paper on one side of tagboard cards.) Prepare three cards for each number from 2 to 10 by coloring different arrangements of squares (See Figure 18.)

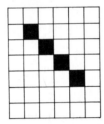 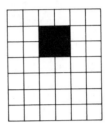 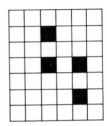

Figure 18. Set cards.

   Procedure: Child tries to find the cards which have the same number. Guidance would include asking the child to find cards with the same number and helping the child name the number. Guidance would also include encouraging the child to check to make sure the cards are the same by placing cubes over the squares first on one card, and then on the other two. It is important that the child use the *same* cubes on all cards to stress the idea that the cards all represent the same number.

   Suggestions and Variations: It is not wise to include all of the cards at once with preprimary children. Cards for number three through six might be enough to start. It is helpful to color code each set of cards. For example, the cards for number 4 might have green squares, while the cards for number 5 might have blue squares. If the cards are color coded, it is particularly important to use the blocks for checking, so that children pay attention to the number aspects of the cards and not just the color.

2. *Activity:* Numeral call (PP–P)

   Materials: Twenty 3″ × 5″ tagboard cards, each with a picture of a set of objects pasted on one side (sets 1 through 9).

   Procedure: Two or three children may work with the materials. Cards are placed face down in a deck. Children take turns taking a card and naming the number corresponding to the set which is on it. A child who names the set correctly, may keep the cards. A child who cannot name the set must return the card to the bottom of the deck.

Suggestions and Variations: Catalogues and magazines are good sources for pictures of sets of objects. The cards will last longer if they are covered with contact paper or if they are laminated.

3. *Activity:* Snack time (PP–P)

Materials: Cups, cookies, straws, napkins; any of the items which are used at snack time.

Procedure: Children can be selected to help pass items to the rest of the children. Earlier, in the section on matching one to one, it was suggested that children determine the correct amount of any item simply by matching items with children. Later, helpers can count the children and then count out the required number of items. In this way they use a different skill: counting.

Suggestions and Variations: Young children should be encouraged to use the matching-one-to-one method before they switch to the counting method. It's a good idea for one child at each table to be responsible for the children at the table. In this way the numbers do not get so large. Four-year-olds may have a difficult time counting out items for a group of 25 children, but if there were four tables of children, a child would be better able to cope with counting six items.

4. *Activity:* Outdoor play (PP)

Materials: All outdoor equipment.

Procedure: Use opportunities to help children recognize the number properties of sets of outdoor equipment. For example, perhaps there are five old tires, six swings, and three tricycles. Children can also be encouraged to count the number of "cupcakes" they make out of sand in the sandbox, the number of rungs they climb on a ladder, the number of times they catch a ball, and so on.

5. *Activity:* Beanbag toss (PP–P)

Materials: Several beanbags or small balls. A basket or box to toss beanbags into.

Procedure: Guidance would include helping children set up an area for the beanbag toss game. Obviously, nothing should be in the path of the thrown object. The game should be limited to two or three children at a time. A chalkboard or piece of paper can be used to keep score. Every time a child is able to toss the beanbag into the container, a tally is placed beside the student's name. At the end of the game, the tallies are counted to see who is the winner.

6. *Activity:* Group time (PP–P)

   Materials: Children in class
   Procedure: Take a couple of minutes to count all the children with brown hair, red shoes, blue slacks, blond hair, curly hair, straight hair, etc.

ACTIVITIES TO HELP CHILDREN DEVELOP COMPETENCE IN READING NUMERALS AND IN ASSOCIATING THEM WITH THE NUMBERS THEY REPRESENT

1. *Activity:* Numeral concentration game (PP)

   Materials: Twenty 3″ × 5″ tagboard cards. (Write one numeral on each card so there are two cards each for every numeral from 0 to 9. Store the cards in a small box or clasp envelope.)
   Procedure: Two or three children may play. Cards should be placed face down. Children take turns turning over two cards at a time. If the cards are identical, the child may keep them. If they are not identical, the child must return them face down to the center of the table. The game continues until all pairs have been picked up.
   Suggestions and Variations: An individual child can use the materials. The child searches through the cards and matches up the pairs. Regular playing cards may be used.

2. *Activity:* Numeral draw card game (PP)

   Materials: Forty 3″ × 5″ tagboard cards. (Write one numeral on each card to make four cards for every numeral from 0 to 9. Store cards in a small box or clasp envelope.)
   Procedure: Two or four children may play. Shuffle cards and deal four to each child. Place remaining cards in the center of the players as the deck. Players take turns drawing one card from the deck and discarding one card from their hand. Players who have three of a kind may place cards from his hand on the table. If a player draws the fourth of a kind after placing three down, the fourth may be added to the group of three. The game is won either by the first player to run out of cards by placing them on the table or by the player holding the fewest cards when the deck runs out.
   Suggestions and Variations: Three-year-olds in particular have trouble playing games because it is difficult for them to follow rules, even when these are very simple. Therefore, games are best to use

with older preprimary and primary children rather than young preprimary children.

3. *Activity:* Sandpaper numerals (PP)

Materials: Medium coarse sandpaper and 4″ × 5″ squares of cardboard cut from cardboard boxes. (Cut numerals out of the sandpaper and glue them with rubber cement or white glue onto the cardboard squares. Store the cards in a box or clasp envelope.)

Procedure: Encourage children to run their fingers along the outline of the numerals. Provide the name of the numeral verbally as you stop by to work with the children.

Suggestions and Variations: Cut squares out of newsprint the same size as the cardboard the numerals are mounted on. Provide paper clips for holding the newsprint over the numeral. Provide crayons for children to make rubbings of the numerals. Children can make one for each numeral and staple them together to make their own books.

Indoor-outdoor carpet samples may be used instead of sandpaper.

4. *Activity:* Felt numerals and felt cutouts (PP–P)

Materials: Felt board, felt numerals, and felt cutouts. (Select felt cutouts so that different quantities of each type are available. For example, six ducks, three stars, one rabbit, eight circles, seven apples, four squares, and five rectangles might be provided.)

Procedure: Children can be encouraged to place the numerals and cutouts on the felt board. Guidance should include providing the numeral name and helping to match the numerals with the proper sets.

Suggestions and Variations: A "felt" board can be made by attaching a piece of cotton flannel to a section of cardboard with rubber cement. Flannel can also be attached with staples, thumb tacks, or tape to a low bulletin board, the back of a book shelf, or the side of a metal cabinet. Provide only one or two of each felt numeral. A complete set is too many to have out at once.

5. *Activity:* Junk and numeral cards (PP–P)

Materials: Ten 3″ × 5″ tagboard cards with the numerals 1 through 10 written on them with a felt-tipped marker; a box of objects such as bottle caps, acorns, golf tees, paper clips, corks, etc. (Provide different quantities of some of the objects. For example, one might provide one clothespin and one small pencil, two acorns, two golf tees, three corks, four paper clips, five dried beans and five paper fasteners, etc.)

Procedure: Child classifies objects and puts identical ones together. Child matches numeral cards with sets having that number property. Guidance would include questions such as "Which ones are alike?" "How many are in this group?" and "Which card would you place with this group?"

6. *Activity:* Set board (PP–P)

   Materials: Use the set board from the set board activity on page 176. Make numeral cards to fit over the squared sections of the board.
   Procedure: Encourage the child to match the numeral cards with the sets on the board. The teacher can stop by to watch, or check the board when the child finishes.

7. *Activity:* Rook deck pick-up (PP–P)

   Materials: Rook deck cards.
   Procedure: Two children may play. Cards are placed face down on the table. Children take turns turning over one card at a time. First child to call out numeral name gets to keep the card. Child who has the most in the end wins.
   Suggestions and Variations: For younger children, do not include cards with numerals over 10 until they can identify the first ten with ease and can count to 20.

8. *Activity:* Puzzle cards (PP–P)

   Materials: A set of puzzle cards with numerals 0–9 on one-half and corresponding sets and with dots or pictures of objects or animals on the other half. (For instructions on making puzzle cards, see Activity #2 in activities for sight vocabulary in Chapter IV.)
   Procedure: Place in a box in math center. As this is a self-correcting activity, no particular instructions are necessary. Sets may be extended to 12 for older children.

ACTIVITIES TO HELP CHILDREN GAIN COMPETENCIES IN COMBINING AND SEPARATING SETS

1. *Activity:* Pegboards (PP–P)

   Materials: Pegs and peg-boards.
   Procedure: The teacher should ask a child who is working with the peg-board questions such as "How many pegs would you have if you put the two red ones and the four blue ones together?" or "How many would there be altogether if we put two pegs in each row?" or "How many would you have left if you took the three blue ones out

of the board?" or "How many groups of two do you think you could make from the pegs you have in the board?"

2. *Activity:* Cubes (PP–P)

   Materials: Any type of commercial cubes. (Those available in colors are better for this than plain ones because the different colors differentiate between sets.)

   Procedure: Encourage children to combine and separate the blocks in different ways. The same questions used with the peg-board activity are appropriate here also.

3. *Activity:* Jar lids and beans (K–P)

   Materials: Twelve baby-food jar lids, ten cardboard discs cut to fit loosely inside ten of the lids. (Label each with a numeral so there is one each for the numerals 1 through 10.) Any type of dried beans. Small containers with a lid for the beans; larger box to hold both lids and the container of beans.

   Procedure: The child starts with the lid labeled "1" and works up through the lid labeled "10." The child places as many beans in the lid as the label says. The child must then separate these beans into the two non-labeled lids in as many different ways as he can. The child should make drawings of his discoveries.

   Suggestions and Variations: The teacher can prepare paper with circles to represent the lids already drawn so the child's task of recording is simplified. Children then need only to draw pictures of the beans. Young children will often form twice the number of combinations for a number because they will consider $4 + 1$ and $1 + 4$ to be different ways to make "5." This introduces children to the concept of commutativity.

   The use of three lids rather than two can be used to introduce children to the idea of associativity. The materials can also be altered in order to stress addition of equal sets (multiplication). Provide 30 lids and 30 cardboard inserts. Label the inserts to make five each for numerals 1 through 6. Prepare dittoed record forms as shown in Figure 19.

   Children fill the lids with beans according to the numeral in the lid. The child counts the number of beans in lids in each row to determine what one group of one equals, two groups of one equal, three groups of one equal, etc.

4. *Activity:* Pill bottles (K–P)

   Materials: Ten cylindrical plastic pill bottles with plastic slip-on lids; slips of construction paper or tagboard cut to stand in middle

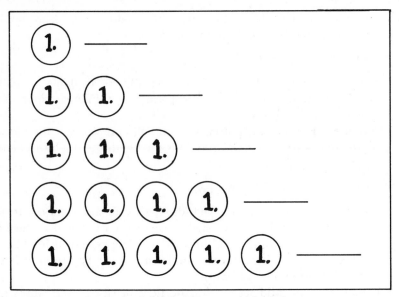

Figure 19. Record form for jar lids with numerical labels.

and act as separator; small beans or pebbles; container for beans or pebbles.

Procedure: Print numerals from 2 to 10 on dividers and place one in each bottle. Child counts number of beans indicated by numeral in each bottle, puts beans in bottles, and places lid on each. Child shakes bottles. If dividers are correct size, some beans should fall on each side. Child should then count the number on each side, and make a record of any discoveries by either drawing or writing them.

ACTVITIES TO HELP CHILDREN GAIN COMPETENCIES IN WORKING WITH BASE TEN

1. Activity: Peg-boards (PP–P)

Materials: Any of the commercial peg and peg-board materials.

Procedure: The structure of the materials encourages children to regroup in tens. As children fill rows with pegs, the teacher can sometimes ask them to count all the pegs. Perhaps they have filled one row and have placed three pegs in the next. By asking that they count all the pegs, they begin to get the idea that 13 is made of 1 group of tens and 3 ones. The teacher should even verbalize this by saying, "Oh, 13 has one group of tens, and 3 ones." Later, the teacher can ask children to make different numbers, such as 15, 21,

25, etc. In this way children will gain an idea of the composition of these numbers in terms of groups of tens and ones.

Suggestions and Variations: Teachers should remember that for a long time, young children (3-year-olds in particular) just enjoy placing the pegs in the pegboard. They often make groups of different colors. During this first exploratory stage, teachers should be careful not to force children to conceptualize the mathematical concepts that may be apparent in what they are doing. When it appears that children have had sufficient time to explore, and at the point where they are filling each row before placing pegs in the next row, the teacher can ask the children how many pegs there are in each row. The child needs to have a solid understanding that there are ten pegs in each row before he can appreciate the composition of numbers larger than ten.

2. *Activity:* Base-ten cards (K–P)

Materials: Make a set of tagboard cards with the same dimensions as the pegboards, or smaller ones made to scale. Make dots on each card to correspond to any numbers from 11 to 99.

Procedure: Child names the number represented by the dots on the cards by stating the number of tens and ones drawn in. For example, the sample card shown in Figure 20 would be called "2 tens and 1 one."

Child can also be asked to give the counting name for the number, which in this case would be twenty-one.

Suggestions and Variations: Children can work with these cards on a one-to-one basis with an adult or with each other. A game can be

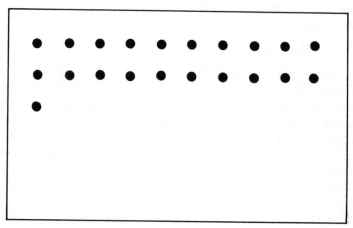

Figure 20. Base ten cards.

played by turning all cards face down in a pile. Children can take turns turning a card over and naming it. They may keep those they name corectly. The winner is the one who has the most at the end of the game.

3. *Activity:* Popsicle-stick numbers (P)

   Materials: At least 100 popsicle sticks; rubber bands.
   Procedure: Ask the children to pick a number. Once they have decided what number they would like to make, they count out that many popsicle sticks. They then group these in tens by placing a rubber band around each bunch. They can *see* what their number looks like in base ten. The teacher should provide labels such as "two tens and three ones."

ACTIVITIES TO HELP CHILDREN DEVELOP COMPETENCE IN ADDITION, SUBTRACTION, MULTIPLICATION, AND DIVISION FACTS

1. *Activity:* Dominoes (P)

   Materials: Commercially made dominoes or teacher-made domino cards.
   Procedure: Two children may play. The dominoes are divided between them. Each child selects a number between 1 and 10. The children alternate turns and may place one domino at either end of the line of dominoes to make their number. They may use any fact they can to make their number. For example, if a child's number is 6, and one of the end dominoes is 2, a child could make 6 by matching the 2 with a 4 and saying, "4 and 2 make 6," or by matching the 2 with an 8 and saying, "8 take away 2 makes 6." The first child to run out of dominoes wins.

2. *Activity:* Mixed-up odometer (P)

   Materials: A die; a sturdy box lid at least 2″ deep and with one side at least 10 inches long; fifty tagboard cards 2″ × 1½″ with a numeral from 0 to 9 written on each so there are five cards for each numeral; five small metal notebook rings. (Use a paper punch to make one hole in the top of each numeral card and five holes at equal intervals on one side of the box lid. Mix up the numeral cards and then attach ten to each of the five metal notebook rings. Attach rings and numeral cards to holes punched in lid so numerals face out.)
   Procedure: Two children may play. Children take turns tossing the die into the box lid. The child must make the number shown on

the die in any way he can with the numeral cards by using any addition, subtraction, multiplication, or division fact, and may use one or more cards. When a card has been used, it is flipped over the box lid. A child who can keep making the number on the die may keep flipping the cards. When a child can no longer make the number, all the cards are flipped back and it is the other child's turn to throw the die. A tally is kept for each child to indicate the number of ways the number was made on each turn. The child with the most tallies at the end of five or ten rounds wins.

3. *Activity:* Multiplication race (P)

   Materials: Pair of dice labeled with numerals; small plastic discs in various colors or other small objects suitable for markers; game board made of heavy cardboard. (Draw "road" or "track" to wind around board. Mark road into small segments so that the road contains at least 150 segments. Label the end segments "start" and "finish.")

   Procedure: Two or four children may play. Children take turns throwing the dice, determining the product of the two numbers thrown, and moving their marker that many spaces. The first child to reach the finish line wins.

   Suggestions and Variations: The same game can be used to practice addition, subtraction or division facts. It is interesting to play using division facts because a player can only make a move after rolling two numbers, one of which can be *evenly* divided by the other.

4. *Activity:* Card train (P)

   Materials: Thirty 3" × 5" tagboard cards numbered from one to nine.

   Procedure: Two or three children may play. All cards are placed in a deck. One card is turned over to start. Then children take turns drawing a card and putting it down next to the last card played. The child must state the answer to the fact represented by the two cards. Addition, subtraction, and multiplication facts may be practiced with this game. Players who cannot state the needed facts accurately must keep the cards they draw. The object is to end the game holding as few cards as possible.

ACTIVITIES TO HELP CHILDREN GAIN COMPETENCIES IN USING PLACE VALUE

1. *Activity:* Finding the tens and ones (P)

   Materials: Popsicle sticks; rubber bands; numeral cards (11 through 50); tens and ones chart made by drawing a line down the center of an 8½″ × 11″ piece of white construction paper and labeling the left side "TENS" and the right side "ONES."

Procedure: Two children can work together, or individual children can work. Child draws a numeral card and counts out that many sticks. Child then groups the sticks in bundles of ten and places the bundles of tens in the tens' space on the chart and the ones in the ones' place on the chart.

2. **Activity:** Odometer race (P)

Materials: Popsicle sticks; rubber bands; sturdy box lid at least 2″ deep and with one side at least 5″ long; 30 tagboard cards 2″ × 1½″ with numerals 0 through 9 written on them (three cards for each numeral); three small metal notebook rings. (Use a paper punch to make holes in tagboard cards and in the box lid. Order the numerals facing out so that "9" is in the back, and "0" is in the front.)

Procedure: Two children may work at once. A child throws the dice, picks up that many popsicle sticks, and groups them into ones and tens using the rubber bands to hold the tens in bunches. Child then flips the numeral cards so they represent that number. Player then passes the popsicle bundles to the other child who throws the dice, organizes the additional sticks into ones and tens and flips the odometer to represent the new number. This continues until the odometer reaches 100. The child holding the sticks when 100 is reached wins.

3. **Activity:** Pegboard (P)

Materials: Pegs and peg-board; pencil and paper.

Procedure: Two children work together. One child places pegs in the peg board to make a number. The second child must write on a paper the numeral which represents that number. The children then exchange tasks. Children gain practice in writing two-digit numerals and thus use the concept of place value.

Measurement

ACTIVITIES AND EXPERIENCES TO HELP CHILDREN DEVELOP COMPETENCE IN INVESTIGATING LENGTH

1. **Activity:** Body drawings (PP–K)

Materials: Roll of butcher paper; crayons.

Procedure: Children place a length of paper on the floor. They then lie on it and have another child or the teacher trace around them. They then color the outline in. Length is highlighted if paper is prepared in a variety of lengths from which children choose one on which they will "fit."

2. *Activity:* Measuring ourselves (PP–K)

   Materials: White paper, 36″ wide or wider. (Cut a length as long as tallest teacher in class. Mount lengthwise on the wall. Colored construction paper cut into 1″ × 3″ rectangles, and 1″ × 12″ rectangles. Use one color for each size strip.)

   Procedure: Children stand with their backs against the paper. The teacher makes a mark just over their heads. The teacher then makes a 1″-wide line from this mark to the floor (a yardstick or meter stick is handy for this). The child then fills in the height-mark with pieces of colored construction paper. Some children will paste all 1″ × 3″ strips on the paper. Others will use all 1″ × 12″ strips, while others will use a variety of sizes. Children will notice how many strips it takes to make their height and the heights of other children. The teacher can help them notice that more strips are needed when mostly smaller strips are used.

3. *Activity:* Dressing up (PP–K)

   Materials: A variety of dress-up clothes, including items that vary in length such as jackets, shirts, skirts, dresses.

   Procedure: Place items in dress-up area for children to play with. Comment on the lengths of the items on the children who are wearing them.

4. *Activity:* Doctor's office dramatic play (PP–K)

   Materials: Stethoscope; old flashlight, etc.; medical scales.

   Procedure: Encourage children to measure themselves with the upright post on the scales during play. Suggest that one child compare height with child not standing on scale and then trade places. Have children compare their heights when standing on the same level. Discuss findings. Record heights on a bar graph mounted on wall.

5. *Activity:* Block play (PP–K)

   Materials: Unit blocks.

   Procedure: Encourage children to play with the blocks. Provide first-hand experiences such as walks and field trips to see roads, bridges, and buildings. Since the blocks are designed on a units basis, children who use them will discover the concept of units. They will invariably use several of the smaller blocks to build a road or the side of a house next to another road or house which was built with larger blocks. In this way they find out that the same length can be built with many different combinations of blocks. Children also gain an idea of linear measurement from block experiences because the blocks "use up" the length or width of the area they are used in. Children are, then, measuring the room in blocks when they build roads or rivers or any other structure which has length.

A plank measures the distance between two blocks.

6. *Activity:* Woodworking bench (PP–P)

Materials: Wood, saws, hammer, nails; six-inch ruler, foot ruler, six-foot carpenter's rule, metal tape measure.

Procedure: Make measurement tools available at wood bench with other woodworking tools and supplies. Children can utilize the tools when making items.

Suggestions and Variations: When young children are involved (3–5 years of age), do not try to have them make accurate measurements. Merely use terms such as "that long," "this much," "longer than," "shorter than," when referring to the length of the measure the wood takes up or in comparing it with other pieces of wood. The purpose of including the measurement tools with young children is just to provide measurement props to enhance the children's carpenter play, nurture their interest in the variety of linear measurement tools, and familiarize them with the characteristics of linear measurement tools. Primary age children will be able to use the tools to actually measure pieces of wood accurately for items they wish to make.

7. *Activity:* Outdoor play (PP–P)

   Materials: Lengths of rope knotted at one-meter intervals; small and large plastic balls.

   Procedure: Two children should play together. One child throws the ball as far as possible. The other child spots the landing. The distance is then measured with the rope.

   Suggestions and Variations: With young children, the distance should be discussed in global terms such as "very long way," "longer than the last time," "three knots this time." With older children the distances can be described in terms of meters (the distance between each knot). Older children can keep records of their ball-throwing and determine how many throws it took them to reach a total of 5 meters, 10 meters, half a kilometer, etc.

8. *Activity:* Plants (PP–K)

   Materials: Plants which grow rather rapidly (beans, coleus); string or yarn; quarter-inch graph paper with columns numbered from left to right indicate the first measurement, second measurement, etc.; crayons.

   Procedure: Encourage children to measure height of plant with string every other day. The child then places the string on a column of the graph paper and makes a mark to indicate the length of the plant. The child then colors in the graph squares up to this mark. The child continues this for as many days as is desirable. The progression in height over time is readily visible on the graph paper.

9. *Activity:* Sticks (K–P)

   Materials: Toothpicks, popsicle sticks, long Tinker-toy sticks, a dowel rod.

   Procedure: Ask child to find out how many toothpicks must be used to make a line as long as the popsicle stick, the Tinker-toy stick, and the dowel rod. Ask how many popsicle sticks are required to make a line as long as the Tinker-toy stick and the dowel rod, etc. Children then solve the problems by actually placing the sticks down end to end.

   Suggestions and Variations: Children can be asked to predict what they think the answers will be. Older children can be asked to measure themselves with the dowel rod and then figure out how many toothpicks, popsicle sticks, or Tinker-toy sticks would equal their height.

10. *Activity:* Measure the parts (K–P)

   Materials: Yarn or string, scissors, construction paper; picture assignment cards with the following body sections drawn on them: (1) heel to knee, (2) heel to toe, (3) knee to waist, (4) waist to shoulder, (5) shoulder to elbow, (6) elbow to wrist, (7) wrist to fingertips. (Indicate the exact area to be measured by marking pictures with red lines. Place a caption at the top of each card naming the section to be measured.)

   Procedure: Children should work in pairs to measure each other, for it would be difficult for them to measure themselves. Measurements should be taken in yarn or string, and a piece should be cut to represent the length of each body segment. These can then be mounted on paper, perhaps from the smallest to the largest, and labeled.

11. *Activity:* The ruler game (P)

   Materials: Forty 4″ × 6″ tagboard cards; colored construction paper strips cut into ½″ × 1″, ½″ × 2″, ½″ × 3″, ½″ × 4″, ½″ × 5″, and ½″ × 6″ strips. (Paste strips onto one side of tagboard cards so each card has one strip; label strips 1″, 2″, 3″, etc.)

   Procedure: Several children can play. Each child is dealt five cards. Remaining cards are placed in deck. Children take turns drawing one card. Children may put cards down any time they have any combination of cards which equals "12." Such a group is called "a ruler." The winner is first child who puts down all cards held. If no player's hand is gotten rid of before the deck is gone, the child who has the most "rulers" wins.

   Suggestions and Variations: The game can be changed to the "yardstick" game or the "meter stick" game depending on what information children need to practice.

ACTIVITIES AND EXPERIENCES TO HELP CHILDREN DEVELOP COMPETENCE IN INVESTIGATING WEIGHT

1. *Activity:* Pan balance (PP–P)

   Materials: A sensitive pan balance can be made from scrap lumber, salad-dressing-jar lids, string, and a strip of peg-board or a yardstick with holes drilled at two-inch intervals. Build a stand with the scrap lumber. The peg-board or yardstick makes the arm of the balance. The lids, suspended with the string or wire, serve as the pans. Also provide an egg carton with the following materials stored separately in the sections: soda-bottle caps, dried beans, washers, paper clips, golf tees, glass marbles, small corks, a ping pong ball, nuts, bolts, paper fasteners, identical buttons.

Procedure: Children can be encouraged to experiment to find things that weigh the same or to discover how many of one item are required to balance another.

Suggestions and Variations: Children's explorations with a pan balance can be quite extensive. A series of directions and questions are listed below. They are clustered to indicate ones which might be placed on one assignment card.

1. Put one bottle cap on one side of the pan balance. Find something heavier than the bottle cap. Find something lighter than the bottle cap.
2. Put a clothespin on one side of the pan balance. Find as many objects or combinations of objects as you can that weigh the same as the clothespin. Keep a record of what you find.
3. 2 bottle caps = ? beans
   2 bottle caps = ? golf tees
   2 bottle caps = ? washers
   2 bottle caps = ? paper clips
   (These may be pictures instead of words.)
4. Put the following objects in order beginning with the lightest:

   bottle cap
   washer
   cork
   golf tee
   bean

5. Find something which is one-half as heavy as a paper clip. Find something that is twice as heavy as a golf tee. Find something that is five times heavier than a paper clip.
6. Can you find a way to balance two washers with four washers?
7. How many bottle caps does it take to balance one cube? How many bottle caps would it take to balance two cubes? three cubes? four cubes? Check to see if your guesses were correct.
8. Find as many pairs of objects as you can which are different in size and shape but that weigh the same. Make a record of what you find.
9. Drop a washer into the pan of water. Does it sink or float?

Find five objects which weigh more than the washer. Predict whether they will sink or float.

Check to see if you were right.

10. Find two objects that are different in size and shape but that weigh the same. Place them both in water. Do they both do the same thing?

Find other pairs and check them the same way.

11. Fill identical pill bottles with sand, salt, and flour. Do they weigh the same? Explain.

12. Fill four different pill bottles with water, corn syrup, mineral oil, and rubbing alcohol. Which liquid weighs the most? The least? Guess and then check your guess with the balance.

2. *Activity:* Store play (PP–K)

Materials: A pan balance or kitchen scale; grocery store set-up, including empty boxes and containers and plastic fruit and vegetables which are typically weighed in the produce department.

Procedure: Take children on a trip to a grocery store before or soon after the grocery store is set up so they can see that some items are weighed for customers. Children will incorporate this knowledge into their store play if appropriate props are made available. Teacher guidance would include suggestions about how much items might weigh, such as ½ lb., 1 lb., etc.

Suggestions and Variations: Young children tend to exaggerate prices and weights of store items. They typically say something weighs "thirty-six-eight pounds." Teachers should not be too vigilant in correcting these unrealistic notions, although suggestions during play that you want ½ lb. of apples, or 1 lb. of grapes are very appropriate. Children then model these more realistic behaviors.

3. *Activity:* Doctor's office role play (PP–K)

Materials: Doctor and nurse play props, including doctor's scales if possible.

Procedure: Make props available for children to play with. Help children think through the items doctors are interested in, such as height, weight, heart rate, etc. Help children read the weight on the scales.

Suggestions and Variations: Young children will not understand how to read pounds or ounces and will not really comprehend what they mean. The purpose of the play is not for children to gain accurate concepts of pounds and ounces, but to introduce them to the concept of weight through activities which have some meaning to them.

4. *Activity:* Cooking (PP–P)

   Materials: Kitchen scales; cooking utensils and equipment; recipe for some food which requires fruit in an amount designated by weight. (For example, applesauce recipes often call for so many pounds of apples.)

   Procedure: Permit children to assemble the ingredients and measure out the correct amount of the weighed item.

5. *Activity:* Shopping for snack (PP–K)

   Materials: Food which is sold by weight. (Carrots, tomatoes, apples, cherries, oranges, and potatoes would be good examples.)

   Procedure: Take a small group of children to the store to shop for fresh fruits or vegetables to be prepared for snack. The adult who accompanies the children should point out to them that the produce must be weighed and should make sure the store worker relays to the children the weights of the items purchased.

6. *Activity:* Objects in ounces (P)

   Materials: Various objects which range in weight from 1 ounce to 16 ounces; a pan balance.

   Procedure: Make materials available to children to work with. Encourage children to find objects which increase in weight by 1 ounce and to put the objects in order as they test them. The teacher should use terms such as ½ lb. and 1 lb. when children use the 8-ounce and 16-ounce weights and should explain that these are other names for these weights.

7. *Activity:* Match a pound (P)

   Materials: Objects such as washers, nuts, screws, marbles, etc., in large enough quantities to make more than a pound of each; pan balance; set of weights.

   Procedure: Two children work together. One child selects an object and fills the pan balance until it contains 1 lb. of the item. The second child must then guess how many of another item would equal a pound and thus balance the first item. The child then places that many objects on the balance to see if the guess was right. If it is not, the child should determine with the weights how many ounces over or under a pound the guess is and write that down on a score pad. The child who has the lowest score at the end of five rounds wins.

ACTIVITIES TO HELP CHILDREN DEVELOP COMPETENCE IN MEASURING AREA

1. Activity: Crazy shapes (K–P)

Materials: Irregular shapes cut from colored construction paper; graph paper (made with ditto).
Procedure: Encourage children to guess which shape they think covers up the most area. Then have them trace the shapes on graph paper and count the number of squares covered by each.

2. Activity: Hands (K)

Materials: Graph paper.
Procedure: Have children trace around their hands and count the number of squares the outline covers. Encourage children to compare hand outlines to see whose is the biggest, whose is the smallest, and whose is the same size.

3. Activity: Blocks and rugs (PP–K)

Materials: Unit blocks; carpet samples of different sizes and shapes.
Procedure: Include carpet samples stored near the block area so children can use them in their block play. Children will use them as rugs on the floors of their houses and find out that it takes more smaller pieces than larger pieces to cover an area.

4. Activity: Setting the table (PP)

Materials: Equipment for dramatic play, including table, chairs, and dishes. (Include place mats of different sizes and shapes in the house play props.)
Procedure: Have equipment available for children to play with. Encourage children to put place mats on the table when they set it for "meals." Children will notice that different place mats cover the table differently or take up more area.

5. Activity: Increasing squares (P)

Materials: Geoboards and rubber bands.
Procedure: Make materials available for children to work with. As children work, suggest they enclose an inch square with a rubber band. Then ask them to extend the lengths of each side of the rubber band an inch at a time, each time noting how many squares are enclosed by the rubber band. Children will notice that as the sides

of the square are increased by one inch, the area of the enclosed square increases much more. They will see how the area of a rectangular figure is related to the length of its sides and will also gain an intuitive grasp of what squaring a number means.

Suggestions and Variations: Be sure to use the correct vocabulary in describing the area enclosed by the rubber band (i.e., one *square* inch, four *square* inches, etc.).

6. *Activity:* Center squares (P)

Materials: Graph paper run from ditto master; make graph paper so squares are one-inch square.

Procedure: Ask the child to pencil around a square in the center of the paper. Ask the child to then find the next biggest square and pencil around it. Encourage the child to keep finding the next biggest square until no more squares can be enclosed. Encourage the child to count the number of square inches enclosed in each square and label them.

7. *Activity:* Corner squares (P)

Materials: One-inch graph paper made with ditto.

Procedure: Ask the child to pencil around a square in the center of the paper. Ask the child to find the next biggest square using the first square as the corner of the second square. Encourage the child to keep finding the next biggest square until no more squares can be made, always using the last square made as the corner of the new one. Encourage the child to count and label the square inches in each square he made.

Suggestions and Variations: If colored pencils or crayons are used to shade in the squares as they are made, center squares and corner squares can be done on the same piece of graph paper.

ACTIVITIES TO HELP CHILDREN DEVELOP COMPETENCE IN MEASURING VOLUME

1. *Activity:* Boxes and blocks (PP–K)

Materials: Set of one-inch cubes; boxes of different shapes, some of equal sizes and others varying in size.

Procedure: Make cubes and boxes available on the classroom shelf in a suitable container. When a child selects this item to work with, the teacher should ask questions which encourage noticing that some boxes hold more cubes than others. If boxes are appropriately selected, children can also notice that although some boxes are different in shape, they hold the same number of cubes.

2. *Activity:*   Blocks clean-up (PP–K)

   Materials: Set of unit blocks; shelves for storing blocks.

   Procedure: As children clean up blocks after playing, they will notice that fewer large blocks can fit into the same space that smaller blocks will fit into. The teacher should point this out occasionally as when helping children clean up from time to time.

3. *Activity:*   Water play (PP–P)

   Materials: Suitable tub for holding water; containers selected so a variety of sizes and shapes are provided. (Make sure some containers vary in shape but are identical in size.)

   Procedure: Provide water play as an activity. Teacher guidance would include asking children questions such as (1) Which one holds more, this one or that one? (2) How many of these little ones does it take to fill that big one? (3) Can you find two containers which are different shapes but hold the same amount of water?

   Suggestions and Variations: As children are able to keep records of their work, they can make charts to represent their findings. They might make a chart representing the containers in the order of the amount of water they hold, or make charts which indicate how the containers are related to each other (how many of one it takes to fill the other).

4. *Activity:*   Cooking (PP–P)

   Materials: Ingredients for recipe; cooking utensils.

   Procedure: Select recipe which requires liquid measurements. Puddings, jello, cakes, and ice cream are good examples. Gather a small group of children to do the cooking. Have children do all the measuring.

   Suggestions and Variations: Some system for selecting cooking groups is usually necessary to insure that everyone gets a fair number of turns. The teacher can divide the children into cooking groups and then make sure the groups take turns, or children can have turns as their names come up on a class list. It's best to keep cooking groups no larger than four members so all children can be actively involved.

5. *Activity:*   House play (PP–K)

   Materials: Empty food containers which illustrate standard liquid measurements. (For example, include milk and cream containers in pint, quart, half-gallon, and gallon sizes. Include plastic ice cream containers in pint, quart, and half gallon sizes. Plastic liquid dish detergent bottles of different sizes can also be included.)

Procedure: Place the empty containers in the play area for children to play with. The teacher can at times play along with children and verbalize the names of the containers.

Suggestions and Variations: The same props can be used in store play, which should be set up so this activity can be combined with house play. While shopping for items and putting them away in the house, children will notice different-sized containers. Teachers can help children notice the different sizes by playing store and asking customers which size they prefer, or by playing in the house and helping make a shopping list which indicates sizes of containers desired (i.e., a quart of milk; a pint of cream).

6. *Activity:* Half-pint card game (P)

Materials: Tagboard cards with sketches and written labels for cups, pints, and quarts. Make the following set of cards:

> 8 cup-cards
> 12 pint-cards
> 12 quart-cards
> 1 half-pint card

Procedure: Three or four children may play. All cards are dealt to players. Players than draw from each other as in the game Old Maid. Players may lay cards on the table in groups which equal a pint, quart, or gallon. The half-pint card may not be combined with any other. The person left holding this card at the end of the game loses.

Suggestions and Variations: Children will need to know the relationship of one liquid measure to others. A chart of such relationships can be helpful, and children can refer to this during the game.

ACTIVITIES TO HELP CHILDREN UNDERSTAND
THAT TIME IS NOT CONTROLLED BY THEIR ACTIONS

1. *Activity:* Time your turn (PP–K)

Materials: Sand timers and design cubes and patterns.

Procedure: Encourage two children to work with the design cubes. Encourage the children to use the sand timer to designate the length of each turn. This will help children develop a concept of time as an arbitrary and objective segment separate from their own actions.

2. *Activity:* Sand timer experiment (PP–K)

Materials: Two sand timers, identical in size.

Procedure: Two children are needed to do this activity. Each child has a sand timer. The children should allow the sand timers to run simultaneously to make sure they take the same amount of time to empty. The children then decide some action to perform while the sand timer is running. One child should perform the action at a fast rate, while the other should perform it at a slower rate. They should watch the sand timers to see if they empty at the same time.

Suggestions and Variations: Children should be asked to predict what they think the outcome will be.

ACTIVITIES TO HELP CHILDREN UNDERSTAND
THAT TIME IS INDEPENDENT OF THE MEASURING DEVICE

1. Activity: Baking (PP–P)

Materials: Ingredients and utensils for cookies, bread, or cake recipes; at least two clocks with different face dimensions (one large and one small); one paper or cardboard clock face with hands.

Procedure: Mix recipe and place in the oven. Set the paper or cardboard clock face at the time the real clocks will read when the food is to be finished baking. Children will notice that the small and large clocks read the same time when the food is finished, particularly if the teacher asks them to check both clocks.

2. Activity: Clean-up time (PP–P)

Materials: At least two clocks, one with a large face, one with a small face. Paper or cardboard clock faces.

Procedure: Warn children several minutes before clean-up time that clean-up will begin at a certain time. Set the cardboard clock for the time you have said. The real clocks should be placed where children can see them easily. The teacher should refer to the clocks when announcing the final clean-up.

3. Activity: Clocks (K–P)

Materials: A variety of clocks—big, small, electric, etc.

Procedure: Children can work with the clocks, setting them all for the same time and then checking to see if they always read the same time regardless of their physical dimensions or characteristics.

Suggestions and Variations: Add a metronome to the clock collection. Children can count the number of strokes of the metronome it takes for the hands of each clock to move from one numeral to another. This helps children understand that no matter what the distance between numerals, it takes the hands of all clocks the same amount of time to move from one numeral to another. Children also obtain practice in telling time in this activity, because as they set the clocks, they will be asking what time it is; or the teacher can set them for certain times.

Geometry

ACTIVITIES TO HELP CHILDREN DEVELOP COMPETENCIES IN IDENTIFYING GEOMETRIC FIGURES AND SOLIDS

1. Activity: Paper shapes (PP–K)

Materials: Geometric figures cut from colored construction paper. (Include triangles, rectangles, circles, squares, diamonds, trapezoids, octagons, and any other figures you wish.)

Procedure: Make figures available in a container on a shelf in the math center. As children work with figures, the teacher can interact to help them find figures that are alike and provide their names.

Suggestions and Variations: After children have had experience identifying figures which are different, variations *within* a type of figure can be provided. For example, a box containing just triangles of different kinds could be available. Several of each kind should be provided so children can search for those that are alike.

2. Activity: A walk (PP–K)

Materials: The neighborhood.

Procedure: Take a few children for a walk to look for different geometric figures and solids. Adult guidance would include providing verbal labels for what the children see.

3. Activity: Shape bingo (PP–K)

Materials: Make bingo cards from tagboard. Make figures with colored construction paper. Make call cards with tagboard and construction paper also.

Procedure: Several children can play. The game is played just like regular bingo. Children should do the calling so they can practice the names of the figures.

4. *Activity:* Containers (PP–K)

   Materials: A variety of boxes and cans representing different solids.
   Procedure: Set up a display using one container for each solid. Make labels to place by each type of solid. Have other containers available in a box nearby. Children can then find containers which are of the same type as those on display. Teacher guidance should include helping children read the labels and note the distinguishing characteristics of each type.

5. *Activity:* Templates (PP–K)

   Materials: Pencils or crayons; paper; cardboard templates. (Use a mat knife to cut figures out of the centers of pieces of cardboard.)
   Procedure: Make templates available in the math center. Children can use them to trace different figures on paper. Teacher guidance would include providing verbal labels for the figures children trace.

6. *Activity:* Block solids (PP–K)

   Materials: Full set of unit blocks.
   Procedure: Unit blocks include cylinders, cubes, etc. As children use the blocks, the teacher can provide names for the different solids.

7. *Activity:* Flattened boxes (K–P)

   Materials: A variety of small pasteboard boxes and tubes; paper and pencil; a ruler.
   Procedure: Allow children to pull or cut all containers apart so they can be flattened. Children should then place the flattened boxes on a piece of paper and trace around them. The ruler can be used to draw in lines to indicate where the sides begin. Children will be able to see how many sides a particular box has, as well as the shape and size of each. (See Figure 21.)

8. *Activity:* Wooden block diagrams (PP–K)

   Materials: One small block of each shape from unit block set; tagboard cut about 8″ × 11″. (Select one block and trace around each of its sides on a piece of tagboard. Repeat for all the different blocks, drawing only one block on each piece of tagboard. See Figure 22.)
   Procedure: Place blocks and tagboard diagrams in a box available to children to work with. Children try to match each tagboard diagram with the block it was drawn from.
   Suggestions and Variations: Sometimes blocks of unusual shapes can be obtained from scrap boxes in a wood shop or lumber yard. These make interesting diagrams.

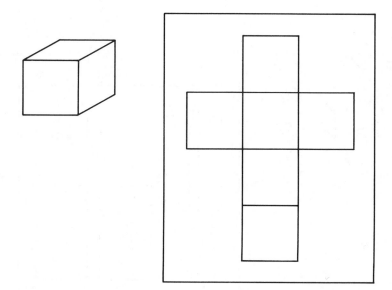

Figure 21. Flattened box.

ACTIVITIES TO HELP CHILDREN DEVELOP COMPETENCE IN CONSTRUCTING GEOMETRIC FIGURES AND SOLIDS

1. Activity: Geoboard construction (K–P)

Materials: Geoboards; colored rubber bands.

Procedure: As children make figures on the geoboards, the teacher should ask questions such as "Can you change that square into two triangles?" "Can you change that square into two rectangles?"

Suggestions and Variations: Assignment cards might be helpful with this activity. Teachers could make sets in different colors to indicate those that go together. The cards for each set could then be numbered on the back so children will know in which order to follow the directions.

2. Activity: Sand constructions (PP–K)

Materials: Empty plastic and metal containers of all sizes and shapes; wet sand in sand table or tub.

Procedure: Make empty containers available to children for use in the sand. Encourage them to pack the containers with wet sand and then dump the contents out. The wet sand will take the shape of the container. Help children notice the features of the sand constructions they make.

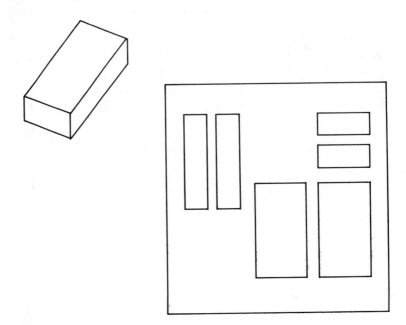

Figure 22. Block surface diagrams.

3. *Activity:* Plasticene constructions (K–P)

   Materials: Plasticene; models for geometric solids (boxes, blocks, cans, etc.)

   Procedure: Make the plasticene and models available for children to use during activity time. Children try to make a plasticene construction to look the same as one of the models. To do this, they must pay close attention to the features of the model and thus become familiar with the attributes of different solids.

4. *Activity:* Peg-board constructions (K–P)

   Materials: Pegs and peg-boards.

   Procedure: Make pegs and peg-boards available to children to use during activity time. Encourage children to use pegs to enclose different geometric figures on the peg-boards. Teachers might again find assignment cards useful. For example, directions might include asking children to make as many different figures as they can that have three sides, four sides, etc.

   Suggestions and Variations: This activity may be used with older preprimary children, although it may be too difficult for them.

5. *Activity:* Tangrams (K–P)

Materials: Paper geometric figures that can be combined to make various figures; tangram assignment cards that illustrate possible figures. (See Figure 23. Geometry; figures and assignment cards should be organized into sets by color coding; make figures and assignment cards of each set out of the same color paper.)

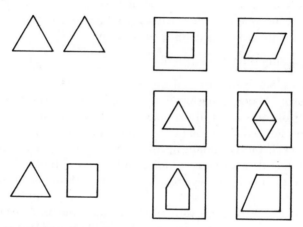

Figure 23. Tangram puzzles.

Procedure: Make materials available for children to work with. The teacher should provide names for the figures children make.

Suggestions and Variations: Put out only three or four sets at one time. After children have explored these for awhile, put out several new sets.

ACTIVITIES TO HELP CHILDREN LEARN TO RECOGNIZE AND NAME COMMON COINS AND BILLS

1. *Activity:* Store play (PP–K)

Materials: Play money or real coins; empty food cartons of various types; shelves or some other arrangement for organizing containers as a store.

Procedure: Encourage children to engage in store play. The teacher can join the play from time to time and provide information about the names of particular coins and bills. For example, the teacher might play the role of cashier. When children offer the money to pay for their purchases, the teacher can say, "That will be 40 cents. Do you have four dimes, or a quarter and a dime and a nickel?" The teacher can then help search for the appropriate coins from among the child's play money.

Suggestions and Variations: For preschool children, the stress should not be on learning the value of money (for example, that 40 cents is 40 pennies, 8 nickels, 4 dimes, etc.), but on recognizing certain coins as being a penny, a dime, or a nickel. The example given above is just one way the teacher might get children to attend to the characteristics and names of specific coins.

2. ***Activity:*** Shopping trips (PP–K)

Materials: Shopping list and money.

Procedure: When going on a shopping trip, make sure you have a variety of coins and bills to take along. Give each child some of the money. For example, one child might be asked to carry the dime and nickel, another might be asked to carry the quarter, and a third might be asked to carry a dollar bill. Tell children the names of the pieces of money they are asked to carry. While on the way to the store, check once or twice to make sure each child still has the money, e.g., "John, do you still have the dime and nickel?" When the actual purchase is made, ask the children to place their money in the cashier's hand: "John, give the cashier your dime and nickel. Joshua, give the cashier your dollar bill." Any change should be distributed among the children to carry back to school, and the coins should be named again as they are given to each child.

Suggestions and Variations: The checking of the money on the way to the store is for the purpose of naming the money again. Be careful not to do this in a way which suggests to children that you do not trust them with money.

3. ***Activity:*** Money poster (PP–K)

Materials: A variety of coins and bills; poster board, clear contact paper, tape, rubber cement.
(Use tape or rubber cement to attach coins to poster board. Cover entire display with a sheet of contact paper so a one-inch edge folds back on the underside.)

Procedure: Place the poster on a bulletin board or other spot in the room where children can see it clearly and easily. Talk with children about the various coins and bills. Name the ones children do not know.

Suggestions and Variations: Small versions of the poster can be made and placed in an appropriate container on a shelf in the math center.

ACTIVITIES TO HELP CHILDREN UNDERSTAND
THE VALUE OF EACH PIECE OF MONEY

1. Activity: How many pennies? (PP–K)

Materials: Nickel, dime, quarter and at least 25 pennies; appropriate container to hold the money.
Procedure: During activity time, work with individual children to help them count out the number of pennies that equals each of the other coins.
Suggestions and Variations: This activity is not appropriate for the younger preschool child because a concept of number and the ability to count to 5, 10, and 25 are required. The activity is appropriate for many older four-year-olds and most five-year-olds.

2. Activity: Money chart (PP–K)

Refer to activity #6 on page 276 ofthe Social Science chapter and to Figure 27 on page 277 of the same chapter.

ACTIVITIES TO HELP CHILDREN UNDERSTAND
THE EXCHANGE RATES OF VARIOUS PIECES OF MONEY

1. Activity: Money chart (K–P)

Materials: Nickels, dimes, quarters and a fifty-cent piece; poster board; contact paper. (Make a money chart similar to the money chart in activity #2 in the preceding section, but instead of using pennies, use nickels. A dime would be shown to be equal to two nickels, a quarter would be shown to be equal to five nickels, and a fifty-cent piece would be shown to equal ten nickels. Other charts can be made to illustrate other exchange values. For example, the values of quarters, fifty-cent pieces, and dollar bills in a combination of dimes and nickels could be illustrated.)
Procedure: Make these charts available to children in the math area. Talk with children about the charts.

2. Activity: Shopping trip (PP–K)

Materials: A variety of coins and a shopping list.
Procedure: When shopping for multiples of one item (five apples,

three goldfish, etc.), find out the cost of each one. Then give each child who is making the trip money for one item, making sure each one has different coins. For example, if an apple costs 12 cents, give one child two nickels and two pennies, give a second child one dime and two pennies, and give a third child twelve pennies. They will discover that each amount of money is the same and will buy the same amount.

Suggestions and Variations: This activity is not appropriate for younger preschool children. It is very difficult for them to understand that one dime and ten pennies are equal in value. They think that more pieces of money equals more money. Older four-year-olds begin to understand that more pieces do not necessarily mean more money, and they can profit from experiences like the one in this activity.

3. Activity: Extra change (P)

Refer to activity #5 on page 275 of the Social Science chapter for this activity.

ADDITIONAL RESOURCES

BOUCHER, J., "The New Mathematics," in Vincent Rogers, ed., *Teaching in the British Primary School*. London: Collier-Macmillan, 1970.

COLLIER, C., and H. LERCH, *Teaching Mathematics in the Modern Elementary School*. New York: The Macmillan Company, 1969.

COPELAND, R., *How Children Learn Mathematics*. New York: The Macmillan Company, 1971.

INHELDER, B., and J. PIAGET, *The Growth of Logical Thinking*. New York: Basic Books, 1958.

Nuffield Mathematics Project. New York: John Wiley, 1962.

PIAGET, J., *The Child's Conception of Number*. New York: W. W. Norton & Company, Inc., 1965.

PIAGET, J., *The Child's Conception of Time*. New York: Ballantine Books, 1971.

STERN, C., and M. STERN, *Children Discover Arithmetic*. New York: Harper & Row, Publishers, 1971.

6

science

PIONEERS in early childhood education saw science as a discipline beyond the ken of young children. That the basis for scientific processes could be established in early childhood was not considered. That young children had a great deal of curiosity and interest in phenomena was ignored. Until about three decades ago, science had either a minor position in the curriculum or was included incidentally as a part of nature study and physical education. While nature study—expanding upon incidental occurrences and observations—often resulted in relevant science learnings, the child's understanding of science was usually limited to recognition of natural phenomena.

Today, science is considered one of the principal areas of the curriculum at the preprimary and primary levels. Partly as a result of Piaget's work on the development of notions of causality and logical thinking, we are now aware of ways in which children gain and organize information. We also know they not only enjoy contact with science study, but that they benefit from guided experiences which involve processes such as observing, experimenting, classifying, and hypothesizing.

This chapter is about science for young children. Its purposes are: (1) to introduce teachers to the nature of science, (2) to relate the implications of children's thinking to the development of scientific knowledge, concepts, and skills, (3) to discuss science skills and concepts appropriate for young children, and (4) to provide teachers with science activities for children at the preprimary and primary levels.

THE NATURE OF SCIENCE

Webster's New World Dictionary[1] defines science as "systematized knowledge derived from observation, study and experimentation carried on in order to determine the nature or principles of what is being studied." Science refers, then, not only to *content*—what is already known about plants, animals, minerals, and forces in the world—but to *process*—a method of inquiry into observed phenomena.

Observed variations in the environment (phenomena) are often the impetus for scientific study. Some things float while others sink. Why? Some objects cling to a magnet while others do not. Why? Some sub-

---

[1]D. B. Guralnik, ed., *Webster's New World Dictionary*, 2nd ed. (New York: The World Publishing Co., 1972), p. 1275.

stances change to a liquid when heated, while others change to a vapor. Why? How can we make sense out of these phenomena? How can we predict what will happen? Scientific inquiry is a means of answering such questions.

Scientific inquiry involves the use of several specific skills combined in certain ways. First, it requires observation and accurate description of phenomena observed. Next, inferences or hypotheses are made on the basis of these observations. These inferences are then tested. Experimentation follows, and then more observations are made. These lead to new inferences and further experimentation.

For example, if one wanted to determine why some objects sink while others float, one must first determine which of these sink and which float. A variety of objects can be classified into two groups: "things that sink," and "things that float." Next, one needs to determine if there is a common characteristic which might account for the difference in the reactions of objects from the two groups. This requires close observation of the objects tested. Are all things that float of one size whereas those that sink are another? Are all things that float light whereas those that sink are heavy? Are all things that float made of one material whereas those that sink are made of another?

The scientist, while testing out a large variety of objects in water, carefully records all observations. On the basis of the observations, hypotheses are formed about why objects react as they do: "It is the weight which makes the difference. Light things float and heavy things sink." The scientist sees a block of wood and a pin. "If weight makes the difference, then the pin should float and the block should sink." But trying it out shows that it is not so in this case. A new question is asked: "When does it make a difference and when does it not?" The scientist continues to observe, record, make inferences, and test until gaining an understanding of the relationship between objects and their tendency to sink or float in water.

The above example includes experimentation as part of the scientific inquiry. Though it is often an important part, it need not always be included. Knowledge of systems, interrelationships, and processes can be the result of scientific inquiry that may or may not require experimentation. Some knowledge comes from observation coupled with analysis and careful recording of factors involved. The manner in which plants grow from seeds is an example of scientific investigation which does not necessarily involve experimentation. Classification of plants and animals by their characteristics is another.

Scientists have accumulated a great storehouse of knowledge about the phenomena they have studied. This knowledge results in information which is useful to others. This ready-made knowledge should form a part of the science program in the schools, although it should never be the complete program. It is important for children to know that certain foods must be refrigerated or that illness will result, that electrical equipment can be deadly if not handled properly, and that life jackets can keep one afloat in water. It would be foolish and dangerous to have children acquire such knowledge through experimentation. Other information may be fascinating and safe for children to obtain, but might be impractical in terms of cost or availability of materials.

When planning science programs for young children, one should consider that science includes both the process of inquiry and the products which result from inquiry. Though it is important for some scientifically obtained information to be passed on for the sake of practicality and safety, it is important for teachers to understand that if children are really to understand science, they must be permitted to *abstract* knowledge on their own, or at least be permitted to *verify* for themselves much of the information they are given.

CHILDREN AND SCIENCE

The basis for an understanding of science can begin in very early childhood. An infant sitting on a rug turns a baby bottle upside down. A few drops of milk spill. The infant pats the wet spot, looks at the bottle, deliberately turns it upside down, watches the milk drip, pats the wet spot again. In a similar manner, infants and toddlers explore the objects in their environments. The analogy to scientific experiments which explore cause and effect is evident.

As children develop language, they bombard adults with questions related to the what, why, and how of everything around them. It is vital to children's understanding of the world that they continue to explore, manipulate materials, ask questions. Generally, young children voice inferences about their observations which, because of their lack of understanding, may be amusing to adults. "Why does it get dark at night?" the adult asks. "So we can go to sleep," the three- or four-year-old child replies.

It's a magical world to young, egocentric children. Events occur just for their benefit. What they say, do, and desire causes things to happen. The sun follows them around. The existence of lakes or snow has no cause or function but to provide them pleasure in swimming, skating, or sledding. And when an older child teaches a younger one, "Step on a crack, break your mother's back; step on a line, break your mother's spine," the second child is very careful about where he steps, fearful that it might really happen.

As children become less egocentric, they begin to look for physical rather than magical or psychological reasons for events. They begin to rely on contiguity of two events in time or space as an indication of cause and effect.[2] The sun shines and the clouds move. Asked why the clouds move, the four-year-old might say, "The sun pushes them away." A reel-to-reel tape recorder is shown to a child. Asked what makes the reels go around, the child indicates by pointing that he thinks it is the moving tape that is causing the motion of the reels.

It is quite reasonable to assume tentatively that events closely related in time or space might have a causal relationship. The problem is that such assumptions can be quite wrong. Another less obvious factor may in fact be the actual cause. In order to be sure we are not fooled by an obvious, but irrelevant factor, we must search for other possible causes. For example, bread left in a warm moist place develops mold. We reason that the warmth and moisture cause the mold. Research using a microscope reveals the presence of spores. Continued microscopic observation over time shows the spores developing into mold. The warmth and moisture are necessary for the growth of the spores, but are not the cause of the mold. The cause of the mold is the presence of spores.

Young children have great difficulty generating hypotheses and testing these systematically so as to discard irrelevant ones. In order to perform such tasks, one must possess mental structures and abilities which Inhelder and Piaget[3] have called **formal operations.** Formal operational structures permit a person to work out mentally all the possible variables which might have a bearing on a phenomenon, and then to plan strategies to test each variable while holding the others constant. Formal operational structures also permit a person to assume or imagine changed conditions in which variables might operate.

Young children are in the **preoperational** and **concrete operational** stages of mental development, not in the **formal operational stage.** Preoperational children have great difficulty just making judgments about actions performed before their eyes. Concrete operational children can make judgments about processes they can see, but these are often not very sophisticated. They also cannot predict the results of actions performed under hypothetically changed conditions, nor can they generate ideas about what these changed conditions might be. It is only when they attain the stage of formal operations at around eleven or twelve years of age that they can function on this level.

[2]J. Piaget, *The Child's Conception of the World* (Totawa, N.J.: Littlefield, Adams and Co., 1969), pp. 256–388.
[3]B. Inhelder and J. Piaget, *The Growth of Logical Thinking* (New York: Basic Books, Inc., 1958), pp. 307–333.

Presumably, the adult working with a child has developed formal operational structures and can provide both experiences and information which will help the child gradually attain more complex modes of thinking. For example, if an adult calls the child's attention to clouds moving when the wind blows and not moving when the wind is still, the child may begin to consider the effects of the wind rather than the effects of the sun as the factor which controls the movement of clouds. Even more important, the child may begin to question any first hunches about the causes of phenomena and search for other possibilities.

One should not expect changes in children's thinking to occur quickly or necessarily in a straightforward, linear fashion. The unique characteristics of young children's thinking limit what they can understand. What seems clear to an adult is not always clear to a child. For example, because spores cannot be seen on the bread without a microscope, a child might assume the spores are part of the microscope and not on the surface of the bread. Or, in the case of flotation, size in relation to weight (density) is a factor which determines whether an object sinks or floats, not absolute size or weight alone. Because younger children are unable to make comparisons of two things simultaneously, it is not possible for them to think of the size and weight of one object in relation to the size and weight of another object. Given the opportunity to explore and experiment, four- and five-year-olds usually come to understand that flotation has something to do with size and weight, although typically they cannot integrate the two ideas into the concept of density. Their concept of flotation is, therefore, incomplete. It is important to note that this notion is on the right track, for their concept is not attached to irrelevant attributes such as material of the objects or their color, which would be characteristic of even younger children.

The teacher should be able to discriminate between confusion resulting from too much information, information obtained in confusing ways, or too little opportunity to obtain information, and confusion which would be expected in terms of the child's level of thinking. Teachers should expect children to be unclear for a time about the actual site of the spores and the concept of density. And teachers should be prepared to provide continued exposure to experiences which will give children a chance gradually to refine and integrate into more accurate concepts the information they obtain.

In addition to limitations in understanding causality, young children have limited ability to reason logically. This has important implications, particularly for children's understanding of hierarchical classification (subclasses within larger classes).[4]

[4]C. B. Stendler, *Readings in Child Behavior and Development,* 2nd ed. (New York: Harcourt, Brace & World, Inc., 1964), pp. 326–327.

One of the ways in which knowledge obtained from scientific inquiry can be organized is through classification. For example, plants and animals are two major classes into which things in the world can be grouped. Within each, there are subclasses, and within these there are more subclasses. This system provides a way to organize a vast amount of information. It also provides an efficient way to learn a great deal of information if one can comprehend the system. The categories can be used as cues to information applicable to all the specific things in the class.

Young children cannot comprehend such systems. They may be able to learn that something is an animal, that it is a mammal, and further, that it is a goat, but the information remains specific and unintegrated in the child's mind. It is not used by the child to predict characteristics of other things similarly labelled (animal, mammal).

Young children do build the system gradually, but the important point is that they *build it* from specific information. The usefulness of the system for adults is that it can be *used* to learn the specifics. For young children, the specifics are used to build the classification system, not vice-versa.

Despite limitations, young children can make considerable progress in understanding science. They can acquire a great deal of descriptive knowledge about the world and begin to develop systems for organizing it. They can observe events. They can test out objects to see how they behave in relationship to a certain event, and they can organize objects according to their responses. If given some help, they can suggest several possible explanations for events they observe, and they can test these out. Although concepts formed by children may not become integrated into completely accurate concepts immediately, or even for a very long time, such incomplete concepts are the stuff from which complete and accurate concepts will eventually emerge.

SCIENCE SKILLS AND CONCEPTS
FOR YOUNG CHILDREN

Although, as we have noted, young children are not yet able to perform the necessary formal operations for true scientific inquiry, we can help them gain the basic science skills. These include:

> observing
> classifying
> hypothesizing
> experimenting
> recording
> interpreting and generalizing

Observation

Observation is the foundation on which scientific inquiry is built. As acutely perceptive as young children are, they need guidance in order to focus their perceptions on significant characteristics and so attain skill in observation. Through comparing and contrasting what they observe, children are helped to see relationships, likenesses, and differences.

Classification

Classification helps us make order out of what we have observed. It is so much a part of our lives that we are not conscious of its importance. Had you not learned both the concept and skill of classification, you would not be able to use the telephone directory or find items in a grocery store. Fortunately, it is unlikely that a child could completely avoid the development of some concepts and skills in classification. Many young children find great satisfaction in sorting objects into like collections. But skill development in classification goes far beyond such simple sorting of objects that are similar in terms of some physical characteristic (size, shape, color, material).

For the young child, the next step beyond sorting objects into groups that are alike is sorting objects which may not be similar in terms of physical attributes, but which may react similarly in some situation. For example, things that sink and things that float, or materials which dissolve or do not dissolve in water may be classified into categories by their reactions. Objects may also be classified in terms of their function, rather than according to physical attributes or reactions.

Classification can also involve subordinate categories within larger categories. For example, within the class of animals are subclasses of mammals and reptiles, and within each of these subclasses there are further subclasses. This skill serves as a powerful tool for helping the scientist organize information. As we have pointed out earlier, however, children generally do not understand the logic of these relationships until they are about eight or nine years of age. It is useful for teachers to indicate that a particular creature is an animal, a mammal, and specifically a cow, but teachers should not expect young children to grasp the relationship of one of these classes to the others.

Hypothesizing

Hypothesizing involves generating possible reasons for observed events. As we discussed earlier, young children have not yet acquired the ability to search for all possible reasons, nor are preoperational children able to deal with two characteristics at the same time. Instead, they tend to make explanations based on the fact that two events occur together in time or space or that two phenomena appear to have something in common; e.g., hard carrots eaten by rabbits and ears that stand up straight.

Without guidance, children tend to be satisfied with such reasons and will not test these. The teacher's role is to help children verbalize what they have observed, give a possible reason, make a prediction based on the reason given, and test to see if the reason is true. For example, after children have separated objects into two piles of things that sink and things that float, the teacher elicits comments about like characteristics of the objects in each pile. Perhaps the children agree that the things that float are lighter than things that sink. This is their hypothesis.

Experimenting

Experimentation is required to test hypotheses. The teacher's next question should be, "How can we tell whether or not light things float and heavy things sink?" A balance scale might be brought in to test the verity of the hypothesis: "Things that float are lighter than things that sink."

Experimenting is the part of scientific inquiry which is most likely to be enjoyed by young children, and it is the most appropriate to their stage of development. A form of experimentation which David Hawkins[5] so aptly terms "messing about" should precede hypothesizing. Hawkins advocates allowing children to explore materials freely on their own before guidance and information are provided. When materials appropriate to the demonstration of a new concept are placed on a table accessible to children for exploration, this exploration leads to observation and hypothesizing. The skillful guidance of a teacher can maximize the learning. Such guidance for preschoolers should take the form of brief interest on the part of the teacher in the children's ongoing experimentation. A few well-chosen questions such as "what would happen if . . .," or well-chosen comments about observations that had gone unnoticed by the child will suffice. As children grow older and enter the primary grades, they gain more interest in taking time out from actual experimentation to think about what they have been doing and to plan what they might do next.

[5]D. Hawkins, "Messing About in Science," *Science and Children,* 2 (1965), pp. 5–9.

Recording

Recording serves two purposes: (1) insuring that the observations made in the science experience are accurately remembered, and (2) communicating findings to others.

Records may take many forms. Drawings, experience charts, graphs, and booklets are all used in recording and communicating descriptions for science experiences and results of experimentation. *Products* themselves, may also be records. A batch of fudge, scrambled eggs, a dead plant, and cornstarch putty are all results of chemical or biological processes. Another such product record may be collections of objects which have been sorted into labelled containers. For example, two containers are labelled with words and pictures "things that sink" and "things that float." Drawing on their experimentation, children fill the two containers with objects that fit the labels. Such records have limitations. The products are difficult to preserve and they will show only the results, not the processes or conditions under which the results were obtained.

For younger children such product records may be sufficient, provided that both process and end results are accompanied by directed conversation which focuses observation on pertinent factors, elicits recall, and helps the children interpret the experience. Teacher's questions during activity and evaluation times are particularly important to help children think and report about what they have done. "John, how did you make the applesauce? What do you think made the apples fall apart?" "Franz, I noticed you didn't have any orange paint; can you tell me what you did to get the orange color in your painting?" Such questions should help children recall observations made, hypotheses tested, actions taken, and the results obtained.

Children's responses to questions about their experiences may be recorded by the teacher on an *experience chart*. An experience chart together with products from the experience may form an attractive and informative display for the enjoyment not only of the entire class but of visitors to the room too.

Children may independently make records by *drawing pictures* to illustrate the process of experimentation, the objects used, and the products obtained. The degree of complexity of such illustrations will, of course, depend on the child's stage of development. Beginners may only draw that which impressed them the most, while the more advanced may cartoon the entire process in sequence.

Graphs may also be made to illustrate changes which have occurred. For example, the growth of plants given differing amounts of light over a three-week period might be illustrated in graphs as shown in Figure 24.

Children who have developed some skill in writing may make *book-*

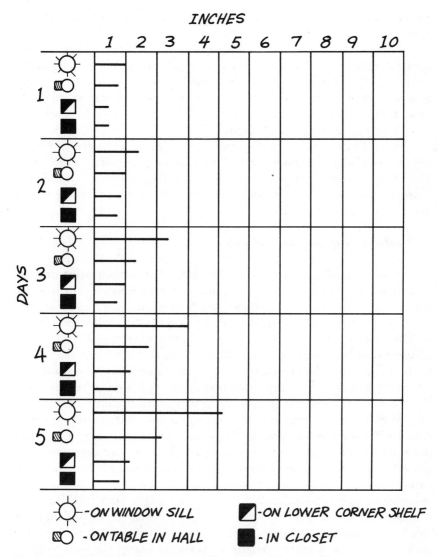

Figure 24. Graph showing plant growth under varying conditions.

lets which record the science experience. In planning such a booklet, children should receive guidance to insure that they include a description of materials used, procedures followed, results obtained, and interpretations and generalizations. Again the expectation for all of these descriptions must be adapted to the stage of development of the child. New words which the children will need for their books may be written on a piece of paper for their later reference or may be added to their word collections (see Chapter IV, Language Arts, Activity 6, Spelling dictionaries, page 154).

Children should use the records they keep. They should be encouraged to trade records and repeat each other's work. Results should be compared. Preschoolers cannot be expected to do this with a great deal of sophistication. Though they may start out wanting very much to do what another child has done, they will typically do it their own way. This should be accepted and encouraged.

As children grow older they will become more interested in following precisely what someone else has done as well as doing it their own way and comparing the two. By doing this, children will form clearer concepts of scientific inquiry and become aware of the variety of factors which may influence results.

Interpreting and Generalizing

These may be considered the culminating steps of scientific inquiry. What has been learned through the processes that were described above is now translated into a concept on which more advanced learning may be built. The teacher should be careful to insure that this step is made. It is not enough to describe the materials, procedures, and results of a science experience; one must also extract meaning from the experience. What do the results tell us about _____? If water travels downhill, then where would we put a bucket in relation to the aquarium we're emptying? If a box of nails spills, is there something we can use to pick them up?

With preschool children, it is important that interpreting and generalizing be done in context, as things happen. Preschoolers cannot sit down and think of the implications of an observed phenomenon. They can relate an observed phenomenon to real situations that have occurred earlier or which occur later. For example, if children are permitted to experiment with magnets and objects, a child might later think of using a magnet to collect nails spilled at the workbench. If a child did not think of it, the teacher might ask, "What could we use to pick up the nails?" Better yet, a magnet might be included among the woodworking tools just for such occasions.

Primary age children are better able to think of implications of information they have obtained than are preschool children. Part of this increase in ability is due to their greater experience in the world. They bring many more experiences to school than a younger child. Part of the increase in skill is also due to progress in ability to think and to understand and use language. This does not mean that primary age children do not need concrete situations in which to apply what they have learned.

What it does mean is that more interpreting and generalizing can be done through talking, reading, and writing.

Science Concepts

Science concepts are the information children gain as a consequence of their inquiry. Although it is our opinion that science programs should be weighted in favor of process over content, children must have something to inquire about. While children in many classrooms have been unable to gain adequate scientific information because they have not been permitted to engage in the processes of inquiry, other children have been unable to gain adequate understanding of science because their inquiry had no direction or content.

When teachers have a clear idea of the concepts they wish children to gain from an experience, the children will be more apt to learn those concepts than if the teacher does not. It is important, therefore, that teachers be well versed in the subject matter of science. Without an understanding of science concepts, teachers cannot arrange an environment from which children can abstract meaning, nor can they give good guidance. This is not to say the teacher is expected to know all the answers. Rather, teachers explore the world of science with children and provide information and guidance to help children both attain concepts which were selected as appropriate goals and also to go beyond these to unforeseen concepts. An effective teacher is one who learns with and from students.

The concepts selected as goals for children should be based on the teacher's knowledge of the children and of the community in which they live. What experiences have the children had? What things do they show an interest in? What kinds of knowledge and skills do they need to function safely and effectively in the community where they live? Questions such as the above should be asked and answered whether the teacher selects activities from this book or from specific commercially produced courses of study.

Experiences which will help children gain concepts from the content areas of science should be provided. All of the activities which follow later in this chapter are designed to involve children in the process of scientific inquiry and to develop the skills which have been described. The activities are grouped into content areas which include biology, chemistry, physics, earth sciences, and astronomy. Since these are rather complex sciences, the content of each in terms of early childhood education is discussed below. Teachers who are not familiar with the concepts outlined in each area will find much good information in the topical books that are listed in the references at the end of the chapter. Many of these are appropriate for use by young children as well as their teachers.

BIOLOGY.   Concepts about plant and animal life are involved when one studies biology. Subjects such as the human body and adaptation of life forms to environment do not readily lend themselves to experimentation and observation; therefore, talks, discussions, books, audio-visual aids, and other informational sources will be the principal means of teaching about these.

Many plants and animals may be brought into the classroom, and the teacher may also capitalize on home experiences or take children on walks to observe plants and animals. Observation and experimentation should be the principal means of teaching these concepts, but informational sources may also be used.

CHEMISTRY.   Chemistry is the study of material things, their properties and their reactions when combined or subjected to changes in temperature and light. Using all the senses to explore the characteristics of a variety of materials is a first step toward discovering their properties. Children should be encouraged to observe changes that occur as materials are combined and as they are exposed to air, water, and variations in temperature.

PHYSICS.   Physics involves the study of force, energy, mechanics, light and optics. It includes the study of machines because they are tools which change the distribution of force. We tend to be unaware of these aspects of our lives because they surround us constantly. The teacher's job is to help children identify what occurs as children work and play and to design activities and experiences which can help illustrate physics concepts.

EARTH SCIENCES.   These areas deal with features of the earth's surface, such as geology, meteorology, ecology, and geography. The last two also belong in the realm of social science, since they deal with the interrelationships between man and his physical environment. Observations of weather, of the surrounding countryside, and of land and water features of interest are most appropriate to the teaching of earth science to young children.

ASTRONOMY.   Astronomy is the study of the solar system, stars, and planets. It might appear that astronomy would be remote to the interests and capabilities of young children. Yet they are well acquainted with astronauts and trips to the moon. Observation of the night sky, sunrise, and sunset, as well as visits to planetariums and use of models of the solar system may all help children gain concepts in the area of astronmy.

ACTIVITIES FOR SCIENCE INSTRUCTION

Biology

ACTIVITIES TO HELP CHILDREN UNDERSTAND PLANT LIFE

1. *Activity:* Inside a seed (PP–P)

   Materials: Large seeds such as beans. Pan or dish of water.

   Procedure: Have children soak beans in water overnight. Have them open the seeds the following day. Children should predict what they will find inside the seed.

   Suggestions and Variations: This is such a simple experiment that children can do it off and on throughout the year. The use of magnifying glasses can increase the children's ability to see details of the seed.

2. *Activity:* Sprouting seeds (P)

   Materials: Vermiculite, sand, potting soil, cotton, cedar chips, shredded newspaper, styrofoam packing chips, water, vinegar oil; aluminum pie tins from frozen pot pies; bean seeds.

   Procedure: Encourage several interested children to plant seeds in pie tins containing one of the media listed above. Each pie tin should be labeled with the medium it contains (this is not crucial, as the appearances are distinctive). Children should watch the seeds for several weeks to see in which tins they grow and in which tins they do not. Teachers should help children think of reasons why some media support growth and others do not.

3. *Activity:* Sprouting seeds to eat (PP–P)

   Materials: Alfalfa seeds, mung bean seeds; two large glass jars (institutional size); wire or fabric mesh to cover the jar mouths.

   Procedure: Help interested children sprout the bean and alfalfa seeds in the jars. Follow the directions on the seed packages. This usually involves placing a layer of seeds in the bottom of a jar, covering the jars with wire or fabric mesh, rinsing daily, and keeping them in a dark place. The volume of the sprouted seeds will be many times that of the original seeds.

   Spouted seeds can be served at snack.

Suggestions and Variations: Guinea pigs and rabbits love alfalfa and bean sprouts.

Sprouted seeds may be used in food prepared by the children, such as chop suey or fried rice.

4. *Activity:* What makes a plant grow? (P)

Materials: Eight or nine slips of coleus; a small pot for each slip; potting soil and several pebbles; graph paper (one-inch run on ditto); string.

Procedure: Help a few children pot the coleus slips, one to a pot. Place all of the plants in the sun and water them for the first few days. Then select one plant to place in each of the following places:

> a sunny place
> a light, but not sunny place
> a place that is sometimes light, and sometimes
> dark (a closet that is opened and closed often)
> a place that is always dark (under a can; inside
> a heavy box)

Then select one plant to treat each of the following ways:

> watered often (every day)
> watered once a week
> watered never

Encourage children to take appropriate care of each plant according to the condition under which it is grown. Plant growth can be measured with the string every other day and marked on a piece of graph paper (each plant should have its own piece of graph paper). The experiment can be continued for several weeks. The teacher should encourage children to check and care for their plants every day and to observe what is happening to their growth and color. The teacher should help children draw conclusions about what plants need if they are to grow properly.

Suggestions and Variations: There may be an appropriate time to suggest that plants that are not doing well be placed in conditions which seem to be more conducive to growth. This helps children see the dramatic effect that such conditions can have.

5. *Activity:* Terrariums (PP–P)

Materials: Glass jars such as gallon pickle jars, candy jars or goldfish bowls; potting soil; a variety of small plants such as ferns, moss, philodendrons, ivy, begonias, African violets.

Procedure: Plants may be removed from their pots by striking sharply against a table and turning the plant with root-structure and soil intact into the palm of your hand; or, if the container is large, the plants may be left in the pots. Arrange plants in the container and surround with moist potting soil. Cover. If container has no lid of its own, use clear plastic. Plants should not be watered until soil looks and feels dry. Water condensation on the glass will indicate the moisture level. Children should be asked to observe changes seen, e.g., water condensation on glass. They may be asked to guess where the water comes from and can be provided with books which explain the water cycle.

Suggestions and Variations: A lizard may be added to the terrarium. Insects will need to be provided as food, if one is. A desert terrarium can be constructed using sand as ground and cactus for plants.

6. *Activity:* Starting plants (PP–P)

Materials: Variety of seeds, some saved from food children have eaten (i.e., avocado, apple, orange), others purchased at the store; variety of vegetables such as sweet potatoes, white potatoes, beets, carrots and turnips; slips of ivy, coleus, and wandering Jew; potting soil, dishes, glasses, pebbles, pots, and water.

Procedure: Encourage a few interested children to do this project. Seeds may be planted in potting soil in dishes or pans. Vegetables should be suspended with toothpicks in water in dishes or glasses. The leafy tops of turnips, beets, and carrots should be trimmed. Avocado seeds require special procedures to start. They are sprouted first in water. Then they are placed in soil so the top of the seed is above soil level. They are slow to sprout, so one should not give up if no roots appear for many weeks.

7. *Activity:* Gardening (PP–P)

Materials: Seeds for lettuce, tomato, pumpkin, zinnias, sunflowers, and spinach; pans; soil; space outdoors for a small garden; spades.

Procedure: The actual procedure will vary depending on climatic conditions. In warmer areas where planting can begin in late April or early May, garden spots can be tilled and lettuce and spinach planted in time for eating before school is out. Tomato seeds can be started inside in March or April and then transplanted to the outside garden in May. Flowers can be planted in early spring. If someone can care for the plants over the summer, the tomatoes, zinnias and sunflowers should be at their peaks when children return to school in the fall.

Pumpkins would be ready later in the fall. In colder regions, frost does not cease until early or middle June. Tomato plants and zinnias can be started indoors from seed before school is out for the summer. On the very last days of school, children can prepare the

Gardening is good science activity for young children.

Even young children should be given real garden tools.

garden plot and transplant the plants, or children can take their plants home to plant and care for during the summer.

Suggestions and Variations: Children can save the seeds from their Halloween Jack-o'-lantern for planting in the spring. It's a good idea to buy additional seed in case the ones from the pumpkin do not germinate.

Garden soil should be analyzed to determine if it is suitable for growing vegetables. A small sample can be sent to the nearest Agricultural Extension Service office for analysis and advice on soil needs.

8. *Activity:*   Decorating the classroom (PP–P)

Materials: Several different kinds of plants including coleus, begonia, spider, and Swedish ivy; materials for a hanging flower pot, if possible (primary children can macrame the cords).

Procedure: Keep these plants in the classroom during the year. Encourage children to care for these, including watering, feeding, trimming, and repotting when necessary. These plants can be the source of clippings for the children's experiments or for plants to take home as gifts, but their primary function is to make the classroom an attractive place to be and to involve children in its care.

ACTIVITIES TO HELP CHILDREN UNDERSTAND ANIMAL LIFE

1. *Activity:*   Caring for animals (PP–P)

Materials: Cages, food, water, and other equipment to care for animals in a safe and sanitary manner; animal books; writing and drawing equipment.

Procedure: Before bringing an animal into the classroom, prepare yourself and the children by reading and talking about the animal, its habits, and the natural conditions in which it thrives. Plan with the children for the care of the animal to protect it from harm and to keep it healthy and happy. When the animal is brought into the classroom, the children should be asked to observe such things as what the animal likes to eat, when and how it sleeps, how it moves, what it likes to do. Children may record their observations by writing stories, drawing pictures, making tape recordings, or, as a group, making an experience chart.

Suggestions and Variations: Gerbils and hamsters are particularly popular for school classrooms. One drawback is that they tend to be nocturnal and sleep much of the time that children are present. Animals other than mammals might be considered. Lizards, poultry, and snakes are interesting to children.

2. *Activity:* Aquarium (PP–P)

> **Materials:** Kit of materials for establishing an aquarium, including the following: five or ten gallon glass tank; sand; assortment of shells, stones, and other decorative materials; filter and pump; charcoal; glass wool; aquarium plants. (Although artificial plants are preferred by many because they are less trouble, real plants should be purchased in order to lay the groundwork for understanding the interdependence of plants and animals.)
> Purchase fish and snails only after the tank has been set up.
>
> **Procedure:** A small group of children may assist an adult in setting up the aquarium. Follow these steps: (1) Put clean sand in the bottom of the tank. If beach sand is used, wash it thoroughly by putting in a shallow pan and letting water run in and over the sides. Swish the sand around with the hand until the water runs clear. (2) Add water until it is about an inch above the level of the sand. (3) Arrange plants and decorative materials. Anchor the plants in the sand, covering the roots. (4) Put about a quarter to a half inch of charcoal in the filter then fill with glass wool packed lightly. Immerse in the water and attach plastic tube. (5) Fill tank with water until about an inch from the top. To avoid disturbing the sand and plants, pour water slowly over a piece of paper against the side of the tank. As the above is being done, discuss with the children why each item is needed: plants because they look pretty and provide oxygen; decorative materials for attractiveness; filter to keep the water clean and provide air. How the pump works should also be explored.
> When the tank is set up, let the water age overnight. Plan a buying trip to the pet store for fish. The pet store owner can advise on which fish are compatible in the same tank. Angel fish, which are showy, will eat guppies, for example. Guppies are a good choice because they are generally hardy, males are easily distinguished from females, they breed readily, and are live-bearers (the birth process may be witnessed). Buy a catfish and a few snails to keep the tank clean. After the tank is installed, children should be encouraged to notice such things as how fish eat and move about, and which part of the tank different kinds of fish seem to like the best. A magnifying glass helps children explore details in an aquarium.
>
> **Suggestions and Variations:** Add books on fish to the table where the aquarium is placed. If the tank has a good balance between fish and plants and fish are not overfed, the water should stay clean for as long as six months. A temperature of between 68° and 80° should be maintained. The tank should be away from direct sunlight to prevent rapid algae growth.

Have children assume responsibility for feeding. To avoid over-feeding, it is wise to use a feeding ring—a small plastic ring which floats on the surface. If feeding the fish is not exclusively the responsibility of one person, a tag with different colors on each side with the word "fed" on one side and "feed" on the other side may be hung near the tank. The teacher must remember to turn the tag "feed" side out before going home or when arriving in the morning. Water will evaporate from the fish tank, and children can be responsible for refilling it. Tap water kills fish because of the chlorine. Letting water stand for a few days will permit the chlorine to escape. Children can store water to refill the tank in open gallon jars. Teachers should provide guidance by asking children where they think the water goes (young children often think the fish drink it). The full water level of the tank can be marked with masking tape so children can see clearly how much water is being lost through evaporation.

3. *Activity:* How our bodies work (P)

Materials: Models, charts, filmstrips, books which illustrate and explain in simple terms the systems of the human body.

Procedure: Invite a pediatrician, pediatric nurse, or the school nurse to visit the class to explain body functions. Such arrangements should be made when a need or interest has been shown by the children. For example, a child is cut and bleeds. As you apply first aid, other children show concern and talk about what has happened. Their conversation reveals curiosity and misunderstanding about why and how a person bleeds. You provide simple explanations but note that questions are being asked which you are not prepared to answer. This interest may indicate readiness for a more extensive explanation by a professional.

Suggestions and Variations: Follow-up conversations should be held to insure that children understand clearly what was said by the visitor. When a child in the class is scheduled to go to the hospital for corrective surgery or has returned to class after a stay in the hospital, such explanations may help to reduce fear and increase understanding of the experience.

4. *Activity:* Healthy bodies (K–P)

Materials: Audio-visual aids, pictures from magazines, paper, paste, scissors.

Procedure: Present information on good health practices. This may be done by inviting a pediatrician, pediatric nurse, or school nurse to talk with the children; or the teacher may utilize audio-visual aids. (Good sources for audio-visual materials are the state and local departments of health, which may maintain an audio-visual library; and the Dairy Council.)

Suggestions and Variations: Make "do–don't "cause–effect", or "good–bad" posters. To start this activity, ask children such questions as "What happens when you stay up to see the late show night after night?" "How do you feel when you've had a good night's sleep?" "Can you make a poster to show us what happens?" For readers, these questions may be on an activity card placed next to a selection of art and writing materials. As a class project, a large sheet of paper divided into two sections may be attached to the wall. The word "sick" and a picture of a pale, listless child may be pasted to the top of one side while the word "healthy" and a picture of a robust, active child appears at the top of the other section. Children are encouraged to paste cut-out pictures or draw pictures of what they think the children do which makes children "sick" or "healthy."

5. *Activity:* Snack (PP–K)

Materials: Food for snack which can be prepared by the children; utensils for preparing food.

Procedure: Select only those foods of high nutritional value, such as fresh fruit juices, raw fruits and vegetables, whole grains and nuts, and milk products. Informally, as children are preparing and eating snack, teachers can talk about the special value of types of food.

Suggestions and Variations: Young children usually like to eat foods they have seen adults eat, foods that they have had frequent exposure to, and foods that are prepared and served in an attractive way. "Preaching" and "lecturing" to children about what they should eat is usually only effective in strengthening their resolve not to eat certain foods.

Chemistry

ACTIVITIES TO HELP CHILDREN OBSERVE CHARACTERISTICS OF VARIOUS MATERIALS

1. *Activity:* Smelling (PP–K)

Materials: Plastic pill containers with lids obtained from a pharmacy; metal photographic film containers with screw-on lids, or other small containers; a variety of common substances which may be distinguished by smell (onions, cinnamon, perfume, coffee, soap, pine needles, etc.).

Procedure: Puncture lids of containers so fragrance can emerge, or use gauze attached by rubber bands as a lid. Be sure substance cannot be seen from outside the container. (Cover clear bottles with aluminum foil or opaque paper.) Mark each with a number or letter and prepare a key (a chart showing the number and a picture of the contents) so children can determine if their guesses are accurate. Children sniff the containers and guess what each contains.

2. *Activity:* Touching (PP–K)

Materials: A variety of materials that vary in texture (sandpaper, velvet, fake fur, pinecone, satin, corduroy, flocked wallpaper, vinyl floor tile, mosaic floor tile, smooth wood, etc.).

Procedure: Place materials in a closed box that has a hole large enough for a child's hand cut in one side. Children reach in through the hole, feel the objects, and talk about the materials. Guidance would include stopping by as children are engaged in the activity and talking about how the materials feel, and providing vocabulary (hard, soft, rough, stiff, slick, etc.). Teachers can also encourage children to guess what the materials are and for what they might be used.

Suggestions and Variations: A texture board can be made by gluing materials to a large piece of cardboard, with the interesting texture side facing out. Children can then feel the materials and also see how their appearance varies with their texture.

3. *Activity:* Snack (PP–K)

Materials: Pudding, apples, celery, carrots, peanut butter, nuts, and other nutritious snack items.

Procedure: Proceed with snack as usual, but talk with children about the different smells and textures of the foods they are served. Two foods with contrasting textures might be served on the same day so children can compare them.

4. *Activity:* Woodworking (PP–K)

Materials: Wood, nails, sandpaper, hammer, saw, plane, and other woodworking tools being used in the woodworking center.

Procedure: Encourage children to use the woodworking center. They will find out that materials have different characteristics such as hardness and roughness. Guidance from the teacher should include calling children's attention to the characteristics and talking about how they determine uses of the material (nails are hard and can be driven into other materials; sandpaper is rough and can make wood smooth, etc.).

ACTIVITIES TO HELP CHILDREN UNDERSTAND THE PROPERTIES OF DIFFERENT TYPES OF SUBSTANCES

1. Activity: Salad dressing (PP–P)

Materials: Vinegar, oil, salt, pepper, lettuce.

Procedure: Select a small group of children to prepare the salad and salad dressing. Help children identify the ingredients, especially the vinegar and oil. Help children note that the vinegar and oil do not mix, but that the oil forms very small droplets in the vinegar for a short time.

2. Activity: Water and oil (PP–P)

Materials: Clear plastic bottles with caps (such as the bottles cooking oil is sold in); water; oil.

Procedure: Fill bottle about ¾ full with water. Add 2 tablespoons oil to the water. Cap the bottle. Place bottle out where children can use it. Encourage children to try and mix the two layers they see in the bottle. Guidance would include asking children what they think the two materials are.

Suggestions and Variations: Food coloring can be added to the contents of the bottle. It is soluble in water and so mixes with it, thus making the oil droplets stand out better. Children should be encouraged to think of other substances (liquid) which could be added to water. As they come up with these ideas, more bottles should be supplied so they can test out their ideas.

3. Activity: Soap bubbles (PP–K)

Materials: Water pans or plastic tubs; newspapers or terry towels, rotary beaters, wire whips, straws; liquid soap, *not* detergent; plastic or oilcloth aprons.

Procedure: Children should wear plastic aprons. Water containers should be placed on newspaper or terry towels so any spills will be absorbed. Children (two or three at a time, depending on space) make bubbles using any of the equipment. Guidance would include asking children what's inside the outer film of the bubble. Teachers can also ask children why they think some of the utensils make big bubbles while others make small ones.

Suggestions and Variations: Cut straws in half to reduce cost of materials. Children do not need a whole straw. Half of one works well.

4. Activity: Air-filled bottle (PP–K)

Materials: Bowl of water; small bottle with lid or cap.

Procedure: Encourage children to cover the bottle with its lid or cap and then submerge it in the water, where the lid or cap should be removed. Children will see bubbles of air emerge from the bottle as it fills with water.

5. *Activity:* Candle making (K–P)

   Materials: Wax, paraffin, coloring; utensils to make candles.
   Procedure: Find directions in craft books or magazines for specific candles to make. Follow directions. Talk with children about how the wax changes, depending on the temperature.
   Suggestions and Variations: As with all activities which require heat, safety must be of primary concern. Special care must be taken when working with hot wax. Follow safety procedures carefully.

6. *Activity:* Cool snack (PP–K)

   Materials: Ice trays, refrigerator with freezing compartment; juice.
   Procedure: Help children fill ice trays and place them in the refrigerator to freeze. Help children remove ice from trays when it is ready and use it to chill their juice. Guidance would include talking about how water changes from liquid to solid when it freezes, and how ice floats on the top of the juice in the cup.
   Suggestions and Variations: Children may enjoy a few ice cubes in the water-play tubs from time to time.

ACTIVITIES TO HELP CHILDREN UNDERSTAND CHEMICAL CHANGES

1. *Activity:* The shape of things (PP–K)

   Materials: Colored construction paper; flat objects such as a pair of scissors, a small book, a sponge, a key, etc.
   Procedure: Encourage interested children to place the objects on the paper, which is then placed in the sunlight. Leave the objects on the paper for several days. The sun will bleach the color where the paper is exposed, but not where the objects have covered it.

2. *Activity:* Rust (PP–P)

   Materials: Iron nails and other iron objects, as well as metals that do not rust; shallow aluminum pie tin with water.
   Procedure: Put objects out for children to see. Encourage interested children to place the objects in water and then observe for a few days to see if any of the objects change.

3. *Activity:* Painting equipment (PP–P)

   Materials: Tricycles, swings, wagons, and any other metal equipment; paint to touch up equipment; brushes and cleaner to clean them after painting.

Procedure: Point out to children any rust spots that appear on outdoor equipment. Involve children in preparing the spots for touch-up and also permit them to help paint the spots. Talk about what causes the rust, and that paint helps keep things from rusting.

4. *Activity:* Photography (P)

Materials: Camera, film, developing materials, and a dark room to work in (or arrange to visit someone else's).
Procedure: Permit children to take pictures with the camera and then help develop the film.
Suggestions and Variations: This activity would be most appropriate for children in the upper primary grades. The contact with chemicals and the timing and care necessary in processing film is too complicated for younger children.

5. *Activity:* Cooking (PP–P)

Materials: Ingredients and utensils to make cakes, cookies, bread, biscuits, etc.
Procedure: Select a small group of children to do the cooking. Discuss the changes that occur in the process of preparing the food and why they occur.
Suggestions and Variations: With young preprimary children, the discussion should focus on changes in appearance (the bread dough was small and then it got big; the bread dough was soft, and the baked bread was hard; the cake batter was wet, and the baked cake is dry, etc.). As children are able to comprehend the information, the discussion can include more and more of the reasons for the change (yeast ferments the sugar and a gas is formed, making the bread rise).

6. *Activity:* Fizz (PP–P)

Materials: Baking soda, vinegar; small dishes; spoons.
Procedure: Have children predict what they think will happen if vinegar and soda are combined. Then permit them to combine the two and see what happens.
Suggestions and Variations: For older children, this activity may be related to what happens when you put baking powder or yeast in baked goods. Buttermilk pancakes may be made. Children can notice what happens when soda is added to the buttermilk and can discuss soda's function in the pancakes.

7. *Activity:* Flat drops (P)

Materials: Medicine droppers, aluminum pie tins; Ivory liquid, salt, food coloring, vinegar; several bowls, water.

Procedure: Provide materials for children (two or three at a time depending on space) to work with. Bowls should be used for different types of water: plain, salted, soaped, colored, etc. Children can make these mixtures and label the containers. Ask children to place drops of each mixture in a pie tin and determine if some are flat and others rounded. Children should be asked to speculate about the causes of their results. Teacher guidance will include adding suggestions and providing information.

Suggestions and Variations: This activity illustrates the action of surface tension. If possible, provide reading material about surface tension. This activity can be illustrated well with drawings. Encourage children to make drawings of their results and label them. Spelling for labels is simplified if the containers for the items to be added to water have been labeled. Children can then copy the needed words.

Provide pieces of waxed paper. Have children place a few drops of water on a piece of waxed paper and roll it around. (The drops will unite into one.) Then drop a few grains of powdered detergent into the drop and observe what happens. (The drop will flatten out and seep through the paper.)

Physics

ACTIVITIES TO HELP CHILDREN UNDERSTAND SIMPLE MACHINES

1. Activity: Wheels #1 (PP)

Materials: Tricycles, wagons, wheeled toys of all sizes. (Include some toys from which wheels may be removed and put on again.)

Procedure: Include a large variety of wheeled toys in the block area, on the playground, and in areas where there is space to run wheeled toys without disturbing other activities. Encourage free exploration and help children verbalize what they observe. For example, a child has a tricycle upside down and is turning the front wheel by moving the pedals by hand. You might comment with mock surprise: "The rear wheels aren't turning!" or you might ask questions such as "What's happening to the front wheel when you do that?"

2. Activity: Wheels #2 (P)

Materials: Sturdy cardboard cartons or plywood cartons (cigar boxes, cheese boxes, etc.); drill and bit; lengths of dowel to extend beyond sides of cartons; plywood circles, jar lids, extra-strength cardboard circles; glue or hammer and thin nails.

Procedure: Discuss with children ways in which wheeled carts might be made from the materials. Holes may be drilled in the cartons close to the base and exactly opposite each other. Holes need to be large enough to allow the dowel to turn easily. Wheels must be fastened on the dowel after it is inserted into holes in the cart. The dowel when attached to the wheels in this fashion is called an axle.

Suggestions and Variations: The trickiest part will be fastening the wheels to the axle. Find the center of the cardboard or plywood circle and, using a bit the same size as the dowel, drill a hole. It would be wise for the teacher to do this in advance. When wheels are fastened to the axle, coat the joint with glue. If jar lids are used as wheels, they should be nailed to the ends of the dowel-axle. Children may work in pairs on this project. Assignment cards may be useful and might take the following form:

Can you make a wheeled cart with the materials on this table?

Before you start, load the box with blocks and push or pull it across the table. Notice how it feels and how hard you have to pull or push. After cart is made, put the same number of blocks in it and again pull or push it across the table.

A display of all sorts of wheels may be set up. Books about wheels may be provided. Children may be interested in speculating about how people managed to move things before there were wheels.

3. *Activity:* Gears and springs (PP–P)

   Materials: Old worn-out alarm clocks, gear-driven toys, music boxes, old watches, etc.

   Procedure: Place these on the table. Tell children that these are items that people have discarded because they no longer work well. Children may find out what made them work by taking them apart. Teachers can encourage children to describe what they see inside. Children may be able to move one gear with their fingers to see what happens to the one attached to it, or to wind up springs.

   Suggestions and Variations: Children may draw pictures or write stories about what they see.

4. *Activity:* Downhill racer (inclined plane) (P)

   Materials: Blocks, flat boards, matched pair of toy cars or balls, ruler, stopwatch.

   Procedure: While children are playing in the block corner, suggest the following, or set up a table with the above materials and an assignment card:

Put two blocks under one end of one of these boards.

Put three blocks under one end of another board.

Allow one car to run down each of the boards.

Measure how far the car goes on the table before it stops.

With a friend, race cars down the inclined boards.

Ask someone to time the cars using a stopwatch. (You will need to mark a finish line on the table with a strip of masking tape.)

Suggestions and Variations: Provide extra blocks so that children may experiment with steeper slopes. Commercial toys such as trains and racing cars with tracks may be introduced. Set up a display of various inclined planes: doorstops (wedge shaped), axes, wedges of various types, pictures of ramps, dump trucks, etc. Discuss how they help people do work.

5. *Activity:* Ladders (PP–P)

Materials: Portable ladders for climbing on a climbing box.

Procedure: Suggest children adjust their ladders so different inclines are obtained. Talk about which are harder to climb—steep ladders or more slanted ladders. Help children see that the steeper the incline, the shorter the distance to the top (it takes less ladder) but the harder the climb.

6. *Activity:* Circular inclined planes (P)

Materials: Drill, variety of screws, screwdriver, screw-on lids and jars; pieces of soft wood 1″–2″ thick.

Procedure: Make materials available for children to work with. Help children notice that the lines on a drill bit, a screw, and a jar lid slant as they go around, which makes them easier to use.

Suggestions and Variations: Try to find screws that differ in terms of numbers and slant of lines. Have children compare the ease with which each can be screwed into a piece of wood.

7. *Activity:* Levers (P)

Materials: Claw hammer and boards with nails driven part-way in; erasers or other small objects and a triangular-shaped piece of wood with a flat board which may be balanced on it; screws and screwdrivers; a flat square board and a ball which fits in the top of a cup; slingshot and ping-pong balls or balls of styrofoam; basin with sand, a shovel, a toy steam shovel.

Procedure: Allow children to explore freely. They might pull out nails; screw in screws; put an eraser on the lower end of the board resting on the triangular-shaped piece of wood and press down on the board's upper end (catapult); balance the square board on the ball in the cup and see how small blocks can be placed on it without destroying the balance; shovel sand with the toy steam shovel and with the hand shovel; and use the slingshot with styrofoam balls or ping-pong balls (a target such as a shoe box or small basin should be provided for this). In discussion, introduce the word *lever* and talk about what each of these do.

Suggestions and Variations: Not all of the above need be put out at once. It may be preferable to introduce separately such things as the catapult, balance board, and slingshot and to add the shovel and toy steam shovel to the sandbox as a new dimension. A scrapbook of levers may be made with pictures of such things as a steam shovel, a man prying a stone from the ground, a jackhammer, a seesaw, etc. The word *fulcrum* may be added to the vocabulary and the fulcrum identified on the seesaw, the claw hammer, and the catapult.

8. *Activity:* Lifting loads (PP–K)

   Materials: A large pulley; twice enough rope to reach from a low tree branch to the ground; sand or dirt; bucket; hook.

   Procedure: Attach pulley to tree branch. Thread rope through pulley and attach to one end. Leave other end free, but knotted so it can be held easily. Children can fill buckets with sand or dirt and then lift them up by pushing the pulley.

9. *Activity:* Clothesline pulley (PP–P)

   Materials: Clothesline; two pulleys attached to opposite walls of a room, one end high on the wall, and the other end low enough to be easily reached by children; pincer clothespins.

   Procedure: Encourage children to hang up their own paintings on the clothesline to dry. Children can attach their paintings to the low end and then move the rope to send their painting to the high end. The rope goes around the pulleys at each end.

ACTIVITIES TO HELP CHILDREN UNDERSTAND LIGHT, HEAT, AND SOUND

1. *Activity:* Making rainbows (PP–P)

   Materials: Jar and water, prisms, white paper; soap solution and bubble pipes.

   Procedure: Fill jar with water and place it on a window sill where there is sunlight, or hang prisms in a window. Hold white paper in

Simple pulleys can be made from scrap materials.

front of the jar or prism so that the sun shines through onto the paper. Bands of color (a rainbow) will appear on the paper. Ask children to identify the colors and the order in which they appear. Ask them to recall rainbows they have seen. What kind of weather was there when they saw the rainbow? Was it raining? Was the sun shining? Or both?

Give children soap solution and pipes outside on a sunny day. Encourage them to notice and talk about the colors they see in the bubbles.

Suggestions and Variations: The light refraction, which appears as a rainbow, may occur when the sun shines through an aquarium and children may comment spontaneously. Follow up on such spontaneous remarks with the above activity. Attractive art projects may result from this activity.

2. *Activity:* Light spots (PP–P)

Materials: Bowl of water, small hand mirrors.

Procedure: Place bowl of water on floor, table, or shelf where it catches the sunlight. The water will reflect the light onto the ceiling or wall depending on the angle it strikes the water. This may be done before the children enter the room. If children do not spontaneously notice and remark on the spots of light, call attention to them and start a search for the source. Use hand mirrors in similar fashion.

Suggestions and Variations: Have children sort materials such as construction paper, aluminum foil, bottle lids, opaque plastic pieces, and shiny and dull coins into containers marked *reflectors* and *non-reflectors*. Help children decide what characteristics materials must have in order to reflect light.

3. *Activity:* Making things safe (PP–P)

    Materials: Collection of reflectors like the ones found on bicycles; fluorescent materials like those used to mark guard rails or mailboxes; stick-on fluorescent materials like those provided by fire departments to mark clothing, bicycles, and bedroom windows.

    Procedure: Make a display of these items. Discuss with children how the items are used to prevent accidents. Enough stick-on dots can be obtained from the local fire department to mark the children's clothing.

4. *Activity:* Shadows in sunlight (PP–K)

    Materials: Sunlight; children's bodies.

    Procedure: As children play outside, point out their shadows. If children go out at different times during the day, help them note how their shadows change.

5. *Activity:* Heat (P)

    Materials: Test tube and test-tube holder, candle or other source of heat, water.

    Procedure: Put water into test tube and mark level with a rubber band. Hold over the candle flame and watch what happens. Call attention to little bubbles moving through the water as it nears boiling point. Note level of water.

    Suggestions and Variations: In science kits there is a metal ball and a ring mounted on sticks. When heated, the ball will not go through the ring, but when cold it will. As does any activity which involves fire or high heat, this needs to be carefully supervised.

6. *Activity:* Sound is conducted (PP–P)

    Materials: Two tin cans, nails, ten or more feet of wire.

    Procedure: Hammer nails into ends of cans. Wrap wire around nails. Have one child hold one can against an ear while another child talks into the other can.

Suggestions and Variations: Two funnels stuck into the ends of a long piece of hose may be used as a variation of this. For other explorations of sound, see the activities in the chapter on expressive arts. Call attention to vibrations.

ACTIVITIES TO HELP CHILDREN DEVELOP UNDERSTANDINGS ABOUT LENSES

1. Activity: Real lenses (PP–P)

Materials: Hand magnifying glasses, old box-style cameras, binoculars, small telescope, old eyeglasses.

Procedure: Make these materials available for children to explore. They will notice that some of the lenses make objects appear smaller and farther away, whereas other lenses make objects appear bigger and closer. Help the children explore the curvatures of the lenses to see if they can discern the difference.

Suggestions and Variations: It is helpful to tape comic pages from the newspaper (Sunday, colored ones) to a tabletop or to the bottom of a water table and to place different kinds of lenses on them. Children tend to look at the comics through the lenses. This arrangement prevents children from wandering around the room with the lenses and misplacing them.

2. Activity: Magnifying jar (P)

Materials: Glass jar or bottle with rounded sides (mayonnaise jars work well); water; objects to hold behind the jar (word cards, pencil, etc.).

Procedure: Have children fill the jar with water and then hold objects behind the jar and look through it to view them. Objects and writing will appear larger behind the jar because the jar's outwardly sloping sides make the water act like a lens. The teacher should explain to children that glass and water can bend the light rays as they pass through and thus make the object look different.

ACTIVITIES TO HELP CHILDREN UNDERSTAND FORCE AND PRESSURE

1. Activity: Pinwheels (PP–K)

Materials: Pinwheels, either commercially made or made from paper, pins, and pencils. (See Figure 25.)

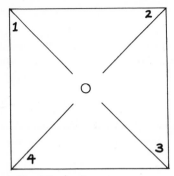 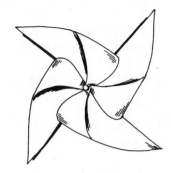

Figure 25. Pinwheels.

Procedure: Take pinwheels outside and hold them in the wind. Talk with children about what makes the pinwheel move. When the wind stops and the pinwheel is still, help children think of other ways to make the pinwheel move. Some possible solutions are blowing on them, using a small electric fan (with a good screen guard), or using the reverse end of a vacuum cleaner.

Suggestions and Variations: On field trips and other outings call attention to windmills, sailboats moving on bodies of water, and clouds moving across the sky. Relate these movements to experiences with pinwheels.

2. *Activity:* Snack preparation (PP–K)

   Materials: Cans of juice, can opener.

   Procedure: Permit a few children to help prepare juice. Start by punching only one hole in the top of the juice can. It will pour with difficulty. Then punch another hole. The juice will now pour easily as air moves in to replace the juice.

3. *Activity:* Vacuums (K–P)

   Materials: Straws and milk or juice; medicine dropper and bowl of water; vacuum cleaner.

   Procedure: Permit children to use the above items in appropriate situations (straws at juice time, dropper and water during activity time, vacuum at clean-up time). Through discussion and questions, help children understand that when air is removed from something, an empty space or vacuum is created, and some other substance rushes in to fill the empty space.

4. *Activity:* Pumps (PP–P)

   Materials: Hypodermic and bulb syringes, pump-type hand lotion or spray bottles, straws, water; old, hand-operated water pump mounted over a tank of water if possible.

Procedure: Encourage children to exlore freely with these various kinds of pumps. As they work, ask questions which will further children's thinking. For example, as a child pushes the plunger down on a hypodermic syringe with the tip held under water, ask, "Do you see what's happening" (Bubbles.) What are those bubbles? A child who doesn't know can be asked to hold an empty syringe with the tip about an inch above one arm and to push the plunger down. What does the child feel?

Suggestions and Variations: These items are good for outdoor water play. When they are used inside, children will need to be reminded to point the water toward the tub!

5. *Activity:* Jumping Jimminy (PP–K)

Materials: Commercial canvas cover to fit over large inner tube. (Makes a small trampoline-like piece of equipment that children can jump up and down on.)

Procedure: Permit children to play on the equipment outside on the ground or, if there is space, inside on a mat. When children jump on the piece of equipment the air in the inner tube is compressed, but then it "bounces back" and propels the child upward. This illustrates how air exerts force on other objects.

6. *Activity:* Inflatable things (PP–P)

Materials: Balloons, plastic bags, inner tubes, inflatable balls; bicycle pump.

Procedure: Allow children to inflate items and then use them. These items illustrate that air has weight and exerts pressure.

7. *Activity:* Water pressure (PP–P)

Materials: Garden hose with nozzle attachment; pipes in a variety of diameters and types which fit together. (One piece of the pipe should connect with a faucet or garden hose.) Tin can with a vertical line of holes punched about one inch apart from the bottom nearly to the top.

Procedure: Pipes and garden hose and nozzle can be made available to children outside in warm weather. Children can discover that the narrower the pipe, the stronger the force of water as it emerges. Children should look at the nozzle to see how it is constructed and notice how it changes the force with which water comes out of the hose. The can with holes can be used for inside water play. A faucet works best to fill it. Children will notice that the water stream from the bottom hole is the longest, while the water stream from the top hole is the shortest. If no faucet and sink are available in the classroom, the tin can can be filled by being dipped into a bucket or pan of water.

8. *Activity:* Water and tubes (K–P)

Materials: Tubs of water; bowls and funnels; pincer clothespins; metal racks (i.e., from felt board or experience charts); wooden building blocks or other materials to use as platforms to raise the height of some water bowls; newspapers to soak up spills; pieces of clear plastic tubing varying in thickness from ¾ in. to ¼ in. (Each piece should be at least 3 ft long. Some longer pieces of the smaller diameter tubing would also be useful.)

Procedure: Materials can be placed out together and arranged so children can explore them. Children will discover lots of ways to combine the equipment to transport water from one bowl to another. Teacher guidance would include questions and suggestions such as "Can you find out through which size tubing water travels the fastest from a given height?" or "Can you find something to stop the flow of water in that tube?" Clothespins can be used to stop the flow of water in tubes as well as to attach them to the metal racks at a height.

9. *Activity:* Sink and float (PP–P)

Materials: Large variety of objects such as washers, ping-pong balls, golf tees, poker chips, paper clips, pins, colored wooden cubes, blocks of wood, plastic fishing bobs, bolts, buttons, spools, corks, rubber jar rings, erasers, pieces of styrofoam, pebbles, etc.; container for water, such as plastic dishpan or water-play table; two smaller containers, labeled with pictures showing something floating and something sinking or with the words "sink" and "float."

Procedure: Place water tub on terry towel or newspaper laid on a table or the floor. Make objects available in appropriate container near water tub. Encourage children to place objects in water to see if they sink or float and then place them into the properly labeled containers.

Suggestions and Variations: Do not provide too many objects at any one time. New objects can be added and old objects removed every three or four days. Encourage children to try to find ways to make sinking objects float.

Younger children will be content to sort objects into sink or float containers rather than seeking reasons for floating or sinking. Teachers should not insist that they do so. Older children will become interested in solving the problem of what determines flotation. At this point teachers should help children generate possible hypotheses through questioning—"How are these objects different from these?" "Do you suppose all of these are heavier than these?" A pan balance can be provided to find out. "Do you think size has anything to do with it?" "Are these alike in any way and different from the others in any way?" Older children might also be interested in altering the condition of the water to see if this affects the flotation of objects in any way. Ice, food coloring, sugar, soap, and salt should be provided so children can experiment. Smaller bowls are helpful at this point so that a great deal of the materials is not consumed. Older children might notice that there are many gradations of sinking and floating. Some objects float, though almost totally submerged. Others float midway, while others are on top of the water. They may want to test objects for these fine distinctions. Children may be asked to see if they can make a ball of plasticene float. Children who live near a port may find it interesting to take a trip to see large ships and find out about *ballast*.

10. *Activity:* Parachute (K–P)

   Materials: Parachute purchased commercially from school equipment company.
   Procedure: Follow suggestions that come with the parachute for ways to use it. Add to the discussion, however, by commenting that air has weight and takes up space and that it resists the falling parachute.

   Astronomy

ACTIVITIES TO HELP CHILDREN GAIN CONCEPTS RELATED TO THE MOVEMENT OF THE EARTH AND SUN

1. *Activity:* Day and night (PP–P)

   Materials: Mounted globe map of the earth; a flashlight or small light bulb.
   Procedure: Begin a discussion with children about what they do during the day and at night. Lead into questions about what causes the change from day to night, and night to day. In a closet, a large packing box or other place that can be darkened, set up the globe and station the flashlight or light bulb in such a way that it will shine most directly on the equator. Show children the approximate area where they live. Have them mark it with a piece of colored

Parachutes help children learn about force and resistance.

tape or a pin. Have the children spin the globe and note where the marked area is in relation to the light.

Suggestions and Variations: The globe and light activity would not be appropriate for young preprimary children, although older preprimary children can understand the idea that at night they are "not where the sun shines." For older primary children, the globe may be moved around the sun (light bulb) in an ellipse to demonstrate where the sun's rays hit at different times of the year (the seasons), or a model of the solar system may be used.

2. *Activity:*   Sunrise, sunset (PP–P)

Materials: None.

Procedure: Ask children to note where they see the sun in the morning and where in the evening. Children could even change the position of plants in the classroom in order to keep them in the sunlight. Children should be helped to relate their observations to the activity of the earth and sun activity (primary age children).

3. *Activity:*   Gardening (PP-P)

Materials: Enough outdoor space to allow for a garden plot; tools for working the garden; seeds for the garden; stakes; string.

Procedure: Help children mark the edges of shadows from trees and buildings in the yard at different times of the day. Help children determine where the sunniest spot in the outdoor space is.

4. Activity: The seasons (PP–P)

Materials: Outdoor environment; pictures of outdoor environment.

Procedure: Help children notice changes in the seasons by commenting about new plant growth, cessation of growth, need for outdoor clothing, frequency and form of precipitation (rain, sleet snow), etc. For preprimary children, the focus should be observation of the indicators of seasonal changes as well as the names for each. Older children should be helped to relate these observations to the changes in movement of earth around the sun.

Suggestions and Variations: Spring flowers and autumn leaves are excellent materials to use for aesthetic displays in the classroom, and can serve to initiate children's interest in other signs of a season.

A large outdoor thermometer mounted where children can see it provides a good ongoing experience which ties in with the study of seasons. Preprimary children should not be expected to master reading the thermometer, but they can understand that "when the red line goes up it's hot outside, and when it goes down it's cold outside." Older primary children can read a thermometer and may keep a graph illustrating the variation in temperature over a period of several months. If a few annual plants of some type are placed outside, children can relate seasonal changes to growing seasons, because they will be able to see the adverse effects of low temperatures on plants.

Earth sciences

ACTIVITIES TO HELP CHILDREN GAIN AN UNDERSTANDING OF WEATHER

1. Activity: Weather station (PP–P)

Materials: Outdoor thermometer, large mounted calendar, drawings and paper to be used to indicate different weather (yellow circle for sunny day; white irregular shaped paper to indicate cloudy day; white irregular shaped paper with black dots to indicate rain; white paper cut to look like a snowflake to indicate snowy days), large cardboard doll, mounted, with paper clothes suitable for all types of weather.

Procedure: For younger children, provide the large cardboard doll and paper clothes. Children observe the daily weather, and dress the doll appropriately. Sometimes the weather will change within a day, so the doll's clothes may need to be changed more than once a day. (Be sure to include all types of clothes for the doll and not design them to indicate the doll is necessarily a boy or girl.) Older preprimary and kindergarten children will be able to place weather pictures on a daily calendar. It has been one author's experience that this activity works best as one of many during activity or work time, rather than as a routine function to be performed at group time. Some children will not become involved in it at all, but others will spend a great deal of time taking care of the weather calendar.

Primary children may keep a record of the weather for each week in a weather book. They may record such items as the daily temperature, whether the sun is shining, whether it's raining or snowing and how much accumulates, and whether it is windy or calm.

Suggestions and Variations: Kindergarten and young primary children can make a permanent weather calendar book from the daily records they keep on the large mounted calendar. At the end of each month, before the new month is put up by rotating the numerals on the calendar and changing the name, children can paste smaller replicas of each weather symbol onto a calendar drawn on construction paper. Because of the visual differences among the various weather symbols, it is easy to see rather quickly whether a month was rainy or snowy, or cloudy or sunny. Children can compare the months. Such records are nice to pass on with the children as they go on to the next grade or, if children are in a multi-age classroom, to retain for the next year. New records can be made for the current year, and these can be compared with those from the previous year. Children could predict the next month's weather on the basis of the last year's record.

Primary children may be interested in listening to local weather forecasts and comparing them with actual weather. Books about weather should be provided for children so that they might gain some understanding of factors that determine weather.

Primary age children might incorporate their weather study and predicting into plans made for class activities. For example, if a walking trip is being considered for some aspect of study, they may want to consider weather conditions in planning when it should be made.

2. *Activity:* Irrigation system (P)

   Materials: A section of the playground, preferably with a small mound where children may be permitted to dig holes and trenches and run water. Pieces of plywood, sheet metal, or masonite approximately 6″ × 8″ × ¼″ may be provided for watergates. Other useful materials are tin cans with both ends removed (be sure there are no jagged edges), small pieces of garden hose, aluminum foil or plastic for lining the reservoir. Trowels or shovels are needed.

Procedure: Digging trenches, watching water run, and building dams are such interesting activities for young children that the provisioning with materials may be enough to start an irrigation project. To further learning, visit an irrigated farm or show pictures of one. Older children may build quite elaborate systems with reservoirs, canals, irrigation ditches, and finally, small trenches between planted rows of "farmland." By using a can or a piece of hose, a road may be built over a canal or ditch. Teachers can help older primary children relate irrigation to weather.

Suggestions and Variations: Vocabulary: *Reservoir*—a lake formed by damming a stream. The amount of water allowed to continue in the stream is controlled by gates in the dam. *Canal*—a man-made stream to carry water to farmlands. Canals are generally quite large and keep a constant flow of water. *Irrigation ditches*—smaller ditches leading directly to the farms. Water from the canals is let into the ditches as needed by lifting gates. *Trenches*—water from the ditches is fed into trenches between the rows of plants. Usually this is siphoned in. *Zanjero* (zan-hā-rō)—the man who lifts the gates to let water into the ditches.

This project is an excellent activity for integrating science, social science, language arts, and dramatic play.

ACTIVITIES TO HELP CHILDREN GAIN SOME UNDERSTANDING OF THE EARTH'S SURFACE AND HOW IT CHANGES

1. Activity: Trips (PP–P)

Materials: Materials will vary, depending on the type of trip taken. They may include permission slips from parents, packed lunches, vehicles for transportation, equipment and supplies (camera and film) to record aspects of the trip, and maps (topographical if possible).

Procedure: Plan a trip for the specific purpose of observing certain land features. Perhaps you can visit a river, or some mountains, a large lake, or the ocean. Kindergarten and primary children can be helped to relate what they are seeing to the features on the map. This task is too abstract for preprimary children.

Suggestions and Variations: Children can use sand or clay to make their own topographical maps. Children often initiate the building of a city or town. Teachers can inquire whether there is a river nearby, or mountains, or a lake. Older children can be encouraged to build maps of places they've seen on trips.

2. *Activity:* Erosion (PP–P)

   Materials: Earth, sand, bucket of water or a hose.
   Procedure: Call attention to what happens when a bucket of water is dumped or a hose is aimed at soft earth. Relate this to the action of rivers and other streams.
   Suggestions and Variations: Children can take walking trips around the school to see if they can locate signs of erosion. Call children's attention to any signs of soil's being removed by the wind (swirls of dust outside) in order to help children understand that wind also contributes to erosion. If children locate areas that are eroding, help them plan what might be done to stop erosion (placing rocks along a vertical gulley in a hill; planting something in bare spots where the wind carries soil away).

3. *Activity:* Rock collection (PP–P)

   Materials: Rocks; books about rocks.
   Procedure: Encourage children to collect rocks and bring them into the classroom. Help them match their rocks to pictures of rocks and label them using the names given in the books. Record where each rock was found.
   Suggestions and Variations: Older children are often fascinated by fossils and prehistoric times. Museum trips, as well as books, may help develop their understanding of these areas.

4. *Activity:* Picture study (P)

   Materials: Photographs, pictures.
   Procedure: Bring in photos of the community as it was a few years ago. Compare and contrast photos with the community as it is today. Sources of such pictures include the children's families, local newspapers, private collections, and local governmental agencies.

ADDITIONAL RESOURCES

Science Books for Young Children

ALIKI, *Fossils Tell of Long Ago.* New York: Thomas Y. Crowell, 1972.
BAKER, SAMM SINCLAIR, *The Indoor and Outdoor Grow-It Book.* New York: Random House, Inc., 1966.

BRANLEY, FRANKLYN, *A Book of Satellites for You*. New York: Thomas Y. Crowell, 1971.

————, *The Sun*. New York: Thomas Y. Crowell, 1961.

BRENNER, BARBARA, *Bodies*. New York: E. P. Dutton and Co., Inc., 1973.

COBB, VICKI, *Gases*. New York: Franklin Watts, Inc., 1970.

CORBETT, SCOTT, *What Makes a Car Go*. Boston: Atlantic Monthly Press Books, 1963.

COURTNEY, WILLIAM, *What Does a Barometer Do?* Boston: Little Brown and Co., 1963.

DARLING, LOIS, and LOUIS DARLING, *Worms*. New York: William Morrow and Co., 1972.

Elementary Science Study, *Budding Twigs*. Newton, Mass.: Educational Development Center, 1968.

————, *Starting from Seeds*. Newton, Mass.: Educational Development Center, 1968.

FICE, R. H. C., and I. M. SIMKISS, *Light, Lenses, and Colour*. Chicago: Educational Teaching Aids, 1966.

FICE, R. H. C., and I. M. SIMKISS, *Magnets*. Chicago: Educational Teaching Aids, 1966.

FREEMAN, MAE, *A Book of Real Science*. New York: Scholastic Book Services, 1966.

————, *Do You Know About Stars*. New York: Random House, Inc., 1970.

FRANK, S., *The Pictorial Encyclopedia of Fishes*. New York: Hamlyn, 1973.

GARELICK, MAY, *What's Inside?* New York: Scholastic Book Services, 1968.

HELLMAN, HAL, *The Lever and the Pulley*. New York: M. Evans & Co., 1971.

MURRAY, SONIA BENNET, *Shell Life and Shell Collecting*. New York: Avenel Books, 1959.

REID, GEORGE, *Pond Life*. New York: Golden Press, 1967.

SAVONIUS, MOIRA, *The All Color Book of Mushrooms and Fungi*. New York: Crescent Books, 1973.

SCHLOAT, WARREN G. JR., *The Wonderful Egg*. New York: Charles Scribner's Sons, 1952.

SELSAM, MILLICENT E., *How Puppies Grow*. New York: Four Winds Press, 1971.

————, *Peanut*. New York: William Morrow and Co., 1969.

————, *All Kinds of Babies*. New York: Four Winds Press, 1967.

SHAPP, MARTHA, and CHARLES SHAPP, *Let's Find Out About Wheels*. New York: Franklin Watts, Inc., 1962.

SHEFFIELD, MARGARET, *Where Do Babies Come From?* New York: Alfred A. Knopf, 1974.

SIMMONS, DIANE, *Gardening Is Easy When You Know How*. New York: Arco Publishing Co., 1974.

SIMON, SEYMOUR, *Water On Your Street*. New York: Holiday House, 1974.

STEPHENS, WILLIAM M., *Islands*. New York: Holiday House, 1974.

SUTTON, FELIX, *The Moon*. New York: Grosset and Dunlap, 1967.

WEBBER, IRMA E., *Travelers All: How Plants Go Places*. New York: William R. Scott, Inc., 1964.

ZIM, HERBERT S., *Reptiles and Amphibians*. New York: Golden Press, 1956.
———, *Rocks and Minerals*. New York: Golden Press, 1957.

Science References for Teachers

BLOUGH, G., and J. SCHWARTZ, *Elementary School Science and How to Teach It*. 3rd ed. New York: Holt, Rinehart and Winston, Inc., 1964.

DURGIN, H. J., "From Curiosity to Concepts: From Concepts to Curiosity–Science Experiences in the Preschool," *Young Children*, 30, no. 4 (1975), pp. 249–256.

Elementary Science Study of Education Development Center, *The E.S.S. Reader*. Boston: EDC, 1970.

ENNEVER, LEONARD, "The New Science." in Vincent Rogers, ed., *Teaching in the British Primary School*. London: Collier-Macmillan, 1970.

HAWKINS, D., "Messing About in Science," *Science and Children*, 2 (1965), pp. 5–9.

HAWKINS, F. P., *The Logic of Action*. Boulder, Colo.: Mountain View Center for Environmental Education, 1969.

McGAVACK, J., and D. P. LASALLE, *Guppies, Bubbles, and Vibrating Objects*. New York: John Day Co., 1969.

PIAGET, J., *The Child's Conception of the World*. Totawa, N.J.: Littlefield, Adams and Co., 1969.

SHAW, P., *Science*. New York: Citation Press, 1972.

VERGARA, W. C., *Science in the World Around Us*. New York: Harper & Row, Publishers, 1973.

7

the social
sciences

THE social sciences should be a strong component of the curriculum. No other area of study so directly affects children's understanding of themselves as persons and as members of groups. Yet when teachers contemplate the teaching of social sciences, they may well say, "How can children so young possibly understand concepts as abstract and remote from their experience as psychology, political science, or geography?" Or, faced with demands to insure that children gain the basic skills of reading, writing, and arithmetic, they may say, "Social science can wait." Acknowledging that many social science issues are highly controversial, the teacher may say, "I dare not teach about that!"

The intent of this chapter is to help teachers take a new look at the social sciences. Hopefully, this new look will help teachers realize that children are persons who live in families and who need assistance in gaining understanding about these relationships; that children interact with groups and can benefit from assistance in this area too; that the social sciences can be used as a medium through which basic skills may be taught; and that controversial subjects may be taught in non-controversial ways.

We hope for a world free from poverty, discrimination, riots, assassinations, crime, and wars, but we do not live in one. To assume that these harsh realities may be avoided when children are young is to stick our heads in the sand. It is a myth that the content of social science is too remote for young children. Information about people and places in the far corners of the world is piped into children's living rooms every day via television. Therefore those children who are not actually involved in these aspects of life hear and see them anyway. Children need assistance not only in understanding what they are experiencing, but also in finding better ways to live with others.

This chapter was written to bring social sciences into the classroom. Its purposes are (1) to help teachers understand the nature of social sciences, (2) to help teachers understand how children learn social sciences, (3) to help teachers formulate social science goals for young children, and (4) to provide activities and experiences for social science instruction.

THE NATURE OF SOCIAL SCIENCE

We live in a world of relationships among persons and between people and their environment. The social sciences have resulted as ways to understand these interactions. The complexity of this endeavor is seen when one enumerates the seven areas of the social sciences and realizes that there are specialties within each. The seven areas and the content of each are discussed below.

Geography: The Physical Environment

The physical features of the environoment affect what people do. The environoment has in turn been affected by people. Land masses have been connected with bridges and tunnels. Streams have been dammed and land has been irrigated to change it from barren to productive. Minerals have been dug from the earth. Ecologists warn that the face of the earth is fragile and that the complex effects of changes must be understood if life on earth is to survive.

Geography, and more particularly the ecological aspects, is also in the realm of science. This aspect of geography appears in the chapter on science. But people also live in communities, build houses, stores, hospitals, schools, roads, and bridges. In this chapter will be found suggestions for helping children understand not only their own communities and cities but communities in other locations too.

Psychology: Individual Needs

Individuals have basic needs. Some, such as food, rest, and maintenance of body temperature, are primarily physical, but there are psychological needs as well. These include the need to be recognized and accepted. What other needs are basic? Which are inherited and which culturally transmitted? How can needs be fulfilled? These are questions which concern every human who interacts with other humans.

Sociology, Economics, Political Science: Institutional Needs

Over time, people have experienced an ever-decreasing isolation from other humans. Proximity to others requires rules and institutions in order for groups of people to live together and to meet their needs. To prevent anarchy, political institutions evolved. To provide goods and services for many people, monetary systems came into being.

Anthropology and History: The Need to Understand Culture and the Past

As generations were born and others died, people began to feel the need to understand the past, to see this as affecting the present, and to consider it as having lessons for the future. It was also recognized that different groups of people living in different parts of the world developed life styles different from the life styles of others. The events of the past were often recorded; but where they were not, traces of past groups have allowed those that followed to make inferences about the life of their predecessors.

CHILDREN AND THE SOCIAL SCIENCES

Young children's thinking is *egocentric*.[1] This characteristic influences their ability to understand the affective objectives and knowledge of social science instruction. Children, in viewing the world from their own point of view, are usually unable to see things as they appear to others. This means that they have difficulty imagining, for instance, what another person's life is like, particularly if it is quite different from their own.

Egocentricity also makes it difficult for children to understand social science, because a major concept in the social sciences is interdependence. If one is egocentric, it is difficult to understand interdependence, because one must appreciate the interaction of at least two things. Often a young child is still unaware that one's very own action of hitting another child is what makes that child cry. Though most preprimary children's understanding of relationships goes beyond this, it is quite limited, nonetheless.

Another difficulty the young child experiences in trying to understand social sciences results from incomplete concepts of time and space and representations of these. When a teacher can show that New York and California are but eight inches apart on a map, it is difficult to imagine that if one were to ride in an automobile, it would take five or six days and nights to go from one state to the other.

The study of social sciences can probably help children reduce their egocentricity and expand their concepts of time and space. Experiences which allow children to see, hear, and think about other people, times, and places gradually increase children's ability to look at things from several points of view. For young children, real-life first-hand experiences and the chance to reproduce these experiences in their play are the most valuable methods for teaching the social sciences. Books, pictures, films, and filmstrips are also valuable resources.

Technical aspects of social science, such as map- and compass-reading, require understanding of symbols, scale, spatial relationships, and directionality. All of these are difficult for preprimary children, and

[1]Hunt, *Intelligence and Experience* pp. 216–217.

it would be wise not to attempt to deal with these until children reach kindergarten age. The younger child can, however, deal with such basic concrete concepts as where buildings and other land features are in relation to each other. For example, it would be very reasonable to ask a child whose house is near a church to describe where the church is in relation to the house. The child might answer that it is between his or her own house, and that of a friend.

Social relations among children and between children and adults are influenced by egocentricity as well as by the tendency of young children's thinking to be dominated by perception rather than by logic. Because of egocentricity, children often appear selfish because they literally see the world only from their own point of view. It is not unusual to see two three-year-olds tugging at the same toy, each yelling, "I want it. I want it." Despite the very strong feelings of each child about wanting the toy, neither seems to understand that the other has strong feelings too.

Because of the dominance of perception in young children's thinking, they judge the "goodness" or "badness" of an act not by the intentions of the person who performs the act, but by the amount of damage that results.[2] A child who accidentally bumps into someone's block building and knocks the whole structure down is likely to upset another child a great deal more than one who intentionally knocks down just a few. The visible damage, not the motivation, is used to judge the act. Adults would judge the intentions and not the actual damage. As adults help children interpret the difference between one situation and the other, children gradually begin to behave differently in the two situations, and as they do, social relations improve. But children must have opportunities to interact with one another if they are to learn how to deal with these interactions, and they must have support and guidance from adults.

As in all curriculum areas, concepts in social science will not appear full-blown. For example, a young child asks, "Are you my friend?" Adults may answer "yes," give the child a smile and a hug and go about their business without another thought. But the concept of "friend" is an abstract concept which the child is still struggling to understand. What is a friend? What do friends do? Do friends sometimes do things you don't like? Can they still be you friends? Time, experiences, and guidance from an understanding teacher will bring answers to these questions. It is important to remember that children have difficulty dealing with abstractions and need as much concrete information as they can obtain.

[2]Piaget, J., *The Moral Judgment of the Child* (New York: Harcourt Brace & World, Inc., 1932), p. 122.

GOALS FOR SOCIAL SCIENCE INSTRUCTION

Spodek[3] indicates that in social science education in the recent past, the structure of the individual disciplines, or specific social sciences, as described above, has been the basis for social science education, but he notes that there is growing dissatisfaction with using these divisions as a basis for organizing programs. One reason for not using the separate social science disciplines as the basis for a curriculum is that no single discipline can provide the integrative function which is consistent with the kind of teaching advocated by this book. In developing our goals, therefore, we have cut across disciplinary lines and have centered on children in relation to the society in which they live.

The principal goal of social science education is to develop individuals who can function effectively in a society. This requires instructional content and experiences which will enable children to understand their immediate environment and, eventually, the larger world.

Generally, social science goals are of two types: knowledge and affective. Knowledge includes information about man's environment, needs, activities, institutions, and undertakings. From the vast body of knowledge about man and his world, knowledge goals must be selected to meet children's needs, interests, and ability to comprehend. Affective goals include the formation of attitudes and values. Attitudes refer to positive or negative inclinations toward persons, objects, or ideas. They are feelings or emotions which may be consciously or unconsciously revealed in behavior.

Since social science is such a broad area of study, the goals for social science instruction can be classified into the following sub-categories: (1) cooperative group living, (2) the family in society, (3) cultural diversity and heritage, and (4) values, customs, and traditions.

Cooperative Group Living

EACH INDIVIDUAL HAS WORTH AND DIGNITY. At the core of our democratic heritage are human dignity and self-worth. Goals for social science instruction should include promoting these qualities in children. Children's feelings of self-worth grow first through interactions with the important adults in their lives and later with peers. As children find that people listen to them, respond with interest and pleasure, and show appreciation for their accomplishments, they feel good about themselves and can then respond to others in a similar fashion.

[3]B. Spodek, "Social Studies for Young Children: Identifying Intellectual Goals," *Social Education*, 38, no. 1, January 1974, pp. 40–53.

FEELINGS CAN BE EXPRESSED IN ACCEPTABLE WAYS. All feelings are facts which do not simply disappear by denying their existence. Joy, sadness, anger, frustration, and inadequacy are feelings experienced by all human beings and need to be accepted as part of life. But children must be helped to express their feelings in ways which will not bring harm to themselves or others.

PEOPLE HAVE RIGHTS. Both as individuals and as groups, people have rights which must be respected. Some of these rights are the right to one's own work, the right to privacy, the right to one's own opinion, and the right to own property. It should be noted that many of these rights are peculiar to the dominant culture in the United States. For example, not all peoples living within our borders hold personal-property rights as a value; instead, the properties they own belong to the group as a whole. Nevertheless, since personal- and public-property rights are basic to the legal and economic structure in the United States, it would probably be helpful for all children living here to gain some understanding of these rights.

PEOPLE HAVE RESPONSIBILITIES. Because people live together, individuals must assume responsibility for their own behavior and for the welfare of the group. Learning to take responsibility for one's own actions and for performing tasks for the welfare of a group is a goal which is closely tied to the goal of dignity and self-worth.

The Family in Society

THE FAMILY UNIT IS BASIC IN A SOCIETY. All children are members of families. Though family structures may be different—two-parent, one-parent, foster, or adopted—children need to become aware of things families have in common as well as the uniqueness of each family. Children also need to understand the interdependence of family members, economic, psychological, and social.

PEOPLE HAVE NEEDS AND DESIRES. Food, clothing, and shelter are basic needs of people. *Needs* may be defined as things that are essential to life. People also want goods and services which they believe will make life more enjoyable. We may term these *desires*. Children should begin to learn to distinguish between needs and desires.

PEOPLE PRODUCE AND CONSUME GOODS AND SERVICES. In a complex society, needs and desires cannot be satisfied independently or even by simple barter. In order to satisfy needs and desires, people produce goods or offer services in exchange for money. In turn, they use the money for purchasing the goods and services they want from others. Children should learn the basics of our economic system.

PEOPLE DO DIFFERENT TYPES OF WORK. Children can begin to develop understandings about the community as they come into contact with persons who provide goods and services. Before going to school, most children will have contacts with mail carriers, grocery clerks, doctors, and nurses. To widen their knowledge of careers, they should be introduced to persons who represent a wide spectrum of occupations such as firefighters, dentists, janitors, law-enforcement workers, and architects. They should also become acquainted with the occupations of their parents. To be aware of the wide range of work roles is important to young children who are looking forward to growing up and assuming one of these roles. It is important too that the teacher support the young child's natural respect for the work of non-professional workers such as garbage collectors and ice-cream vendors. These workers, too, have unique skills and provide services that people want.

PEOPLE TRAVEL IN VARIOUS WAYS AND SEND MESSAGES. Transportation and communication bring people together. Children can learn a great deal about the many ways in which people meet directly and indirectly by means of transportation and communication.

WHEN PEOPLE LIVE IN GROUPS, RULES ARE NEEDED. In order for people to live comfortably together, rules must be established. These rules serve as guidelines for behavior and protectors of security and safety. Young children can begin to make and apply rules in order to live together as a cohesive group.

PEOPLE LIVE IN COMMUNITIES. People tend to cluster their dwellings into communities for mutual protection, help, and convenience. Children should become acquainted with the features of their community. As children become familiar with their own communities and represent them in the form of picture maps, they begin to develop map-reading skills which may become useful to them when exploring communities other than their own. A goal related to this area is to help children notice differences among communities and determine reasons for these differences.

Cultural Diversity and Heritage

PEOPLE COME FROM MANY CULTURES. In the world of today, most children come in contact with people from many different cultural backgrounds, either in their own home towns, when traveling, or from television. Children need to know, understand, and have respect for other people, regardless of the color of their skin, their different forms of speech, or (in the child's eyes) the odd things they do. Basic to gaining this appreciation for cultural differences is positive experience with representatives of different cultures and fundamental knowledge of the history and customs of other peoples.

IMPORTANT PEOPLE, PAST AND PRESENT. Many years ago individuals of strength, courage, and honor contributed to this country. Through their efforts and tenacity, homes, institutions, government, business, and public services were established, the conveniences we rely on were invented, and procedures which save our lives were devised. People of all races and countries had great ideas and performed good deeds. Although young children cannot accurately place such persons in historical perspective, they can nevertheless learn to know their stories.

Today many people are making contributions to the world. Children should also be helped to become familiar with people of current significance. Current events can often be the starting point for teaching about past people and events. All children today are familiar with the astronauts and the excitement that surrounds the space program. This current development in mode of travel could be related to past developments in transportation by ship, train, automobile, and airplane.

PERSONAL HISTORY. Children should be helped to gain an understanding of their own heritage and how the cultures they come from have changed over time. They can also be helped to understand the origin of familiar materials and objects, and how these have changed over time.

Values, Customs, and Traditions

FORMING VALUES. Values are the basis for inner guidance and direction. They are acquired from socializing experiences provided by adult models and demands. Values are established at an early age. Of all the goals in the social sciences, the formation of values is at one and the same time the most important and the most difficult. It is impossible for teachers, who are significant persons in young children's lives, not to impart their values to the child. Yet these values may be in conflict with values the child brings from home. Wise teachers will consider carefully the values they feel it is important for children to acquire in order to become responsible and productive citizens. They should also consider the extent to which their concepts of what makes up a "responsible and productive" citizen diverges from the concept held generally by society and whether or not they should modify their ideas for the sake of children who are members of that society. Furthermore, they will respect the values of the home to the extent that these are not in conflict with their own carefully considered goals. For example, if the value of the home is to get what you can for yourself and keep it from others, and the teacher's value is one of cooperation and sharing, the teacher may respect the wishes of the parents in terms of the child's belongings, yet be happy to see the child begin to share with classmates.

CUSTOMS AND TRADITIONS. Every nation has holidays which have grown out of historical and religious events. The customs and traditions which have grown up around these holidays are part of the rich heritage of a people. In pluralistic societies the richness of this heritage is often lost as persons from different backgrounds intermingle, and the trappings rather than the meaning of the customs are adopted. For example, in the spring of the year, most peoples have a festival which celebrates new life. For Jewish people, it is the Passover which celebrates a life free from bondage. For Christians, it is the Resurrection, in which it is believed that Jesus brought mankind hope for a new life. Easter eggs and Easter bunnies are symbols of new life, but nothing more. Yet for many children all that Easter means is the Easter bunny who brings eggs and other goodies.

A worthy goal for teaching young children is to help them appreciate the meaning of such holidays as well as enjoying the traditions and customs which surround them. The traditions and customs of a people are also seen in their dress, their food and the way it is served, and in their art. Children should become acquainted with a wide variety of these.

METHODS FOR TEACHING SOCIAL SCIENCES

Social science teaching should permeate the entire day. The way in which a teacher organizes the classroom, the amount of freedom and flexibility permitted, the reward versus punishment system, the rules established and enforced, the sharing of materials, and independent versus group activities—all are factors contributing to developing children's social concepts and understandings.

The activities which follow provide a variety of suggestions for teaching in the area of social science, but it may be helpful to consider some general methods that may be used.

Teacher Modeling and Classroom Management

As suggested above, the way the teacher guides the interactions among the children, adults, and the materials in the classroom is the most potent means of teaching in relation to the goals described under cooperative group living and to the establishment of value systems. So powerful a tool is example, that if teachers' actions are contrary to their declared goals, children may remember and exhibit in their actions what their teachers do rather than what they say.

Children can and should be involved in the decision-making process of the classroom. For suggestions on ways to involve children in making decisions about their own work and about the organization of the class, see Chapter II.

Dealing with Controversial Issues

Some values teachers hold may be at variance with those held by the families whose children they teach. This poses some problems. As public servants, teachers are bound to show respect for the wishes of the parents and uphold the rules of the community. Yet, many teachers often feel these are in error and would hope that the children would adopt values which they believe are more consistent with establishing a healthy society in which all people are of equal worth and can live together harmoniously.

The most important principles for the teacher to keep in mind are (1) to avoid taking sides early in a discussion, and (2) to present information on which children can base their own decisions. A current controversial issue is integration. A teacher values cultural diversity and believes that children should have the opportunity to make friends with people from other races. In a conversation a child says, "My father says all Black people are lazy and stupid." Rather than indicating any point of view that the parent is wrong, the teacher might ask, "What do you think?" If the child says, "I don't know any Black people," the teacher might say, "I have a friend who is Black; would you like to meet her?" The most common answer would be in the affirmative and the teacher would arrange for a meeting.

If there are Black children in the class, the teacher might explore with the child the meanings of the words stupid and lazy and then ask if the child thinks that a Black child with whom he or she has played is stupid and lazy. No further comment is needed; the child's response is accepted. If pressed for an opinion on an issue, teachers who are wise will, after having presented appropriate information, explain what they think and why, and then suggest that children talk the issue over with their parents.

Conducting Group Discussions

From time to time issues arise from group living. There is a widespread infraction of a rule on the playground, the use of obscene and abusive language by children has become offensive, some children have been laughed at by others for mistakes. The teacher thinks, "Something must be done!"

It is time for a group meeting in which children can explore and deal with these issues. This does not necessarily include the whole group, but may comprise only those involved in the incident. In such a group meeting, the teacher, as concisely as possible, presents the situation that has aroused concern and elicits from the children their reactions, feelings, explanations, and suggestions for solutions. It is quite appropriate here for the teacher to be honest in verbalizing personal feelings; however, the main role is one of facilitator and moderator: to draw out comments from each child though avoiding going around the circle one-by-one; to remind children that only one can be heard at a time; to reflect the statements of children in order to insure that both teacher and other children understand what the child is trying to communicate; and finally, to draw together and summarize decisions.

Such group discussions need not be limited to discussing problems. They are valuable also in sharing positive feelings arising from the excitement and fun of a trip, a birthday, or any other experience some or all have shared.

Group discussions, then, are a means of helping children understand and verbalize their feelings and realize that they are not alone in having those feelings. The teacher should be wary of making such a situation artificial. Children in this age group are, as we have said, unable to project themselves into another's point of view. They all have had experiences which have evoked feelings, and these events should be the source material for the discussion.

Using Books

At the end of this chapter, you will find some book lists which will be helpful to children in developing social science concepts. Though many of these books may stimulate discussions, the teacher should avoid moralizing. Discussions should be relatively spontaneous, the teacher following the children's cues in guiding the conversation. The books should not be the source of all social science teaching. Although they are a valuable resource, books should not take the place of first-hand experiences when such experiences are possible.

Teacher-Planned Units

The traditional pattern of constructing a unit is to select a topic for study, determine what the objectives are, and then plan actitvities to meet the objectives. Often a culminating activity is also planned, which evaluates the children's progress toward attaining the objectives. Though this has long been a respected and useful way of teaching, particularly in the social sciences, it often results in children's simply giving back to the teacher what it was planned that they shall learn.

We suggest that a far richer experience involves a web structure. That is, an experience is planned that all the children will share. In planning, the teacher considers all the different directions the children's interests might go and tries to provide resources which will help them as they follow their interests. For example, a trip to a dairy farm is planned. Some children might become interested in how the milk gets from the cow to the bottle on their table. Others might be interested in how the cows produce milk. Still others might be fascinated with farm life and how it differs from city life. The skillful teacher will think of other avenues and will be alert for cues from the children which indicate the direction their interest has taken. Research in books, interviews with people, and oral, written, or picture reports may follow from such an experience shared by primary-aged children.

Using Kits

In many schools commercially prepared kits are available. They often contain useful materials. The best use of these materials comes when the teacher is so acquainted with what a kit contains so as to be able to pull from it materials which match the needs and interests of the children.

ACTIVITIES FOR SOCIAL SCIENCE INSTRUCTION

The activities included below are organized to correspond to the goals outlined above. The activities are of two types, (1) those specifically planned and contrived to create a situation in which a concept or skill can be learned, and (2) situations which are likely to occur in the life of a classroom and from which children can learn a great deal if teachers are prepared to utilize them.

Cooperative Group Living

ACTIVITIES TO HELP CHILDREN LEARN THAT THEY AND OTHERS ARE OF WORTH

1. Activity: All of us (PP–P)

Materials: Construction paper, film, Polaroid camera.
Procedure: Take snapshots of the children, or have them take pictures of each other. Place pictures in an album or book made by mounting pictures on construction paper. Place the book in the library with other books so children can look at it.
Suggestions and Variations: Children can label their own pictures and write a sentence about themselves. Teachers can take dictation for younger children.
Encourage children to bring a baby picture of themselves. Place it in photo album with their other picture, or make a complete "baby book."
Take slides of the children engaged in activities at school. Show these to the children some day during story or group time.

2. Activity: This is I (PP–K)

Materials: Butcher paper, crayons, scissors.
Procedure: Make paper and crayons available to children in art area or other area where there is floor space. Encourage children to trace around a friend and then have the friend trace around them. Children can then color in their body drawings. Display body drawings in the classroom or the corridor.

3. Activity: My pictures (PP–P)

Materials: Easels, poster paints, brushes, paper, crayons.
Procedure: Materials should be available in the art center. When children draw figures, teachers can pause to ask who the persons are, what they are doing in this particular scene, etc.

4. Activity: Everyone has a name (PP–K)

Materials: Children's literature.
Procedure: Read the books, *Everyone Has a Name* by Richard Bowmar, and *Your Eyes and Mine* and *Your Skin and Mine* by Paul

Showers. After the stories, talk with children about their names, and those of people they know. Help children see similarities and differences among people.

5. *Activity:* Sing our names (PP–K)

   Materials: Autoharp, piano, or just teacher's voice.
   Procedure: During song time, sing "I See A Boy [Girl] with a Yellow Shirt [dress, pants, shoes] Or, Who Are You?" Any simple tune will do. The teacher looks at the child to whom she is referring. The child sings back, "I am Steve." This is a particularly good song during the first few weeks of school in order to help children learn each other's name.

6. *Activity:* Everyone has a place (PP–P)

   Materials: Some set-up—cubbies, bins, shelves—to serve as individual storage spaces for children's personal possessions.
   Procedure: Designate whose place is whose by labeling them with children's names. Encourage children to store personal belongings in these spaces, and encourage them to respect each other's places.

One's very own place suggests respect for each child.

ACTIVITIES TO HELP CHILDREN HANDLE FEELINGS IN DESIRABLE WAYS

1. *Activity:* Accepting feelings (PP–P)

    Materials: None.

    Procedure: With young children, emotions are often on the surface. Children become angry, sad, and happy very easily. When children express any of these, teachers should accept them. This means the absence of statements like, "Oh come on now, big brave boys don't cry." While teachers should not always accept the behavior which accompanies anger (hitting, hurting, damaging things), they should demonstrate acceptance of the feeling. This can be done by helping the child find a different way of expressing it. For example, if in anger one child begins hitting another, the teacher should stop the hitting and say to the child, "Tell her you are angry that she took your truck away and that you want it back."

    Suggestions and Variations: Primary age children can discuss conflict situations in stories or dramatic presentations and relate any solutions to problems they may have encountered. In dramatic play, children will act out feelings that they have had or they think others have had. They will spank or kiss the doll, kick at the pretend dog, act exasperated at pretend spouses or children. Teachers should observe children during dramatic play and ask appropriate questions perhaps at group time. "John, you sure seemed angry at the baby today. What did the baby do?"

    It is appropriate at times for teachers to model the expression of feelings in dramatic play. The teacher can do this by becoming a participant. The teacher should not dominate the play (give orders, determine roles, etc.) but could ask permission to play and ask to be given a role to assume. Through such role playing it is possible to introduce new ways to express feelings. For example, anger over something the baby did can be expressed in a discussion with a spouse or friend, or verbally to the baby, rather than through physical attacks on the baby.

2. *Activity:* Story time (PP–P)

    Materials: Children's literature.

    Procedure: Select books which focus on feelings (*Snowy Day, A Letter to Amy, Curious George, Where the Wild Things Are, Ping*). After reading the story, ask children what feelings the story characters expressed. Ask children to relate situations in which they have felt as the characters felt.

ACTIVITIES TO HELP CHILDREN UNDERSTAND
THAT PEOPLE HAVE RIGHTS

1. Activity: Everyone has a place (PP–P)

Materials: Same as in activity on page 267.
Procedure: Same as in activity on page 267.

2. Activity: Classroom spaces (PP–P)

Materials: Whole classroom.
Procedure: Arrange the classroom so that children can find a private space to be alone if they want to be. This will not be one child's personal space, but will be used by any child when the need arises and the space is not in use.

3. Activity: Honoring a child's work (PP–P)

Materials: The child's work.
Procedure: Children's names should be placed on their work. The teacher will need to write the names for younger children who do not yet know how. Permission to keep, display, file, or send home, or destroy work should be obtained from each child. On rare occasions it may be necessary for the teacher to go against the child's wishes on this issue. If this is the case, the teacher should discuss this decision with the child.
Children's work should also be protected from destruction by others in the classroom. This will require procedures for helping children store their work in safe places.

4. Activity: Your own opinion (PP–P)

Materials: None.
Procedure: The teacher's behavior in routine classroom situations is the crucial variable here. Whenever possible, children should be allowed their own opinions. It will not always be possible for children to act in accordance with their opinions, but they should be allowed to do so if possible.

ACTIVITIES TO HELP CHILDREN UNDERSTAND
THAT PEOPLE HAVE RESPONSIBILITIES

1. Activity: Clean-up time (PP–P)

Materials: Everything in the classroom.
Procedure: Children should be encouraged to put away and clean up

materials and equipment. Encouragement can be provided first, by organizing the room so everything has a place. Labeling can help insure that children will remember where things go. In addition to these structural encouragements, teachers will need to remind children to put things away too. During the first weeks of school, teachers should talk with children about putting things away, and why it is important. When a child forgets, a gentle verbal reminder such as, "Oh, Sue, you will need to put the puzzle back before you start painting. I'll wait here at the easel while you go do that," will help. During general clean-up after activity time, teachers should pitch in and help. Comments such as, "I'll get these things here; can you get the blocks over there?" or "What can I do to help?" or "Can you help me here?" are appropriate.

2. *Activity:* Snack (PP–P)

   Materials: Items for snack.
   Procedure: Children should be involved in the preparation and serving of snack. Snack is usually an enjoyable activity for children, and teachers should not overlook the importance of having children become responsible for preparation, serving and clean-up associated with it.

3. *Activity:* Classroom jobs (PP–P)

   Materials: Materials in the classroom.
   Procedure: All classrooms have routine tasks which must be performed; plants need to be watered, animals need to be fed, materials need to be straightened, lunch money needs to be collected. Children can assume responsibility for these tasks. Refer to page 25 of Chapter II for suggestions for scheduling this work.

4. *Activity:* Completing tasks agreed upon (PP–P)

   Materials: Classroom materials and equipment.
   Procedure: Teachers and children will make agreements about work to be completed. Maybe a young child has agreed to finish a boat made of wood. Perhaps an older child has decided to read a certain number of pages in a book. Children should be expected to finish the work they have agreed to do. There will be some work about which no such agreements are made, and decisions about whether to complete this work may be left up to the child.
   Suggestions and Variations: Teachers must use good judgment in expecting children to live up to agreements. First, teachers should offer good guidance at the time of the agreement so as to avoid setting unreasonable expectations. In addition, teachers should keep

in mind that children's ability to think and plan ahead and then carry out such plans is related to their developmental level. A three-year-old can be expected to follow through with cleaning up one last play area before going on to a new one if the child and the teacher have just talked it over. But a three-year-old cannot be expected to decide on Monday what to do during activity time on Tuesday, Wednesday, Thursday, and Friday. On the other hand, it would not be unreasonable to expect a second grader to plan out activities for a week at a time, although some would no doubt be tentative. Of course, the second grader has the advantage of being able to write down such plans.

ACTIVITIES TO HELP CHILDREN LEARN ABOUT FAMILIES

1. Activity: Dramatic play—house (PP–K)

   Materials: Toy refrigerator, stove, cabinets, table, chairs, bed, chest of drawers, trays, measuring cup, spoons, bowls, pans, dishes and other items common to a house. (See page 101 for dramatic play.)

   Procedure: Encourage children to play in the house area. As children play, take cues from what you hear and observe, and build toward a recognition of interdependent family roles based on such cues. For example, one child says, "You be the mother; you stay home and keep house while I go to work." The second child shows some reluctance to take this kind of "mother" role. The teacher might then suggest that both "mother" and "father" go to work, and ask what kind of work each parent does.

   Suggestions and Variations: As children show interest, housecleaning implements, tools, clocks, old radios, and other items might be added, and the children might assume roles of house cleaner, appliance fixer, cook, etc. "House" play should reflect children's own families. If boys assume traditional female roles or girls take on male roles, there is no cause for alarm. Trying on various roles is one way to find one's own sex role.

2. Activity: The family (PP–P)

   Materials: None.

   Procedure: In a group meeting ask children to talk about their families. Who lives in each child's house? Children may include goldfish, dogs, cats, and other pets as family members. Later, show pictures of different types of families, ranging from those with one parent and one child to families with parents, grandparents, several children, and a menagerie of pets. Discussion may cover such questions as to what makes a family? Can one person be a family? Why do we live in families? Such a discussion could occur at story time after the children have listened to a story related to families.

3. *Activity:* Family jobs (PP–K)

Materials: Felt board; cut-out pictures of family members and of work tools and objects—garden hose, dishes, washing machine, hammer, etc.; pictures of kitchen, yard, laundry, and other areas of the home. (Pictures should have strips of sandpaper or felt pasted on the back for use on felt board.)

Procedure: Make materials available for children to work with during activity time. As children match people and objects they work with, the teacher can help them discuss how this work is accomplished in their own families. Usually, two or three children will gather around to talk and compare how their families divide up work.

4. *Activity:* Different kinds of families (PP–K)

Materials: Felt board; figures for all possible family members (children, mother, father, aunt, uncle, grandmother, grandfather, etc.) backed for use on a felt board.

Procedure: Have materials available for children to work with. Stop by occasionally and talk with individual children about the members in their own families.

Suggestions and Variations: Be sure to include figures from a variety of ethnic backgrounds, particularly if children in the class are from different ethnic groups.

5. *Activity:* Family pictures (PP–P)

Materials: Construction paper or picture album; pictures from home.

Procedure: Ask children to bring pictures of their families. Designate one page in the book for each child's pictures. Help children secure their pictures in the book and label them. Store the book in the library corner.

Suggestions and Variations: Old Christmas card order books (from card shops) or wallpaper sample books make excellent photo albums for a class. They are free and have sturdy covers and bindings.

6. *Activity:* Family survey (P)

Materials: Paper, pencils, crayons, graph paper.

Procedure: Ask children to collect data about their families.
Data might include:
(1) family members

(2) family occupations

(3) family size

Have children report back to class what they have found out. Help a small group of children make graphs which summarize the data. For example, a graph illustrating family size might look like the one shown in Figure 26.

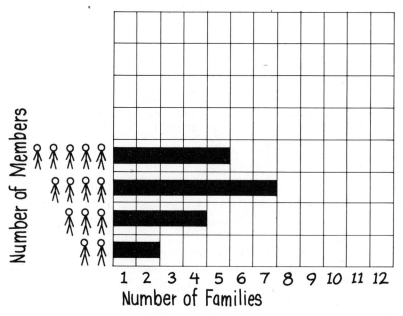

Figure 26. Graph of family size.

Children can be helped to see how to indicate on the graph that fewer families had two and three members than had four and five members.

ACTIVITIES TO HELP CHILDREN UNDERSTAND
THAT PEOPLE HAVE NEEDS AND DESIRES

1. Activity: Your house and mine (PP–K)

Materials: Pictures.

Procedure: Mount pictures of homes where children can see them. These might include a house, apartment, trailer, houseboat, igloo, hut, etc. Discuss differences and similarities among the homes with children who stop by to look.

Suggestions and Variations: Have a flannel board with cut-out items of different kinds of houses. Allow children to show the kind of houses in which they live. Take a walk in the community to look at different types of homes. Make the children aware of the materials that are used in construction of various types of homes. Include such materials as long grass, bamboo, sticks, leather, stone, wood, and brick. Discuss parts of a house, such as roof, eaves, windows, doors, rooms, chimneys. The land area around houses can also be mentioned. Encourage children to construct houses from such materials as blocks.

2. *Activity:* Where we live (K–P)

Materials: Paper, pencils, butcher paper.
Procedure: Ask children to find out what type of home (apartment, duplex, single-family home, mobile home) they live in. Help children make a graph to illustrate their data.

3. *Activity:* What families buy (K–P)

Materials: Paper, pencils, crayons.
Procedure: Encourage children to ask their parents what things their families buy. Have them report back to the class. Help children make a list of all the items families must buy, such as food, clothing, household items, etc.
Suggestions and Variations: Invite to the class people who produce some of the items children have determined that families buy. Preferably, the visitors should be parents of the children. In this way, children can begin to understand that families must produce in order to consume.

4. *Activity:* Fixing things (P–PP)

Materials: Glue, plastic wood, tape, contact paper, oil can, screwdriver.
Procedure: Involve children in the care and repair of classroom equipment. If books are torn or worn, or if puzzle pieces are lost, fix or replace them and have children help. Children love to tighten screws and oil squeaky tricycles or doors. Children should be helped to understand that more needs and desires can be met if equipment is cared for properly.

ACTIVITIES TO HELP CHILDREN UNDERSTAND PRODUCTION AND CONSUMPTION AND THE USE OF MONEY

1. *Activity:* Cashier and customer (PP–K)

Materials: Dramatic play area set up as a store; cash register or money box; play money.

Procedure: As children play, encourage them to take roles of cashier and customer. Explain what each does (young children often think the cashier gives money to the customer because they see the change). Information about what the cashier and customer do can be illustrated well if the teacher enters the play in one of these roles.

Suggestions and Variations: Trips to a store to purchase items needed for the class will help children understand the cashier-customer relationship better.

2. *Activity:*   Supermarket visit (PP–K)

Materials: None.

Procedure: Take a small group of children to the supermarket to see produce and other items being delivered. Then permit children to observe at the check-out counter. They will notice people buy items they saw being delivered.

Suggestions and Variations: If you live where it is feasible, it would be helpful for children to visit a vegetable farm in order to understand where the food comes from that they see being unloaded from the delivery trucks at the store.

Allow children to purchase produce they have seen being delivered to the store. These items can be prepared for snack.

3. *Activity:*   Orchard and applesauce (PP–P)

Materials: Usual preparation for a trip. Saucepan, paring knife, hot plate, bowl, spoon.

Procedure: Take a group of children to an apple orchard to see apples being picked (and perhaps pick their own). Purchase some apples and take to school to make applesauce.

Suggestions and Variations: Similar trips can be taken to a maple-sugar farm, an orange grove, a dairy farm, or a vegetable farm.

4. *Activity:*   Coin names (PP–K)

Materials: Real money coins.

Procedure: Have materials available for children to work with during activity time. As children examine the coins, help them name them—penny, nickel, dime, quarter.

Suggestions and Variations: If possible, permit children to use the coins in dramatic play as they engage in buying and selling commodities.

5. *Activity:*   Extra change (P)

Materials: 16 nickels, 9 dimes, 3 quarters.

Procedure: Two children may play. The coins are mixed up in a box and blindly divided between the two children. The children must arrange their coins in pairs or groups that are equal. For example, they can pair a dime with two nickels because each is the same amount of money. They might also pair a group of three nickels and one dime with a quarter. The child who has the most extra change loses the round. Play five rounds to a game. The child who wins more rounds wins the game.

6. *Activity:* Money chart (PP–K)

   Materials: 40 pennies, 1 nickel, 1 dime, 1 quarter.
   Procedure: Make a chart to illustrate the exchange of each coin in terms of pennies. Cover the chart with contact paper. Display it where children can refer to it easily. Figure 27 shows a sketch of such a chart.

7. *Activity:* Foreign currency (P)

   Materials: Foreign currency.
   Procedure: Invite a money collector in to share a small foreign currency display with children; or ask children to check at home to see if they can bring a piece of foreign currency. Explain the value of the foreign currency by relating it to U.S. currency.

ACTIVITIES TO HELP CHILDREN UNDERSTAND THAT PEOPLE DO DIFFERENT KINDS OF WORK

1. *Activity:* Visiting nurse (PP–P)

   Materials: Tape measure, tongue depressors, cotton swabs, mask, scales, nurse's cap, thermometer.
   Procedure: Invite a nurse to visit the classroom and discuss the nurse's role and the kinds of tools it requires. The nurse should demonstrate the use of each tool. Set up props in the housekeeping corner. Encourage dramatic play.
   Suggestions and Variations: Give each child bits of gauze, band-aids, cotton, and adhesive tape to make a collage. They will talk about the medical uses for these items as they use them. Teachers can interact verbally and add information as needed.
   Invite other people in to talk about their work. Encourage such visitors always to bring tools and equipment associated with their work, because this helps young children understand better what it is that the person does.

2. *Activity:* Visiting people at work (PP–P)

   Materials: None.

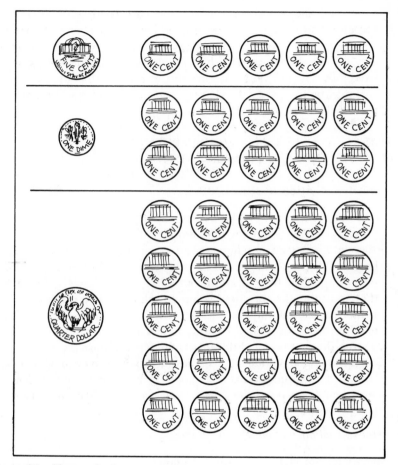

Figure 27. Money chart.

   Procedure: Make the usual trip preparations, including notes from
      home and briefing of the people to be visited. Any type of worker
      may be visited. Those that are popular with young children include
      police officers, firefighters, medical workers, road equipment opera-
      tors, glass blowers, delivery workers, and farmers.

3. *Activity:*   What parents do (PP–K)

   Materials: Paper, pencils, magazines, scissors, glue, construction
      paper.

   Procedure: Ask children to find out what kind of work their parents
      do. They can then cut out a picture of someone engaged in that
      type of work and paste it in a construction-paper book. This can
      become a class book.

Suggestions and Variations: Because in any community there may be parents who for periods of time do not work, it might be wise to suggest this activity as something children may want to pursue, or may not. In this way, those children whose parents do not presently have jobs will not be forced into an uncomfortable situation. Parents may be invited to the classroom to demonstrate and discuss the type of work they do.

ACTIVITIES TO HELP CHILDREN UNDERSTAND TRANSPORTATION AND COMMUNICATION

1. *Activity:* Getting to school (PP–K)

Materials: Large sheet of butcher paper, glue, pencil; cut-outs of buses, cars, trains, bicycles, and figures walking.
Procedure: Attach butcher paper to a space on the wall at a low height. Place cut-outs in a container near the butcher paper. Place pencils and glue there also. Encourage children to select the cut-out that indicates the way they travel to school. They can write their names on the cut-outs and glue them in the appropriate column on the paper. In this way children will make a picture graph depicting the number of children arriving at school each way.
Suggestions and Variations: Children can be provided with magazines to find a picture of their mode of travel. They can cut it out and then place it on the graph. The graph might appear like the one in Figure 28.

2. *Transportation models* (K–P)

Materials: Model cars, trains, airplanes, boats, etc.
Procedure: Set up an area which can be used for displaying models. Ask children to bring in any models they have at home. Books can be selected to accompany the display. While talking with children who view the display, teachers can help them notice details of the models and understand how each is used.

3. *Activity:* Wheels (PP–P)

Materials: Blocks, box, wagon.
Procedure: Encourage children to compare the effort required to move a box of blocks with and without the aid of a wagon. Relate this experience to the construction of most modes of travel. All vehicles carry heavy loads. All (with few exceptions) have wheels.

Figure 28. Graphs of modes of travel to school.

4. *Activity:* Airplanes (PP–P)

Materials: None.

Procedure: Make field trip arrangements as usual. Take the children (all or a small group) to an airport. They should see airplanes; people arriving and departing; planes being loaded, unloaded and cleaned. Go inside a plane. The children can compare the baggage cart with their own experience in moving blocks at school.

Suggestions and Variations: Trips to visit trains, boats, and trucks might also be planned. Primary age children may like to obtain schedules for the different modes of travel so they can compare the time each takes to reach the same destination.

5. *Activity:* Truck traffic (K–P)

Materials: Books, pictures; pencil and paper.

Procedure: Read books to children which are about different kinds of trucks. Display pictures of different types of trucks. Then, allow a small group of children to go sit by the street (accompanied by a high-school student or other adult) and observe the number of each kind of truck that passes by. The teacher can help the children make a graph which illustrates their findings. Through questioning, the teacher might also try to help children think of reasons why they saw certain types of trucks and not others. Questions would include "Where do you think the dairy refrigerated trucks are going?" "Where would the cement truck have been going?"

6. *Activity:* Writing letters (PP–P)

   Materials: Paper, crayons, pencils, envelopes, and stamps.
   Procedure: Make materials available to children in the writing center. Encourage children to write a letter to someone in their family. Teachers may need to take dictation from young children. Somewhat older children will need to know how to spell some words. These can be written on scraps of paper and then copied by the child. When the letters are finished take the children to a nearby mailbox and mail the letters.
   Suggestions and Variations: Draw a picture to be mailed home. If a holiday or special day is approaching, make cards for the occasion. When picture or card is completed have children deposit in a mailbox.
   Take the children to visit a post office. They can see what happens to a letter in preparation for delivery. Encourage children to make a cardboard mailbox for the classroom to use in dramatic play. Letters can be "mailed" to friends in the class. Try to arrange for the children in your class to write letters to children in a class at a different school or to children in another class at the same school.

7. *Activity:* Using the telephone (PP–P)

   Materials: Toy telephones; real telephones (in school office).
   Procedure: Toy telephones can be placed in the dramatic play area for use by children. Children can also be asked to do telephoning for the class on real phones when this seems appropriate. For example, primary age children can call stores in order to locate a particular item needed by the class, or may call a museum to check its visiting hours.

8. *Activity:* Talking machines (PP–P)

   Materials: Two-way radios, intercom system, walkie-talkie, etc.
   Procedure: Try to use any of the above to help children understand how people can talk with each other across distance. A visit to the school office to see the intercom system would be interesting. A police officer who visits the class, can show children a two-way radio.

Young children learn about communication systems by pretending to use them.

9. *Activity:* Talk to keep (PP–P)

   Materials: Records and record player, tape and tape recorder.
   Procedure: Make materials available to children. Talk to them about how these devices make it possible for us to preserve talk. Tape children's songs, stories, and poetry in order to preserve it.

10. *Activity:* Audio codes (K–P)

    Materials: Any devices for tapping out messages (pencil tapping on the table, musical triangle, etc.).
    Procedure: Let children experiment with making up codes and sending messages to each other.

11. *Activity:* Radio and TV stations (K–P)

    Materials: None.
    Procedure: Arrange for field trips to the stations for small groups of children. Be sure children have some notion of what happens at a radio and TV station.

ACTIVITIES TO HELP CHILDREN UNDERSTAND
HOW INDIVIDUALS LIVE TOGETHER IN GROUPS

1. *Activity:* Classroom ground rules (PP–P)

   Materials: None.
   Procedure: As problems arise, discuss with children how they can

be solved. Help children develop rules for the class. Rules might include what a child is to do when finished with a piece of equipment. Another rule might specify when certain activities can occur (maybe hammering can only occur during a specific half hour). Teachers will need to initiate some rule-making at the beginning of the year, but other rules may be permitted to emerge.

2. *Activity:* Interdependence (PP–P)

   Materials: None.

   Procedure: Be alert to everyday activities in which interdependence may be stressed. Discuss what might happen if the teacher did not help children or children did not help the teacher. Encourage children to note how each member of the class is dependent on other members to keep the room clean.

3. *Activity:* Traffic signs (PP–K)

   Materials: Red, yellow, and green construction paper, egg cartons, glue.

   Procedure: Place circles (2½″ diameter) of red, yellow, and green construction paper, the tops of egg cartons, and glue on a table. In morning planning circle, tell children that materials for making traffic signs are on the table. Ask them to recall which color is at the top, which in the middle, and which at the bottom. Also discuss what each color means. Discuss why we need traffic signals. Encourage children to use their signals with roads made of blocks or while playing outdoors with wheel toys.

   Suggestions and Variations: Before introducing above materials, take children for a walk to the nearest traffic signal to observe it. Help children discuss the signals and their contribution to safety.

4. *Activity:* School safety procedures (P)

   Materials: Traffic pattern schedules for the school in case of fire; outdoor playground schedules for school; lunchroom facility schedules for the school.

   Procedure: Arrange to have children obtain the above schedules from the school office. Help them discuss the relationship of these schedules and procedures to comfort and safety of all classes who use the school.

ACTIVITIES TO HELP CHILDREN UNDERSTAND THAT PEOPLE LIVE IN COMMUNITIES

1. *Activity:* Our neighborhood (K–P)

   Materials: Blocks, boxes, wrapping paper, felt marker, construction paper.

Procedure: Encourage children to make their own maps, beginning with their home and the neighbor's house. Give children large sheets of manila paper and crayons. A discussion of their street should precede this experience.

Suggestions and Variations: Have a small group of children who live in close proximity lay out a representation of their street. Give the children strips of masking tape to place on the floor in the block area. After completion of their street, allow the children to walk from each other's homes following the map layout.

Encourage children to make a drawing of the school and nearby places on a large strip of wrapping paper placed on the floor. Begin with the school, trace the route, put in key places. The teacher should help children label certain streets.

Encourage children to discover directions from school to home, to neighborhood market, to library, etc. Have the children also note distance in blocks from school to home, to the store, to a friend's house.

Children might be asked to bring in pictures of their homes. Have children pin the pictures of their homes in the appropriate space on the map.

Take the children to the top of a tall building or tower so they can look down on the entire community. This enables children to see in one glance the whole area that is mapped.

2. *Activity:* Model in blocks (PP–P)

Materials: Unit blocks.

Procedure: Encourage kindergarten and primary aged children to try to make a model of the room out of unit blocks. Once they have made the three-dimensional model, primary children may like to draw it as a two-dimensional model.

3. *Activity:* Sand map (PP–P)

Materials: Sand table and sand; tin cans, blocks, small vehicles.

Procedure: Encourage older children to build cities, or a model of their classroom in the sand.

4. *Activity:* Hidden treasures (PP–P)

Materials: Paper, pencils, toy trucks, balls, jump ropes, etc.

Procedure: Hide small play items on the playground. Draw maps to indicate their location. Give maps to the children to use in trying to find the items.

5. *Activity:* Trip map (K–P)

Materials: Paper and pencil.

Procedure: Plan a short trip near school to see something, gather pebbles, etc. Draw maps for the children to use to find their destination. Have the adult accompanying the children help them refer to the map to find their location.

6. *Activity:* North, south, east, west (P)

Materials: Masking tape.

Procedure: Tape a large cross to the floor. Mark the directions with a large N for the north, S for the south, E for the east, and W for the west. Children will inevitably ask about the cross on the floor and the teacher can explain it.

Suggestions and Variations: This activity should not be used with children until they have the concept of left and right in terms of their own bodies.

Using part of the block area in the classroom, tape long pieces of dark-colored shelving paper on the floor. Let these represent the streets around the school. Have a small group of children construct the school building in this space using the blocks. Help the children orient their block building in relation to the true layout of the building. Talk with children about where the entrances are located and which direction is east or west.

Bring a compass into the classroom for children to use.

Cultural Diversity and Heritage

ACTIVITIES TO HELP CHILDREN UNDERSTAND THAT PEOPLE COME FROM MANY CULTURES

1. *Activity:* Pictures of people (PP–P)

Materials: Portfolio of pictures.

Procedure: In the picture file and on bulletin-board displays, include pictures of Blacks, Orientals, Indians, Mexican-Americans, and others who have distinctive appearance, dress, and hair styles. The pictures should represent people from a variety of ethnic groups, in ordinary dress and hair styles as well as in dress and hair styles reflecting their cultural heritage.

2. *Activity:* Indians (PP–P)

Materials: Artifacts such as beaded or concho belts, jewelry, woven rugs, pottery, and baskets made by Indians who live in your area.

Procedure: Invite a professional person or leader who is Indian to visit your class. Ask the guest to tell the class about his or her place of birth, schooling, occupation, family. (It is important to demonstrate to children that Indians are people whose lives are similar to those of their families. Few live by choice in tepees, hogans, or adobe huts with no modern conveniences.) An Indian visitor who was reared on a reservation may talk about a life quite different from those of the children in the class. The man in the photo on page 286 is a member of the Mohawk Indian tribe and he discussed Indian tribes and their locations with the children.

Suggestions and Variations: Follow the visit by making a display of Indian artifacts. If the museum in your community has a display depicting Indians living as they did years ago, arrange for a field trip. Study other ethnic groups in similar ways.

3. *Activity:*   Posted pictures (PP–P)

Materials: Bulletin boards on walls of classroom; pictures of children with different hair coloring, skin color, hair length, dress, etc.

Procedure: As children stop to look at the pictures during activity time or the beginning of the day, ask them questions which will help them compare their own characteristics to those of children pictured. Children can learn in this way that though children differ in terms of some characteristics, they are alike in many others (i.e., all have hair, all have eyes, ears, legs, etc.).

ACTIVITIES TO HELP CHILDREN UNDERSTAND IMPORTANT PEOPLE, PAST AND PRESENT

1. *Activity:*   Black Americans (P)

Materials and Procedure: Use the *Boning Profile of Black Americans* and the *Gallery of Great Afro-Americans* to stimulate discussion regarding Black Americans. Show the pictures and relate the historical evidence to the children. At a later date, ask children to relate some of the contributions that certain Blacks have made.

Suggestions and Variations: Children may be interested in using the overhead projector and the transparencies to make silhouettes of the Black Americans discussed, and then to use the silhouettes to make a book.

2. *Activity:*   Getting to know past Americans (PP–P)

Materials: Pictures and books.

Procedure: Introduce some famous Americans to the children by displaying their pictures. Such persons as George Washington, Frederick Douglass, Abraham Lincoln, Crispus Attucks, Susan B. Anthony, Amelia Earhart, and George Washington Carver would be

A Mohawk Indian tells children about Indian tribes.

appropriate. Read stories about these persons to the children and talk about why they were important people.

Suggestions and Variations: Be sure to select stories at an appropriate level for the children in your class.

You may be able to find poetry and songs about these important people that the children could learn.

3. *Activity:* Current important people (PP–P)

Materials: Magazines, newspapers, other sources of pictures and reading materials about current events.

Procedure: Display pictures and place reading materials where children have access to them. Discuss with children the deeds the people in the pictures are performing and why their actions are important. Encourage older children to collect newspaper and magazine articles and pictures and bring them to class.

It is wise to plan for visitors to stay to talk with individual children.

ACTIVITIES TO HELP CHILDREN UNDERSTAND
THEIR OWN PERSONAL HISTORY

1. Activity: My special day (PP–K)

Materials: Cake, ice cream, other birthday celebration items.
Procedure: Celebrate the child's birthday in some appropriate way, such as serving the special treats at snack and singing *Happy Birthday*. Inquire about how old the child is with this birthday.

2. Activity: All of us (page 266)

Family pictures (p. 272).
Materials: Same as in previous discussion of activities.
Procedure: These pictures of the children and their families can help them understand their own histories. Pictures of grandparents may be useful here also.

3. Activity: Family historians (K–P)

Materials: None.
Procedure: Invite relatives of the children to come and share their

recollections of childhood with the children. Parents can describe what they did as children—their favorite games, things they liked to do, eat or see. Also, parents might be able to give the children information about the history of the school building, such as what stood on the site before the building, how the area has changed, etc.

4. *Activity:* Where did it come from? (PP–P)

   Materials: Common items in the classroom; children's personal possessions.

   Procedure: Talk with children about the items. Help them think about where the materials for making the item came from, where the item was before it came to the classroom or the child's house, and where it might end up some day.

   Values, Customs and Traditions

ACTIVITIES TO HELP CHILDREN FORM VALUES

1. *Activity:* Classroom purchases (PP–P)

   Materials: None.

   Procedure: Involve children if possible in decisions about classroom purchases. If children are involved, there are bound to be differences of opinion among them regarding what should be purchased for the classroom. These discussions provide excellent opportunities for children to think about and discuss what they think is important and why, and for them to begin to appreciate that people have different values.

2. *Activity:* Open-ended story (K–P)

   Materials: Stories involving choice and decisions.

   Procedure: Select a story children have not previously heard in which the principal character must make a decision whether or not to do something. For example, in *Pet Show* by Ezra Jack Keats,[4] Archie must make two decisions: (1) whether or not to say something when the little old lady shows up with *his* cat and (2) what to do when the judges award her a prize for the cat. The teacher might stop and ask the children what they think Archie did when the little old lady shows up at the pet show. After accepting the children's answers without giving any indication of right or wrong, the teacher completes the story. Discussion following the story's end

---

[4]E. Z. Keats, *Pet Show* (New York: Collier Books, 1972).

may center on the children's speculation of why Archie acted as he did. Teachers should avoid moralizing, however.

ACTIVITIES TO HELP CHILDREN UNDERSTAND CUSTOMS AND TRADITIONS

1. Activity: Foods (PP–P)

Materials: Magazines, scissors, paste, construction paper, food.

Procedure: Have students bring old magazines to school or collect some yourself. Allow children to look for food pictures in the magazines that are part of Black, Indian, Oriental, Mexican, and other cultures. Recipes or picture books may be made by cutting out and pasting pictures of these foods on construction paper. Staple or sew sheets of paper together for a booklet to add to the reading center.

Suggestions and Variations: Ask minority or foreign children to bring to class food representative of their culture. Have a tasting party. On another day, take children on a trip to a local supermarket. Help children to identify foods at the market that are typical of certain cultures. If possible, purchase a few of the foods to prepare at school.

Try to include interesting and representative foods for snack from time to time and discuss their significance to different groups. At holiday time, help children prepare foods which are traditional for the holiday (pumpkin pie, cranberry sauce, plum pudding).

2. Activity: Christmas and Hanukkah (PP–P)

Materials: Pictures, books, food items.

Procedure: Read the book *A Day of Winter* by Betty Miles. Relate to the children that Christmas and Hanukkah come during the winter season. Discuss with the children how their families spend these holidays.

Suggestions and Variations: Make and decorate Christmas cookies or cupcakes. String cranberries or popcorn for a tree. Such a tree might be a natural one growing in the school yard. The cranberries and popcorn can be eaten by the birds.

Christmas music and dances from many lands may be used.

Stories of Christmas in many lands may be told (Sinter Klaas of Holland, Las Posadas of Mexico, Los Tres Reyes of Spain, or Babushka of Russia).

3. Activity: Costumes (PP–P)

Materials: Pictures or real items which illustrate dress for special occasions in different cultures.

Procedure: Display items or pictures if a person from the culture cannot come to class to explain them. Talk to children about the items and the special occasions when they are used. Wedding apparel is usually quite distinctive and of interest to children.

4. *Activity:* Cultural literature (PP–P)

Materials: Literature pertaining to such countries as China, Japan, Thailand, Canada, Mexico, Austria, Denmark, Russia, Scotland, and Sweden. Select books which are stories about customs and traditions in these countries.

Procedure: Read stories to the children. Discuss the story with the children. Questions might include:
   (1) What did these people do that we do not do? Or that we do?
   (2) What do they have in their homes that we do not have? Or that we have?
   (3) What was the special occasion in the story?
   (4) How would we celebrate the special occasion?

Suggestions and Variations: Help older children locate the countries on a globe or map. Relate differences in customs and traditions to differences in climate and terrain where appropriate. For example, traditional festival foods depend on their availability in the area.

Introduce songs, dances, and games of children of other lands. Invite a parent or other resource person from another country to visit the classroom and tell about the customs and traditions there.

5. *Activity:* Films and filmstrips (PP–P)

Materials: Appropriate films and filmstrips depicting people of other countries celebrating special occasions. Equipment and space to show films or filmstrips.

Procedure: Films or filmstrips may either be shown to the whole group at story time or they may be viewed by small groups during activity time. Discussion of the films and filmstrips should follow viewing.

Suggestions and Variations: In perhaps no other area of study are films and filmstrips more useful than in helping children understand customs and traditions of other people. They should be used as frequently as possible. Teachers should also watch local television listings to find similar presentations on TV. A note sent home with the children indicating the time and channel of the program will help insure that the child will be able to watch it.

ADDITIONAL RESOURCES

Children's Books

BAKER, BETTYE F., *What is Black?* New York: Franklin Watts, Inc., 1969. The author poses questions about the things in the world that may be black. A positive concept of blackness is provided the child. The general tone is to present blackness as a positive rather than a negative thing.

BALIAN, LORNA, *I Love You, Mary Jane.* New York: Abingdon Press, 1967. Mary Jane is a big lovable shaggy dog who has a birthday party for the neighborhood children. The party is a wonderful success with balloons, games, ice cream and, best of all, Mary Jane's special gift to each guest.

BARTLETT, ROBERT M., *Thanksgiving Day.* New York: Thomas Y. Crowell Co., 1965. This book provides a brief history of giving thanks at harvest time. It begins in ancient Greece and proceeds to the present with emphasis on the Pilgrims and their Thanksgiving celebration.

BEIM, JERROLD, and LORRAINE BEIM, *Two is a Team.* New York: Alfred Knopf, Inc., 1945. The author relates the teamwork of two young boys. They get into trouble as they race their new wagons. As a result, both boys get a job and work as a team in order to pay for the damage.

BEIM, JERROLD, *Swimming Hole.* New York: William Morrow and Co., 1951. This is a story depicting prejudices in children. Steve, a Caucasian boy, does not want to play at the swimming hole because there are two Black boys with the group. The other boys leave Steve alone until he gets a sunburn which turns him bright red. Then Steve realizes that color is only skin deep. The story is warmly told with nice illustrations.

BROMBALL, WINIFRED, *Peter's Three Friends.* New York: Alfred Knopf, Inc., 1964. This is a story about how friendships might develop. Peter and his three friends share some interesting experiences.

BROWNER, RICHARD, *Every One Has a Name.* New York: Henry Z. Walck, Inc., 1961. A delightful book which has illustrations of animals and a text that rhymes. Human relations are stressed, and the message is that although people may look different, everyone is of worth and has a name.

BUCHHEIMER, NAOMI, *Let's Go to the Post Office.* New York: Putnam and Sons, 1964. The author provides an overview of how mail is sorted, canceled, tied into bundles, put into pouches and loaded onto mail trucks.

BUCKLEY, HELEN, *The Little Boy and the Birthdays.* New York: Lothrop, Lee and Shepard, 1965. A little boy discovers that it is important for him to remember the birthdays of others, just as he hopes they will remember his. This book relates an understanding of mutual exchange and respect for one another.

BUCKLEY, HELEN, *Grandmother and I.* New York: Lothrop, Lee and Shepard, 1961. A young girl experiences times when grandmother's lap is better than anyone else's.

CHANDLER, EDNA W., *Five Cent, Five Cent.* Chicago: Albert Whitman, 1967. This is a story about a Liberian child. Kolu learns how to earn money, while

Jack learns that money comes through working rather than trying to take it. Concepts of work and honesty are expressed.

CLARK, ANN NOLAN, *In My Mother's House*. New York: The Viking Press, 1941. Authentic illustrations and account of life among the Tewa Indians of New Mexico. Ms. Clark has done a number of books on various Indian tribes and Mexican families in the Southwest.

COHEN, MIRIAM, *Will I Have a Friend?* New York: The Macmillan Company, 1967. Jim is very apprehensive about his first birthday in school and asks his father, "Will I have a friend?" All seem to be friends and pay no attention to Jim. Then at rest time, Paul notices Jim and afterwards they play together.

CROSBY, BONSALL, *It's Time*. New York: Harper & Row, Publishers, 1964. Mabel Ann and Patrick are very good friends until the subject of sharing comes up. Then both want to have what the other one has. Each child wants all the toys. They finally learn the benefits of sharing.

ETS, MARIE H., *Just Me*. New York: The Viking Press, 1965. The author relates the experiences and the love shared between father and son. A little boy imitates all the inhabitants of the farmyard and woods. But he runs as only he alone can do to meet his father.

——, *Gilberto and the Wind*. New York: The Viking Press, 1963. Gilberto has many experiences with the wind. Sometimes it does what he wants it to; sometimes it doesn't. The wind and Gilberto grow tired and fall asleep.

EVANS, EVA K., *People are Important*. New York: Capital Publishing Company, Inc., 1957. The author portrays that people are more important than their customs will ever be. The differences among people in language, dress, food, types of dwellings, and ways of doing things are explained. To understand that our ways may seem strange to others is the first step in getting along with the people of the world.

FOSTER, DORIS V., *A Pocketful of Seasons*. New York: Lothrop, Lee, and Shephard Co., 1971. This book relates seasonal changes. A boy picks up something from each season for his pocket.

FREEMAN, DON, *Corduroy*. New York: The Viking Press, 1968. The author tells the story of a toy bear named Corduroy and a little Black girl, Lisa, who wishes to buy him. Feelings are stressed in the book.

GREENE, CARLA, *Doctors and Nurses*. New York: Harper & Row, Publishers, 1963. The author relates the things that people must study in the area of medicine. She also focuses on how doctors and nurses help people who are sick.

GREENE, CARLA, *Railroad Engineers and Airplane Pilots*. New York: Harper & Row, Publishers, 1964. A book which contains information about railroad engineers and airplane pilots. Their roles are carefully explained.

HAWKINSON, JOHN, and LUCY HAWKINSON, *Little Boy Who Lives up High*. Chicago: Albert Whitman and Co., 1967. This story is about Ricky, who lives in an apartment building. Ricky notices the differences in the view when he is in his high-rise apartment and when he is walking on the street. The environment of the city is vividly portrayed.

HILL, ELIZABETH, *Evans' Corner*. Chicago: Holt, Rinehart and Winston, Inc., 1967. The author depicts the need in a child to share and help others. Evans is a little boy who longs more than anything in the world for a place to call his own. He discovers a corner in his apartment and begins to collect items for his corner. His mother helps him realize that this alone cannot make him happy, but that he must help others too.

HOBAN, RUSSELL, *Bedtime for Francis*. New York: Harper & Row, Publishers, 1968. A badger acts like a child as she tries to put off going to bed.

HOBAN, RUSSELL, *A Birthday for Francis*. New York: Harper & Row, Publishers, 1968. Jealous Francis, feeling left out, turns her back on the preparation for her sister's birthday. But she becomes generous at the party and exchanges words with her sister.

HOETHE, LOUISE and RICHARD HOETHE. *Houses Around the World*. New York: Charles Scribner's Sons, 1973. The authors discuss and illustrate all kinds of houses from various parts of the world. They emphasize how houses differ, depending upon the climate, building materials, and nature of people.

HOLSCLAW, CORA, *Just One Me*. Chicago: Follett Publishing Co., 1967. The author illustrates the imagination of a Black boy. Jimmy's father always told him he could be anything he wanted to be. So Jimmy wonders what it would be like to be a tree, the wind, or an airplane. But Jimmy decides, "If there's just one me, that's what I really want to be."

KEATS, EZRA JACK, *Peter's Chair*. New York: Harper & Row, Publishers, 1967. The author conveys to the reader the idea of a little boy's growing up. Peter seemed to resent the idea that his little sister was going to use his cradle and then his crib. In his moment of frustration he decided to move. He moved outside and took his chair. Peter soon discovered that he did not fit into the chair. He was too big.

————, *Whistle for Willie*. New York: The Viking Press, 1964. This is a story of a little boy who wanted to be able to whistle for his dog the way big boys can do. Peter eventually learns how to whistle after much practice.

————, *A Letter to Amy*. New York: Harper & Row, Publishers, 1968. This delightful story for preschoolers is about a Black boy who is having a birthday party and sends Amy an invitation. He has quite a time trying to mail the letter, but finally succeeds. When the party begins, Amy is not present, and Peter is sad. But finally Amy appears.

————, *Pet Show*. New York: Collier Books, 1972. There is to be a pet show and Archie cannot find his cat. A little old lady shows up with Archie's cat and wins a ribbon for the cat with the longest whiskers. Archie's substitute pet is a germ in a jar. He wins a prize for the quietest pet. He also wins a friend in the little old lady.

KESSLER, ETHEL, and LEONARD KESSLER, *The Big Red Bus*. Garden City, N.Y.: Doubleday and Co., 1964. The author illustrates a bus ride. The scenes and flow of traffic are clearly explained. The author also brings out the way it feels to be riding in a big bus.

KIRN, ANN, *Two Pesos for Catalina*. Chicago: Rand McNally, 1961. When Catalina finds a tourist's bracelet and returns it, she is given two pesos as a reward. Much of the story revolves around her trying to decide what to buy at the market in Taxco. Aspects of Mexican rural life are shown. A glossary of Spanish terms is included.

KRAVETZ, NATHAN, *Two for a Walk*. New York: Oxford University Press, 1954. The author shares the experiences of John and Tony as they visit a grocery store, a barber shop, a pet shop, a construction site, and a fire station.

KUSKIN, KARLA, *Just Like Everyone Else*. New York: Harper & Row, Publishers, 1959. The adventures of a boy named Jonathon are shared. He gets up, gets dressed, eats breakfast, and goes to school. He follows the same routine as most children of his age.

LENSKI, LOIS, *Davy Goes Places*. New York: Henry Z. Walck, Inc., 1961. This story is about a boy who goes to visit his grandpa. This visit, which is very delightful for him, involves rides on many different vehicles.

LIANG, YEN, *Tommy and Dee Dee*. New York: Henry Z. Walck, Inc., 1953. The eighth day of the twelfth Chinese month is exciting for Dee Dee and his sister, Bao, for this is the beginning of the Chinese New Year Festival. The children have a delightful day eating, decorating the house, shopping for food and presents. They also see a parade and fireworks at night. Tommy does the same kind of thing, but in another country.

MCCLOSKEY, ROBERT, *Blueberries for Sal*. New York: The Viking Press, 1966. This book tells the story of a little girl and her mother as they go blueberry hunting in Maine. During their hunt they meet a mother bear and a cub.

MCGOVERN, ANN, *Why It's a Holiday*. Eau Claire, Wisconsin: E. M. Hale and Co., 1960. The author explains why certain days are legal holidays. She tells the story of many religious holidays and other special days.

PAPAS, WILLIAM, *No Mules*. New York: Coward McCann, Inc., 1967. This book relates the experiences of an African boy, Faan, who has difficulty going shopping with his mule, Solo.

PATTERSON, LILLIE, *Christmas in Britain and Scandinavia*. Champaign, Ill.: Garrard Publishing Company, 1970. The author discusses Christmas traditions in all the Scandinavian and British countries. She explains and shows pictures of decorations, songs, and food. Excellent information.

REICH, HANS, *Children and Their Mothers*. New York: Hill and Wang, 1964. This is a book of excellent photographs of children with their mothers in countries in Europe, Asia, Africa, and North and South America.

ROTH, EUGENE, *Children and Their Fathers*. New York: Hill and Wang, 1962. The book shows pictures of children and their fathers from different countries.

ROWE, JEANNE, *City Workers*. New York: Franklin Watts, Inc., 1969. Various kinds of work are illustrated in this book. The book provides children with some understanding of the different types of work that need to be done in a city.

SANDBERG, INGER and LASSE SANDBERG, *The Boy with Many Houses*. New York: Delacorte Press, 1968. A boy who has lived in a number of different houses, tries to build one for himself. He gets into trouble with the cleaning lady, his mother, father, sister, and brother. Finally his brother helps him build a house in the yard.

SCHWEITZER, BYRD BAYLOR, *Amigo*. New York: The Macmillan Company, 1963. 1963. Francisco wants a dog whom he plans to call Amigo. His parents tell him they cannot afford to feed a dog. Finally, his mother suggests a prairie dog. The story switches to a prairie dog who wants a human boy. Amigo and Francisco meet and each thinks he has tamed the other.

SCOTT, ANN HERBERT, *Sam*. New York: McGraw-Hill Book Company, 1967. This is a sensitive story which dramatizes a childhood experience. Sam is a little boy who wants to play, but his family does not want to play with him. He finally sits and cries. His mother knows what is wrong with him, and she solves the problem when she takes him into the kitchen with her and gives him a job.

SHOWERS, PAUL, *Your Skin and Mine*. New York: Thomas Y. Crowell Co., 1965. This book explains to the young child that everyone is covered from head to toe with a protective covering that keeps out germs, helps you feel, and keeps you warm or cold. The text tells clearly and simply how melanin gives color to the skin, that skin comes in two layers, and what happens when the skin is cut or damaged.

SIMON, NORMA, *Hanukkah*. New York: Thomas Y. Crowell Co., 1966. A description of this holiday is given with ritual and customs as observed all over the world.

————, *What Do I Say?* Chicago: Albert Whitman and Co., 1967. Manuel's home life and school day are depicted in attractive illustrations and in easy-to-read answers to the question "What do I say?"

UDRY, JANICE, *What Mary Jo Shared*. Chicago: Albert Whitman and Co., 1967. It is sharing time at school. Mary Jo has not known what to share, because everything she wants to share is always shared by someone else. One day Mary Jo shared her father with the children.

UDRY, JANICE, *Let's Be Enemies*. New York: Harper & Row, Publishers, 1961. John is unhappy because his friend is too bossy, and when John tells him this, the two boys say they will stop being friends. Instead, they agree it would be more fun to go skating together.

WABER, BERNARD, *Just Like Abraham Lincoln,* Boston: Houghton Mifflin Co., 1964. A small boy has a neighbor who looks just like Abraham Lincoln and who tells him stories about Abraham Lincoln.

YASHIMO, TARO, *Seashore Story*. New York: The Viking Press, 1967. Japanese children vacationing at the seashore ask to hear a story of Urashima, an ancient fisherman. This story is told to the children several times at their request.

————, *Umbrella*. New York: The Viking Press, 1958. Momo is a Japanese girl living in New York. On her third birthday she is given an umbrella. There is a long wait for a rainy day when Momo can enjoy the sound of the rain on her umbrella.

YOUNG, MARGARET, *Martin Luther King, Jr.* New York: Franklin Watts, Inc., 1968. The story of Martin Luther King and his fight for freedom and equality for Black Americans.

ZOLOTOW, CHARLOTTE, *The Quarreling Book*. New York: Harper & Row, Publishers, 1963. Gruffness and anger are passed along from person to person until a little dog starts a chain of happiness that reverses the trend. This is a pleasant picture book that hints about emotional maturity.

Social Science References for Teachers

BONING, R., *Profiles of Black Americans*. Rockville Center: Dexter and Westbrook, LTU, 1969.

DESART, H., and T. UNABELLE, "Geographic Readiness in the Kindergarten," *Journal of Geography,* 60 (1961), pp. 331–335.

EMMONS, F., and J. COBIA, "Introducing Anthropological Concepts in the Primary Grades," *Social Education,* 32 (1968), pp. 248–250.

GOODMAN, M. E., *The Culture of Childhood.* New York: Teacher's College Press, Columbia University, 1970.

JAROLIMEK, J., "Skills Teaching in the Primary Grades," *Social Education,* 31 (1967), pp. 222–223; 234.

KRANZ, P. L., and R. OSTLER, "Adult Expectations of Children—Do As I Say, Not As I Do," *Young Children,* 29, no. 5 (1974), pp. 277–279.

MITCHELL, L. S., *Young Geographers.* New York: Bank Street College of Education, 1971.

MOYER, J. E., *Bases for World Understanding and Cooperation.* Association for Supervision and Curriculum Development, 1970.

MUGGE, D. J., "Are Young Children Ready to Study the Social Sciences?" in *Elementary School Journal,* 68, no. 5 (Feb. 1968).

PRESTON, R. C., "What Social Studies Content for Primary Grades?" *Social Education,* 29 (1965), pp. 147–148.

SEEFELDT, C., "Is Today Tomorrow? History for Young Children," *Young Children,* 30, no. 2 (1975), pp. 99–106.

SPODEK, B., "Social Studies Programs in the Kindergarten," *Young Children,* 20, no. 5 (1967), pp. 284–289.

————, "Social Studies for Young Children: Identifying Intellectual Goals," *Social Education,* 38 (1974), pp. 40–53.

The Weewish Tree. A magazine of Indian America for young people. American Indian Historical Society, 1451 Masonic Avenue, San Francisco, California 94117.

appendix

KEY FOR ACTIVITY ORGANIZATION ACROSS CONTENT AREAS

Blocks
p. 133, #1
p. 180, #5
p. 196, #3
p. 198, #2
p. 202, #6
p. 202, #8
p. 204, #3
p. 236, #4
p. 282, #1
p. 283, #2
p. 284, #6

Dramatic Play
p. 101, #1
p. 133, #4
p. 133, #2
p. 173, #7
p. 180, #3
p. 180, #4
p. 194, #2
p. 194, #3
p. 198, #5
p. 205, #1
p. 271, #1
p. 274, #1

Sand and Water Play
p. 198, #3
p. 203, #2
p. 243, #7
p. 244, #8
p. 244, #9
p. 248, #2
p. 283, #3
p. 232, #4
p. 232, #3
p. 238, #1
p. 239, #2
p. 242, #4
p. 250, #2

Small Motor
p. 67, #1
p. 68, #2
p. 69, #3
p. 70, #7
p. 70, #8
p. 71, #9
p. 145, #3
p. 151, #1

p. 152, #4
p. 182, #1
p. 183, #2
p. 183, #3
p. 197, #1
p. 203, #1
p. 237, #6
p. 237, #7

Large Motor
p. 95, #1
p. 96, #2
p. 96, #3
p. 97, #2
p. 174, #3
p. 179, #4
p. 191, #7
p. 201, #2
p. 235, #1
p. 237, #5
p. 238, #8
p. 243, #5
p. 245, #10
p. 278, #3

index